Praise for
The Five Stages of Collapse

Profound insight combined with wry humor is such an incendiary
weapon I am tempted to call *The Five Stages of Collapse* an "Orlov
Cocktail." His delivery of hard truths laced with irony saturates us in
seldom reported but extremely relevant facts about the world. He is
one of the best writers on the scene today, working at the top of his
game. There is more to enjoy in this book with every page you turn,
and in very uncertain times, Orlov's advice is, at its core, kind-spirited
and extraordinarily helpful.

— Albert Bates, author, *The Biochar Solution*

Even if I believed collapse were impossible I'd still read everything
Dmitry Orlov writes: he's that entertaining. Unfortunately, however,
collapse of some sort or other, of some degree or another, is almost
guaranteed. Orlov does us all a great service by teasing apart the kinds
and degrees of collapse so that we can prepare for what is likely and
"dig in our heels" to prevent what is unsurvivable.

— Richard Heinberg, Senior Fellow,
Post Carbon Institute,
author, *The End of Growth*

At a time when most talk about the prospect of collapse tends to wander off into vague generalities, Orlov's latest book offers a welcome
dose of clear thinking. Compulsively readable, firmly grounded in
real-world examples, and laced with his usual mordant wit, *The Five
Stages of Collapse* deserves space on the bookshelf of anyone concerned
about the future of industrial civilization.

— John Michael Greer, author, *Green Wizardry*

D1430425

THE FIVE STAGES
of COLLAPSE

SURVIVORS' TOOLKIT

Dmitry Orlov

new society
PUBLISHERS

CATALOGUING IN PUBLICATION DATA:

A catalog record for this publication is available from the
National Library of Canada.

Cover design by Diane McIntosh and Matt Harter.
Cover and interior illustrations by Mark David Paterson,
used by kind permission.

Printed in Canada.
First printing March 2013.

Paperback ISBN: 978-0-86571-736-7 eISBN: 978-1-55092-527-2

Inquiries regarding requests to reprint all or part of *The Five Stages of Collapse*
should be addressed to New Society Publishers at the address below.

To order directly from the publishers, please call toll-free
(North America) 1-800-567-6772, or order online at www.newsociety.com

Any other inquiries can be directed by mail to:

New Society Publishers
P.O. Box 189, Gabriola Island, BC V0R 1X0, Canada
(250) 247-9737

New Society Publishers' mission is to publish books that contribute in fundamental
ways to building an ecologically sustainable and just society, and to do so with the
least possible impact on the environment, in a manner that models this vision. We
are committed to doing this not just through education, but through action. The
interior pages of our bound books are printed on Forest Stewardship Council®-
registered acid-free paper that is **100% post-consumer recycled** (100% old growth
forest-free), processed chlorine free, and printed with vegetable-based, low-VOC
inks, with covers produced using FSC®-registered stock. New Society also works to
reduce its carbon footprint, and purchases carbon offsets based on an annual audit
to ensure a carbon neutral footprint. For further information, or to browse our full
list of books and purchase securely, visit our website at: www.newsociety.com

MIX
Paper from
responsible sources
FSC® C016245

Contents

Introduction: Collapses in General 1
What is collapse? 6
When will collapse occur? 10
What are the stages of collapse? 13

1. Financial Collapse 17
The root of the problem 18
The wrong math 21
Defaults big and small 24
The end of money 26
Options for cashing out 32
Alternatives to money 39
How we did it 43
Chits, specie and stock-in-trade 46
A likely endgame 48
Cold-starting instructions 49
Beware financial despotism 50
Monetary mysticism 54
The untrustworthy and the trustful 57
Götterdämmerung 61
Case Study: Iceland 63

2. Commercial Collapse 73
Cascaded failure 75
Liar word: efficiency 78
Life upside down 83
The many advantages of gift 90
Money corrupts 94
Opportunities for gift-giving 96
Meanwhile in Soviet Russia 98
The new normal 99
A cultural flip 101
Case Study: The Russian Mafia 105

3. **Political Collapse** 123
   Anarchy's charms 125
   The nation-state fades out 139
   National language 142
   Taking care of your own 146
   State religion 147
   Life after the nation-state 150
   The problem of excessive scale 151
   The proliferation of defunct states 157
   Government services disappear 162
   Denationalization of currency 165
   What governments are good at 169
   Warfare becomes self-defeating 169
   The end of law and order 171
   The end of the welfare state 176
   Virtualized politics 179
   Case Study: The Pashtuns 189

4. **Social Collapse** 195
   The limits of community planning 197
   The new rules 200
   Social reclamation 202
   Religion as organizing principle 203
   Charitable giving and taking 208
   What society? 209
   Case Study: The Roma 211

5. **Cultural Collapse** 227
   Humans and other animals 230
   The limits of language 233
   Spoken memory 236
   The isolated human 239
   The primacy of family 241
   Case Study: The Ik 245

   Afterword 261

   Endnotes 265
   Bibliography 267
   Index 269
   About the Author 281

Collapses in General

Collapse is a socially awkward subject. Serious men sometimes discuss it, in a spare moment or over drinks, in hushed tones. The topic is very rarely broached in mixed company, and hardly at all when there are children present. For certain specialists—scientists, engineers and, more recently, those working in finance—collapse is fast becoming the elephant in the room. The enforced silence causes these specialists much frustration, since it is becoming increasingly difficult for them, based on the data at their disposal, to formulate, in their own minds, a scenario that does not culminate in collapse. Others—businessmen, politicians, economists, social scientists, psychologists, educators—find such thinking overly negative.

The contrast between these two groups is a contrast between two radically different modes of thought. The first is trained to think in measurable physical quantities and principles—systems theory, thermo-dynamics and so on. They investigate facts and the results cannot be positive or negative in and of themselves, only accurate or inaccurate. How these results apply to society is, most unfortunately, no more than a secondary consideration. To the second group, society remains at all times both the subject and the object; they hold it front and center and always view as secondary the physical considerations and principles, which they generally have not been trained to understand, and which they regard as a matter of opinion. To them, the topic of collapse is cir-cumscribed by its direct and immediate effect on society—not the long-term reality of collapse, but the effect collapse as a topic of discussion will have on present society. Seen in this light, the subject seems overly negative, disturbing, distressing, depressing, defeatist—rather than in-spiring, comforting, enlightening, uplifting or empowering.

There is one very strong point of agreement between the two kinds of specialists. They both tend to agree that dwelling on the topic of collapse is not conducive to furthering their careers. Those who do mention it tend to leaven their utterances with phrases such as "unless we," or "we must"—making sure to recast collapse as something that is either preventable or avoidable. About the only people who are capable of discussing collapse unguardedly, without looking over their shoul-ders, are retired specialists and tenured faculty, and the latter only if their research is not dependent on grants. At the opposite extreme are those who have discovered that collapse is a growing market niche and cater to it with all manner of products and services, from survivalist bunkers and equipment to wilderness survival training to books that promote financial instruments to hedge against collapse. Somewhere in the middle are people who work within communities that are, in fact, collapsing, and who do not have the luxury of ignoring this reality and its social and medical consequences. They often find themselves conflicted by the cognitive dissonance of the shocking daily reality they must confront and the compulsory optimism they must simulate in order to remain employed.

At a more personal level, the topic of collapse can be corrosive to marriage and family life. A common pattern is for the husband to do some reading and become convinced that collapse is underway. Sud-denly radicalized by this dramatic shift in his worldview, he comes to believe that extraordinary preparations are called for as a matter of the highest priority. Such preparations may include prematurely abandoning one's career; acquiring a homestead, possibly in a foreign land; cashing out of investments, retirement funds and other savings in order to acquire tools, supplies and other inventory; learning to farm, garden and hunt; homeschooling his children; leaving behind any friends or acquaintances who remain skeptical on the topic of collapse; and so on and so forth. Meanwhile, the wife wants to continue living the life she had always wanted: living close to her friends and family, vacationing in the tropics in wintertime, shopping at fashionable boutiques, sending the children to private schools and summer camps and entertaining other successful couples at home. To the husband, collapse becomes an overarching consideration, preparing for the family to survive it of paramount importance; to the wife it is an unbreachable topic of conversation compulsively reintroduced by her increasingly odd, alienated and socially embarrassing husband. She begins to wonder whether she married the right man. After all, somebody's husband *always* does well no matter *what* happens. To a woman, surviving collapse can seem as simple as not worrying about it while making sure to avoid marrying a loser. This is a conservative evolutionary strategy, and most of the time it works. How well it will work during the collapse of global industrial civilization—well, we'll just have to see.

It is something of a pattern that the male concerns himself with the big picture, such as who to elect president, while the wife sweats the little stuff, such as what washing machine to buy or where to send the children. But there are instances in which this pattern is reversed and the wife becomes collapse-aware while the husband chooses to remain in denial. In either case, in many families one spouse gets the picture and is prepared to make major changes in the living arrangement but the other is non-receptive. The constraints multiply if they have children, because living arrangements that are likely to become necessary adaptations post-collapse look substandard to a pre-collapse mindset. For instance, in many places in the United States, bringing up a child in a place that lacks electricity, central heating or indoor plumbing may be equated with child abuse, and authorities rush in and confiscate the children. (In the course of collapse, until these same authorities become overwhelmed, they will try to evacuate entire families to emergency refugee camps rather than let them survive and adapt to life without electricity, central heating, indoor plumbing, government services or police protection, even in parts where such a lifestyle was considered perfectly normal as little as a century ago.) If there are grandparents involved too, misunderstandings multiply.

Another, even greater chasm exists at the social level, between collapse as a topic of dispassionate, academic discussion peppered with terms from systems theory and other lofty branches of higher learning and collapse as personal experience—lived by those who have already gone through it to one extent or another. During its early stages, collapse affects the most vulnerable: the poorest, least protected, least privileged communities, families and individuals. Collapse dispossesses industrial and service personnel even while educated professionals may, for a time, do better than ever. In its early stages collapse may seem like a morality play, a story of punishing the least capable and the least prepared while rewarding the diligent and the successful—to the delight of social Darwinists dreaming that they, being the fittest, will survive. But their delight is sure to be short-lived: like a flood that inundates the lowlands first, then reaches the higher ground and washes away the hills, collapse eventually reaches everybody, and just as in a real flood, what makes survival possible is cooperation, not competition. People who see collapse as a lofty pursuit for themselves and a dire experience for all those other, unlucky persons, those who are less capable and less prepared, simply need to await their turn—then they too will be humbled.

All of this makes it a rather tall order to expect most people to take any significant steps to do anything at all about collapse as families, communities, societies or nations. Social inertia is an awesome force and many people are almost genetically predisposed to not want to understand that collapse is inevitable. Many others understand this truth on some level but refuse to act on it. When they are touched by collapse, they take it personally or see it as a matter of luck. They see those who prepare for collapse as eccentrics; some may even consider them to be dangerous subversives. This is especially likely to be the case with regard to people in positions of power and authority, because they are not exactly cheered by the prospect of a future that has no place for them.

Certain individuals—unmarried men, mostly—have perhaps the greatest freedom of action in preparing for collapse. There seems to be a certain personality type that is more likely to survive collapse unscathed, physically or psychologically, and be able to adapt to the new circumstances. Survivors of shipwrecks and similar calamities share several common traits. A certain degree of indifference or detachment is definitely helpful, including indifference to suffering. Possibly the most important characteristic, more important than skills or preparation or even luck, is the will to survive. Next is self-reliance: the ability to persevere in spite of loneliness and lack of support from anyone else. Last on the list is unreasonableness: the sheer stubborn inability to surrender in the face of seemingly insurmountable odds, opposing opinions from one's comrades or even force.

This should not come as a complete surprise, for there are two distinct components to human nature: the social and the solitary. While most people are strictly social, with all of their motivations, norms, constraints and rewards deriving from their interactions with others, there are also quite a few loners, people who motivate themselves, derive their rewards directly from nature and whose only constraints are self-imposed. The solitary part of human nature is definitely the more highly evolved, and humanity has surged forward through the efforts of brilliant loners and eccentrics. Their names live on forever precisely because society was unable to extinguish their brilliance or thwart their initiative through social inertia. On the other hand, our social instincts are atavistic and result far too reliably in mediocrity and conformism. We evolved to live in small groups of a few families, small enough to easily accommodate a few brilliant eccentrics, and our recent experiments that have gone beyond that limited scope seem to rely on herd instincts that may not even be specifically human. When facing imminent danger, large groups of humans have a tendency to panic and stampede, and on such occasions people regularly get trampled and crushed underfoot: a pinnacle of evolution indeed! And so, in fashioning a survivable future, we would do well to put our emphasis on individuals and small, cooperative groups rather than on larger entities, be they existing, pre-collapse communities, regions, nations or humanity as a whole.

Those who feel the need to be inclusive and accommodating, to compromise and to seek consensus, need to understand the awesome force of social inertia. It is an immovable, crushing weight. "We must take into account the interests of society as a whole" implies that "We must allow ourselves to remain blocked by other people's unwillingness or inability to make drastic but necessary changes; to change who they are." When it comes to larger groups, any meaningful discussion of collapse is usually off the table. The topics under discussion center around finding ways to perpetuate the current system through alternative means: renewable energy, organic agriculture, starting or supporting local businesses, bicycling instead of driving and so on. None of these things is bad, but focusing on them ignores the bigger question of the radical social simplification that is required. It seems unlikely that we can achieve this radical simplification in a series of controlled steps; that would be like asking a demolition crew to demolish a building brick by brick, one floor at a time, instead of following the standard procedure of mining it, blowing it up and bulldozing and hauling away the debris, then laying down a new foundation. It seems far more reasonable to expect that social complexity will be demolished in the traditional quick and dirty fashion rather than dismantled gradually and deliberately.

What is collapse?

This book is about collapse. Not whether collapse will occur or when, but rather, what it looks like, what to expect and how we should behave should we wish to survive it. Such information may be of minimal interest to hardcore collapse skeptics. However, should any of them wish to further educate themselves on this subject, here are some pointers to resources and avenues of approach that should make the process simpler, though by no means easier, since the main impediment to grasping its significance is not intellectual but psychological.

To make the case for the imminent collapse of global industrial civilization, it is necessary to prove two things. The first is to account for the Earth's finite endowment of fossil fuels, metal ores, other industrial and agricultural inputs, fresh water and fertile soil, and to demonstrate that many of these resources are either past their all-time peak of production or will soon achieve it. The second is to prove that, as these resources become too scarce to allow the global industrial economy to grow, the result will be collapse rather than a slow and steady deterioration that could continue for centuries without reaching any conclusive, historical endpoint.

The first task has been carried out by a number of people, but a particularly good book on the subject is Richard Heinberg's *Peak Everything*,[1] which calmly lays out the facts for why the twenty-first century is a century of declines in energy, agricultural output, stable climate and population. While Heinberg weaves together a convincing story, Chris Clugston, in his 2011 self-published book *Scarcity*,[2] takes a more direct approach. Clugston undertook a thorough study of US government data on nonrenewable natural resources, focusing on the raw materials needs and primary energy sources of industrialized economies. In his 2012 update, Clugston shows that only one essential industrial input—bauxite for aluminum smelting—now remains sufficiently abundant to provide for continued economic growth. Consequently, the rate of improvement in the global material living standard (measured as per capita GDP) has slowed from around 2 percent per year during the second half of the twentieth century to just 0.4 percent this decade, and is poised to turn negative. Based on Clugston's projections, the increasing scarcity of the nonrenewable resources required to maintain industrial civilization will most certainly trigger a global societal collapse by mid-century.

While the first task is a relatively simple matter of laying out the numbers, which are available from reputable sources that are difficult to argue against and can be grasped by anyone with a head for numbers and a general understanding of the functioning of industrial economies, the second task is much harder, because the only way to address it is through mathematical models. The first of these models is the World3 model used in the 1972 book *Limits to Growth*. World3 is a relatively simple model that ran on a computer less powerful than a smartphone and included just five variables: world population, industrialization, pollution, food production and resource depletion. This model predicted economic and societal collapse by mid-twenty-first century. The 2004 *Limits to Growth: The 30-Year Update*[3] confirmed that, thirty years later, the initial predictions are still in excellent agreement with reality. Though your instinct may be to mistrust the predictive abilities of mathematical models in general, this wariness should be tempered somewhat when the model in question is shown to have been correct decades later.

Mathematical models can be fearsomely complex, requiring many hours of supercomputer time for a single run and able to defy anyone's attempt to understand them at a sitting. Such models inspire skepticism by their sheer complexity: with so many formulas and parameters, there has to be a mistake in there somewhere! Luckily, modeling collapse, at the simplest and most intuitive level, does not require such complexity, thanks to the Seneca Cliff model proposed by Professor Ugo Bardi of the University of Florence in Italy. Bardi's goal was to create a "mind-sized" model that could be easily understood at a glance by someone even slightly conversant with mathematical modeling. Bardi got the inspiration for the name of his model from a quote by the Roman philosopher Seneca: "It would be some consolation for the feebleness of our selves and our works if all things should perish as slowly as they come into being; but as it is, increases are of sluggish growth, but the way to ruin is rapid."[4]

Bardi started with a very simple model of resource use and depletion with just two variables: resources and capital. Resources are transformed into capital at a rate that is proportional to both the amount of remaining resources and the amount of capital. Also, capital decays over time. This model can be run via a simple spreadsheet or by using a very short and simple computer program, and the result is a symmetrical bell curve: the amount of capital, representing the size of the economy, grows gradually, reaches a peak, and then declines just as gradually, as the resource base is depleted. (The bell curve is ubiquitous, serves as the basis of probability and statistics, and is also known as the Hubbert Curve, which is used to model oil depletion.) Bardi then added a third variable to the model, which he labeled "pollution," and which represents the overhead of running an industrial civilization: not just pollution but also its infrastructure, its bureaucracy and so on. Pollution represents all that has to exist for an industrial economy to function but does not contribute to its productive capacity. A fraction of capital, proportional to both the amount of capital and the size of this third variable, is diverted to it. Just like capital, it also decays over time. This model produces an asymmetric, lopsided curve, in which the upward slope is gradual but the downward slope is steep and cliff-like. In this model, capital does not gradually decay as resources run short; it collapses.

To appreciate why this is so at an intuitive level think of the infrastructure of industrial civilization: its highways and bridges, its oil terminals, refineries and pipelines, its airports, seaports, electrical grid and so on. As the economy expands, all of these have to expand alongside it, and maintain reserve capacity to avoid bottlenecks, shortages, traffic jams and blackouts. But when resource scarcity forces the economy to start contracting, they cannot contract with it, because they have all been built at a certain scale that cannot be reduced retroactively, and have been designed to be efficient and realize economies of scale only when utilized at close to full capacity. Even as they are used less, their maintenance costs remain the same, swallowing up an ever-larger portion of the economy. At some point maintenance costs become unbearable and maintenance is foregone. Shortly thereafter they become nonfunctional, and with them the rest of the industrial economy.

Further insight into the mechanics of collapse can be gained by looking at the role of finance in the day-to-day functioning of the global economy, because it expands by systematically betting on future growth—borrowing from the future, which is assumed to be more prosperous than the present except for minor, temporary setbacks. This borrowing is used not just to finance expansion but to finance all of the shipments that make up global trade: every international shipment starts with a letter of credit issued by a commercial bank in one country and honored by another commercial bank in another country. If the economy stops growing for an extended period of time, these bets on future growth no longer pay off, a large number of loans turn into bad, nonperforming loans and many banks become insolvent and are no longer able to issue letters of credit, while other banks, though still solvent, no longer want to take the risk of honoring their letters of credit. Global trade stops, which in turn disrupts global supply chains, causing shortages of components and other industrial inputs, which then halt manufacturing processes. Before too long, the global economy passes a point of no return beyond which there can be no recovery, because the supply networks and trading relationships that held it together have broken down.

All of these explanations for why collapse is exceedingly likely may be compelling, but for many people they are about as taxing on the brain as the subject of collapse itself. Thankfully, there is also a third way, which is, as time goes on, turning out to be far more productive in informing people about collapse than either the resource numbers or the mathematical models: personal experience. Entire countries, such as Greece, are finding themselves in the throes of what can quite uncontroversially be labeled as financial, commercial and political collapse: there are runs on banks as people try to cash out and expatriate their savings; pharmacies run out of medicines and many other imports run short; nationally elected officials are replaced with political appointees whose candidacies are vetted by the country's creditors. In other countries, such as the United States, such effects are not yet felt, but many people are nevertheless starting to recognize that their future will not resemble the past: younger people realize that their college degrees will not lead to a career or even to a good, permanent job; older people realize that they will not be supported in retirement; long-term unemployed people realize that their careers have ended prematurely. Many of these people already understand that something has gone terribly wrong, but most of them are not yet aware of just how thorough a transformation their country is about to undergo.

When will collapse occur?

Supposing you are convinced that collapse is underway, a natural next question to ask is, When is it going to happen? Unfortunately this question, reasonable though it is, has no definitive answer. You see, predicting *that* something is going to happen is a lot easier than predicting *when* something will happen. Suppose you have an old bridge: the concrete is cracked, chunks of it are missing with rusty rebar showing through. An inspector declares it "structurally deficient." This bridge is definitely going to collapse at some point, but on what date? That is something that nobody can tell you—neither the inspector, nor anyone else. If you press him for an answer, he might say something like, "If it doesn't collapse within a year, then it might stay up for another two. And if it stays up that long, then it might stay up for another decade. But if it stays up for an entire decade, then it will probably collapse within a year or two of that, because, given its *rate of deterioration*, at that point it will be entirely unclear *what is holding it up*."

You see, the timing estimates are inevitably subjective and, if you will, impressionistic, but there are objective things to pay attention to: how much structure is left (given that large chunks of concrete are continuing to fall out of it and into the river below) and the rate at which it is deteriorating (measurable in chunks per month). Most people have trouble assessing such risks. There are two problems: the first is that people often think that they would be able to assess the risk more accurately if they had more data. It does not occur to them that the data they are looking for are not available for the simple reason that they do not exist. And so they incorporate more data, hoping that these are relevant, but only making their estimate even less accurate.

The second problem is that people assume they are playing a game of chance, and that it's a fair one; something Nassim Nicholas Taleb, author of *The Black Swan*,[5] calls the "ludic fallacy." If you drive over a structurally deficient bridge every day, it could be said that you are gambling with your life; but are you gambling, exactly? Gambling normally involves games of chance: a roll of the dice, a flip of the coin, unless someone is cheating. Fair games form a tiny, insignificant subset of all possible games, and they can only be played in contrived, controlled, simplified circumstances, using a specially designed apparatus that is functioning perfectly. Suppose someone tells you that he just flipped a coin ten times and all ten were heads? What is the probability that the next flip will be heads too? If you think 50 percent, then you are discounting the very high probability that the game is rigged. And this makes you a sucker.

Games played directly against nature are never fair. You could say that nature always cheats: just as you are about to win the jackpot, the casino gets hit by an asteroid. You might think that such unlikely events are not significant, but it turns out that they are: Taleb's black swans rule the world. Really, nature doesn't so much cheat as not give a damn about your rules. And these rules are all you have go by: a bridge is sound if it corresponds to the picture in the head of its designer. The correspondence is almost perfect when the bridge is new, but as it ages a noticeable divergence takes place: cracks appear and the structure decays. At some more-or-less arbitrary point it is declared unsafe. But there is no picture in anyone's head of it collapsing, because, you see, it wasn't designed to collapse; it was designed to stay up. The information as to when it will collapse does not exist. There is a trick, however: you can observe the rate of divergence; when this goes from linear to exponential (that is, begins to double) then collapse is not far off, and you might even be able to set an upper limit on how long it will take. If the number of cement chunks falling out of your bridge keeps doubling, you can compute the moment when every last piece of the bridge will be in the river, and that is your upper bound.

Still, your forecast will be subjective (or, if you like, based on your luck as a forecaster) because you are still just playing the odds. If you find that the deterioration in your bridge is linear (one chunk falls out per month) then you extrapolate that it will remain linear; if it is exponential (twice as many chunks as in previous month) then you extrapolate that it will remain exponential, and, if you are lucky, it will.

But the odds of it remaining one or the other are strictly in your own mind: they are not predictable but subjective. Calling them "random" or "chaotic" doesn't add any meaning: the information you are looking for simply does not exist.

To summarize: it is possible to predict that something will happen with uncanny accuracy. For example, all empires eventually collapse, with no exceptions; therefore, the USA will collapse. There, I just did it. But it is not possible to predict when something will happen because of the problem of missing information: we have a mental model of how something continues to exist, not of how it unexpectedly ceases to exist. However, by watching the rate of deterioration, or divergence from our mental model, we can sometimes tell when the date is drawing near. The first type of prediction—that something will collapse—is extremely useful, because it allows you to avoid putting at risk that which you cannot afford to lose. But there are situations when you have no choice; for instance, if you are born into an empire that's about to collapse. And that is where the second type of prediction—that something will collapse real soon—comes in very handy, because it tells you that it may be time to pull your bacon out of the fire.

Let me stress again: the process of coming up with such predictions is subjective. You might reason it out, or you might base it on a certain tingling sensation in the back of your neck. Still, people like to theorize: some declare that the events in question are random, or chaotic, and then go on to formulate mathematical models of randomness and of chaos. But the timing of large-scale, "improbable" events is not random or chaotic, it is unknown. With regular, small-scale events, statisticians can cheat by averaging them over. That is useful if you are selling insurance—insuring against rare events you can foresee. Of course, a large-scale event can still wipe you out by putting your reinsurer/underwriter out of business. We have fire insurance and flood insurance (not so much any more; in the US flood is such a bad risk that it is now underwritten directly by the taxpayers) but there can be no collapse insurance, because there is no way to objectively estimate the risk.

Plugging in everyone's favorite Yogi Berra quote: "Making predictions is hard, especially if they are about the future." Well, I beg to differ: making predictions about the past is just as difficult. The USSR collapsed unexpectedly in 1991, taking the "experts" by surprise. The root cause of the collapse remains veiled in mystery; the reason for the exact timing remains a complete mystery. Expert Kremlinologists were geared up to bet on minor power shifts within the Politburo, expert economists were entirely convinced about the superiority of free-market capitalism over a planned socialist economy, expert military strategists could debate the merits of the Strategic Defense Initiative (there aren't any), but they were all blindsided when the whole Soviet thing just folded up and blew away. Similarly, most political experts in the US were confident in their estimation of the odds that Obama would or would not be reelected in November 2012; what they couldn't give you were the odds that the elections wouldn't be held and that nobody would be elected president. Mind you, these odds were not zero, and we can be sure that such a day will come; we just don't know when.

What are the stages of collapse?

Let us suppose that you are convinced that collapse is going to happen, by mid-century at the latest. You will still need to come to terms with it, to get over the shock, terror, grief, fear and other unhelpful emotions. Elizabeth Kübler-Ross defined the five stages of coming to terms with grief and tragedy as denial, anger, bargaining, depression and acceptance, and applied them quite successfully to various forms of catastrophic personal loss: death of a loved one, sudden end to one's career and so forth. Several thinkers, notably James Howard Kunstler and John Michael Greer, have pointed out that the Kübler-Ross model is also quite terrifyingly accurate in reflecting the process by which society as a whole (or at least the informed and thinking parts of it) is reconciling itself to the inevitability of a discontinuous future, with our institutions and life-support systems undermined by a combination of resource depletion, catastrophic climate change and political impotence. But so far little has been said specifically about the finer structure of these discontinuities. Instead, we find a continuum of subjective judgments, ranging from "a severe and prolonged recession" (the prediction we most often read in the financial press) to Kunstler's "Long Emergency"[6] to the ever-popular "Collapse of Western Civilization," painted with an ever-wider brushstroke.

For those of us who have already gone through all of the emotional stages of reconciling ourselves to the prospect of social and economic upheaval, it might be helpful to have a more precise terminology that goes beyond such emotionally charged phrases. Defining a taxonomy of collapses might prove to be more than just an intellectual exercise: based on our abilities and circumstances, some of us may be able to specifically plan for a certain stage of collapse as a temporary, or even permanent, stopping point. Even if society at the current stage of socio-economic complexity will no longer be possible, and even if, as Joseph Tainter points in *The Collapse of Complex Societies*,[7] there are circumstances in which collapse happens to be the correct adaptive response, it need not automatically cause a population crash, with the survivors disbanding into solitary, feral humans dispersed in the wilderness and subsisting miserably. Collapse can be conceived of as an orderly, organized retreat rather than a rout. It may even be useful to think of collapse as a transition: a transition that has already been planned for us (so no further transition planning activities are needed) and will consist of the collapse of finance, consumerism and politics-as-usual, along with the collapse of the societies and cultures that are entirely dependent on them.

In an effort to introduce a helpful taxonomy of collapses, I have defined my five stages of collapse to serve as mental milestones as we gauge our own collapse-preparedness and see what we can do to improve it. Rather than tying each phase to a particular emotion, as in the Kübler-Ross model, the proposed taxonomy ties each of the five stages to the breaching of a specific level of trust, or faith, in the status quo. Although each stage causes physical, observable changes in the environment, these can be gradual, while the mental flip is generally quite swift. It is something of a cultural universal that nobody (but a real fool) wants to be the last fool to believe in a lie.

Stage 1: Financial collapse. Faith in "business as usual" is lost. The future is no longer assumed to resemble the past in any way that allows risk to be assessed and financial assets to be guaranteed. Financial institutions become insolvent; savings are wiped out and access to capital is lost.

Stage 2: Commercial collapse. Faith that "the market shall provide" is lost. Money is devalued and/or becomes scarce, commodities are hoarded, import and retail chains break down and widespread shortages of survival necessities become the norm.

Stage 3: Political collapse. Faith that "the government will take care of you" is lost. As official attempts to mitigate widespread loss of access to commercial sources of survival necessities fail to make a difference, the political establishment loses legitimacy and relevance.

Stage 4: Social collapse. Faith that "your people will take care of you" is lost, as local social institutions, be they charities or other groups that rush in to fill the power vacuum, run out of resources or fail through internal conflict.

Stage 5: Cultural collapse. Faith in the goodness of humanity is lost. People lose their capacity for "kindness, generosity, consideration, affection, honesty, hospitality, compassion, charity." Families disband and compete as individuals for scarce resources. The new motto becomes "May you die today so that I can die tomorrow."

I have taken the list of human virtues from Colin Turnbull's *The Mountain People*, which I discuss in detail in the case study on the Ik, which follows the chapter on cultural collapse. The motto is from Alexander Solzhenitsyn's *The Gulag Archipelago*.

As we can easily imagine, the default is cascaded failure: each stage of collapse can easily lead to the next, perhaps even overlapping it. In Russia following the Soviet collapse, the process was arrested at Stage 3: there was considerable trouble with ethnic mafias and even some warlordism, but government authority won out in the end.

While attempting to arrest collapse at Stage 1 or Stage 2 would most likely be a waste of energy, it is probably worth everyone's while to dig in their heels at Stage 3, definitely at Stage 4, and it is quite simply a matter of physical survival to avoid Stage 5. In certain localities—those with high population densities, as well as those that contain dangerous nuclear and industrial installations—avoiding Stage 3 collapse is rather important, to the point of inviting international peacekeepers or even foreign troops and governments to maintain order and avoid disasters. Other localities may be able to prosper indefinitely at Stage 3, and even the most impoverished environments may be able to support a sparse population subsisting indefinitely at Stage 4.

Although it is possible to prepare directly for surviving Stage 5, this seems like an altogether demoralizing thing to attempt. Preparing to survive Stages 3 and 4 may seem somewhat more reasonable, while explicitly aiming for Stage 3 may be reasonable if you plan to make a career of it. Be that as it may, I must leave such preparations as an exercise for the reader. My hope is that these definitions of specific stages of collapse will enable a more specific and fruitful discussion than the one currently dominated by such vague and ultimately nonsensical terms as "the collapse of Western civilization."

CHAPTER 1

Financial Collapse

STAGE 1: Financial collapse. Faith in "business as usual" is lost. The future is no longer assumed to resemble the past in any way that allows risk to be assessed and financial assets to be guaranteed. Financial institutions become insolvent; savings are wiped out and access to capital is lost.

Looking at the first three stages of collapse—financial, commercial, political—it is clear why financial collapse should, and to some extent already has, come first. Commercial collapse results from the disruption of the physical flows of products and services; political collapse occurs when governments are no longer able to fulfill their obligations to their citizens in the wake of commercial collapse; but all that is required for financial collapse is for certain assumptions about the future to be invalidated, for finance is not a physical system but a mental construct, one resembling a house of cards that, to stretch this metaphor just a little, can remain stable only while continuously adding more cards, in the sense of continuous credit expansion supported by economic growth. But we are entering a time when a wide variety of physical constraints are making themselves felt around the world, from the depletion of fossil fuel resources, metal ores, phosphate, fresh water and arable land, to massive disruptions because of droughts, floods and heat waves brought by accelerating climate change, to the political instability and upheaval which sweep the world in the wake of each food price spike. All of these elements combine to make a rosy projection for global economic growth untenable. In turn, an extended period of economic stagnation followed by a sustained, perhaps terminal contraction is fatal to a financial system that constantly requires more debt, and more growth.

The mitigation strategy adopted by governments in the US, Europe and elsewhere since the financial crisis of 2008 has been quite accurately characterized as "extend and pretend"—extend government-backed loan guarantees and pretend that economic growth will resume shortly. This state of affairs is perhaps best summarized by the following, now-famous quote by Jean Claude Juncker, prime minister of Luxembourg, president of the Euro Group and Europe's longest-serving elected leader. In 2011, Mr. Juncker said, "When it becomes serious, you have to lie." What I believe he meant is this: finance is about the promises we make to each other, and to ourselves. And if the promises turn out to be unrealistic, then economics and finance turn out to be about the lies we tell each other. We want to continue believing these lies, because there is a certain loss of face if we don't. And so we continue to listen to them, and to try as hard as we can to believe in them. Of course, the economy will recover later this year, maybe the next, and as soon as the economy recovers all of our overly optimistic financial bets about the future will start paying off again. Yes, this is just a financial problem, not a social or a political one; we just need to shore up the financial system by injecting taxpayer funds. These are all lies, but they make us feel better, for the time being.

The root of the problem

At a more fundamental level, the root cause of financial collapse is usury. It may at first seem hopelessly naïve and idealistic to look at the problem of global financial collapse from what you might assume to be a moralistic and religious angle, but we will find that term is both relevant and precise. Usury—the lending of money at interest—is forbidden in the Bible, is forbidden in Islam and has been forbidden or constrained for long stretches of history. It was, for instance, banned in England since the earliest times. In the thirteenth century, Henry III confiscated usurers' possessions, then turned the usurers over to the Duke of Cornwall for flaying or disemboweling. In the fourteenth century, Edward III enacted a law that made usury a capital crime. Two centuries later, Henry VIII granted an exception for loans made at less than 10 percent interest; loans made at lower rates were not collectable by law, but the note-holder was not beheaded. This exception proved to be temporary, and Mary I, who came along thereafter, maintained a strict "Off with their heads!" policy when it came to usurers. And so it went, on and off, until 1694, when William and Mary II entered into a contract to secure a permanent loan and pledged the kingdom to pay interest on it forever. The law of Henry VIII and Elizabeth, which limited the rate of interest, remained in effect until 1854, when all the usury laws were repealed. In 2011, according to a House of Commons report, the financial sector contributed 9.4 percent of the "gross value added" in the UK economy, which is still thought to be growing at a fraction of a percent—though if the financial sector's contribution were subtracted rather than added, as I believe it should be, the economy would be shrinking. Perhaps England's goal is to give future generations a reason to thank them for their willingness to serve as a warning unto others, in which case they just might succeed.

The idea that wealth increases over time is contrary to the laws of physics. Gold, along with one or two more obscure metals and some gems, does not tarnish, but neither does it grow over time; it simply holds its value better than other objects. But everything else in the universe decays with time, losing energy and becoming more diffuse. There can be exceptions but, according to the laws of thermodynamics, these are local and temporary.

We may detest this state of affairs as much as we like, but there is precious little we can do to change it. On the contrary, we have become dependent on global finance, which is based on fiat currencies (ones unsupported by any traditional, fixed store of value such as gold, silver or land) that are loaned into existence by banks, at interest. Our savings, our pensions, the government services that keep us safe, the planting of crops for the food we eat, the financing of international trade for the imported goods on which we depend—all of these would perish if lending at interest were to cease, making the elimination of usury an act of economic suicide for any Western nation.

Nor is it possible to limit the rate of interest, because market participants require the ability to charge an interest rate that corresponds to their notion of the riskiness of the debt: the "risk premium." The reason the interest rate on Spanish sovereign debt is currently spiking to over 7 percent (a rate many consider exorbitant) is because that is the rate the market demands, because in order to sell its debt Spain must compensate bond investors for the high risk of Spanish sovereign default. In effect, Spain must insure its creditors against its own default, and when the cost of that insurance becomes too great, Spain will no longer be able to continue borrowing and will be forced to declare default. But anyone who looks at the risk premium as a sort of insurance is sketchy on the concept of insurance: insurance is where we pay someone to insure our possessions; usury is where we pay others to insure their own possessions while we remain uninsured.

Another logically faulty way to view interest on loans is as the lender's reward for not having the use of his money for the term of the loan. Well, you can't have your cake and eat it too. But if you lend that cake out at interest, the choice is between eating it or having a cake and a half as a reward for not eating it. A more normal way to behave is: if you are hungry, eat your cake; if not, share it. But to reward someone for abstinence in service of greed—the definition of miserliness—is to cultivate a vice. While we are on the subject of vice, let's not overlook the fact that lending at interest encourages laziness: the lender doesn't have to work at all, while the borrower works less, knowing that he will keep even less than what he earns once the interest is paid.

Clearly, from a moral perspective, usury does not have a leg to stand on. But moral considerations may be unjustified altogether, and usury best viewed as a form of systemic, institutionalized violence. The best way to look at lending at interest is as a form of extortion: whenever you have two groups, one that has all the money and another that has none but needs money to live, the former can extort payments from the latter for temporary use of the money. Just as with any racket, the lender's goal is to turn an episode of extortion into an arrangement of permanent tribute, by ensnaring the borrower in perpetual debt that can never be repaid and making him the lender's indentured servant.

The most reasonable overall take on lending at interest is this one: usury is a lamentable product of human weakness and a vice, but, as with most vices, impossible to eradicate, and must therefore be controlled. Thus, we set a usury rate—a maximum rate of interest—at slightly below the projected economic growth. Then the rate of growth of debt cannot exceed the rate of growth of the economy as a whole. This approach poses an interesting question as to what to do when economic growth stalls and reverses: does the usury rate remain stuck at zero, or does it go negative? The question is largely academic, since the usury rate has been repealed in many states in the US, and remains stuck far above the economic growth rate in the ones where it is still in effect. It is a vestige of a bygone era, when people still remembered the meaning of the word "usury." But enough moralizing; a bit of simple math is enough to explain why usury makes financial collapse inevitable.

The wrong math

An argument can be made that lending at any rate of interest above zero percent eventually leads to a deflationary collapse followed by a quick but painful bout of hyperinflation thrown in at the very end. A positive interest rate requires exponential growth, and exponential growth, of anything, anywhere, can only produce one outcome: collapse. This is because it quickly outpaces any sustainable physical process in the universe, outside of a few freak cases such as a sustained nuclear explosion, where the entire universe blows up, taking all of us with it, along with all of our debts.

Here is a thought experiment that illustrates this point. Suppose we solve every technical problem on Earth and go on and colonize space, found space colonies and take over the solar system, and the galaxy, and other galaxies, and the entire universe (which may not be infinite, which would give us another cause for eventual collapse, but let's ignore that for the moment). As everyone knows, space empires aren't cheap, and to get our space empire started we borrow some money, at an introductory low rate of interest (after somehow convincing the lenders that building a space empire is a low-risk proposition). Suppose we expand this empire at close to the speed of light (since it requires infinite energy to accelerate a finite mass to the speed of light). A space empire expanding even at the speed of light in all three dimensions will only grow as t^3 (time cubed). (Let's ignore the fact that initially, while taking over the solar system and the Milky Way galaxy, which are both flat, our empire will only be able to expand in two dimensions.) Meanwhile, our empire's debt will grow as D^t (debt raised to the power of time). And here is the problem: it is a mathematical certainty that as time passes (t increases), debt grows faster than empire for any initial amount of debt. Exponential growth outpaces any physical process.

$$D^t \gg t^3$$

Suppose the empire's engineers struggle mightily with this problem and, after taking on even more debt to finance research and development, eventually invent "warp speed," which flouts the laws of physics and allows our space empire to expand faster than the speed of light. But to their surprise, debt just keeps increasing. Eventually they discover the answer: even at "warp-10," which is ten times the speed of light, debt is still increasing faster than the empire:

$$D^t \gg (10t)^3$$

One brilliant engineer (who happens to be a fan of the band Spinal Tap) hits on a brilliant idea and invents "warp-11." Everyone is hopeful that this invention will give the imperial growth rate "that extra push over the cliff" and allow it to catch up with its ballooning debt. But this too is to no avail, because...

$$D^t \gg (11t)^3$$

Perplexed, the engineers wander back to their drawing boards. Then one remembers a film he saw once—*The Adventures of Buckaroo Banzai Across the 8th Dimension*—and is struck by a brilliant thought: what if they were to actually invent the circuitry that allowed Buckaroo to penetrate solid matter and travel across eight dimensions instead of just three? Then their space empire could expand across eight dimensions at the same time! They get to work, and quickly cobble together the Oscillation Overthruster (Buckaroo's fully automatic 12-volt cigarette lighter socket plug-in unit, not Dr. Lizardo's bulky foot-operated floor-mounted kludge). A bit more effort is required to compensate for strange hyper-relativistic effects when using the Overthruster at "warp-11" (Buckaroo's was only tested at just over Mach-1) but once they get the hang of it their space empire starts expanding across eight dimensions at eleven times the speed of light, quickly conquering and enslaving the Red Lectroids of Planet 10, along with billions and billions of others. Alas, it soon turns out that even this rate of growth is nowhere near fast enough to keep up with their debts, because…

$$D^t \gg (11t)^8$$

After some more fruitless exploration, the engineers decide to overcome their innate distrust of mathematicians and invite one to join the team, hoping he might be able to explain why this keeps happening to them. The mathematician asks for cocktails to be brought in and, once he sees that the engineers are sufficiently inebriated to take the edge off the bad news, he grabs a cocktail napkin and furiously scribbles out a proof (here omitted for clarity). His proof attempts to demonstrate that exponentially expanding debt will eventually outpace the rate of growth of anything finite that grows at any finite speed across any finite number of dimensions. He then goes on to say that "things get much more interesting once we move into the infinite domain," and, even more enigmatically, "we can always renormalize it later."

Shocked, they dismiss the mathematician and, grasping at straws, hire a shaman. The shaman listens to their problem and tells them to wait until sundown for an explanation. Then he asks them to shut off electricity everywhere and to join him outside in the middle of the parking lot and form a circle around him. Once their eyes adjust to the darkness, he points to the sky and says: "Look at the darkness between the stars. See it? There is nothing there. Now look at the stars. That is all there is."

Since the engineers all happen to know that what they can see is limited by the age of the universe and the speed of light, not the size of the universe, which, for all they know, could very well be infinite, they dismiss the shaman, turn the lights back on, drink some more, then nurse their hangovers. One of them (a bit of a class clown) writes "It's Debt to the Power of Time, Stupid!" on a placard and pins it up on a wall next to their cubicle farm. But then another one, a fan of *The Time Machine*, the 1895 novella by H. G. Wells, hits on yet another brilliant idea. What if they invent a time machine, and go back in time to settle the empire's debts? With that, the math would finally work in their favor, because they could go back in time and pay each loan off with just the principal. Being short of cash, they try taking out another large loan to finance the development of the time machine, but their creditors balk, declaring the project "too risky." And so the empire defaulted on its debts. Shortly thereafter, it turned out that it was no longer able to secure the financing it needed to continue interplanetary oxygen shipments, and they all died of asphyxiation.

Conclusion: borrowing at interest is fine provided you have plans for a time machine and enough cash on hand to actually build one, go back in time and pay off the loan with just the principal; it is not recommended otherwise.

Coming back to the root cause of financial collapse: usury (lending at interest) is only viable in an expanding economy; once economic growth stops, the burden of usurious debt causes it to implode. It is no accident that Dante's *Inferno* consigned usurers to the lowest pit of the seventh circle of Hell. Usury has been banned in many places and during many periods of time. Currently, in the US, some states set a usury rate, which, theoretically, if tied to that state's rate of economic growth (if any), could help prevent defaults. But then some states set a ridiculously high rate (20 percent in Massachusetts) and others don't set one at all. The correct usury rate is zero percent, because growth can never continue ad infinitum, and it is impossible to predict with any accuracy when it is going to falter, stop and reverse.

Defaults big and small

Everybody knows that default will come eventually, but nobody knows with any certainty when it will come, putting a lie to the entire notion that there are such things as "risk of default" or "risk premium." These are just reflections of the animal spirits of the beast of international finance. We do know a few things: that a national default is inevitable if a country's sovereign debt is very high but its economy is dwindling in size; that once it defaults its creditors will be forced to accept a huge loss in spite of whatever "risk premium" they were able to extract; and, perhaps most significantly, that forcing that country to pay a "risk premium" brings the day of its sovereign default that much closer in direct proportion to the size of the risk premium it is forced to pay. Charging a "risk premium" is a risk mitigation strategy designed to bring about the very thing it is supposed to mitigate against.

Sovereign collapses have occurred before. For example, Russia's sovereign default, which happened in August of 1998, was a relatively minor event. However, it precipitated the collapse of a large hedge fund, Long-Term Capital Management, which had positioned itself, via a very large number of financial contracts, to reap profits based on certain assumptions as to risk. When Russia invalidated these assumptions, due to the huge sums involved in these contracts, LTCM's inability to fulfill the contracts put the entire global financial system on the verge of locking up. The mechanism by which this happens whenever any one sufficiently large part of the system fails may seem mysterious, but it is not complicated in principle. Every market participant enters into contracts with the others, accepting small amounts of risk based on their perceptions of what that risk is. Their expectation is that small shifts will cause them to either gain or lose much less than a penny on the dollar. But when one of them fails, some number of them stand to lose not just a fraction of a penny, but the entire dollar. Since that dollar is, in turn, borrowed (the game for all of these financial players is to turn a tiny amount of capital into a huge pile of debt, and then trade on that debt), the result is cascaded failure. In 1998, the US Federal Reserve was able to step in and organize a rescue of LTCM. It was the first such rescue, but by no means the last.

But look at the "risk premium" behind the Russian default: Russia was raising money in international financial markets by selling short-term financial instruments called Government Short-term Obligations. Each time these instruments matured, the Russian government would pay them off by rolling them all over and then selling some more of them. For this to work, the interest rate had to go up each time. The default of 1998 occurred when these obligations could no longer be rolled over, even at 300 percent interest, because by that point even a very dim-witted trader could see that Russia was simply running a pyramid scheme. Three things are notable here: first, that such pyramid schemes can go on and on, until some critical mass of people panics; second, that once that panic occurs the collapse of the pyramid scheme comes very suddenly; third, that any such collapse doesn't affect just the pyramid itself, because it is a piece of a larger, global pyramid. To arrest the collapse before it engulfs the planet and reaches the point of no return, central banks and governments must step in and issue huge amounts of new debt (in effect, absorbing the risk premium).

When ten years later, as a result of the subprime mortgage crisis in the US, Lehman Brothers was forced to declare bankruptcy, the amount of new debt that had to be issued to paper over the losses and keep the financial system from collapsing has been truly staggering.

Susan George, in *Whose Crisis, Whose Future?*[8] estimates that at the rate of one dollar per second, the financial bailouts of 2008 will take half a million years to pay off. Such numbers may sound impressive, but it is far more important to understand that we are by no means at the end of the crisis that started in 2008. The bailouts have become a structural feature of global finance. The system is no longer self-stabilizing. Its sustained existence requires a continuous, concerted intervention: bailouts, "quantitative easing," "liquidity injections" and so on—all euphemisms for printing money and handing it out to insolvent financial institutions to allow them to continue functioning. Left to its own devices, the financial system would collapse instantly. Nor are these interventions sustainable: the position of the governments that are continually backstopping and papering over the losses in the financial system becomes more and more untenable every time they step in. Although at present the United States is still able to borrow at record low rates, this is not because its debt is any more repayable than Greek or Spanish debt; it is because the markets think that it will be last to default; the United States has been described as "the best-looking horse at the glue factory." It is the place where big money goes to die. With the US Federal Reserve now committed to endless money-printing and financial asset-buying, the prospects for the US dollar grow dim, and since it is still the reserve currency throughout much of the world, with it grow dim the prospects of other paper currencies around the world. A case in point: Bank of Russia has more than enough foreign currency reserves to buy up every single ruble in circulation, but such a defense in depth against a run on the ruble becomes ineffective if the foreign currency reserves themselves plummet in value, causing the ruble and the dollar to plummet together, like star-crossed lovers jumping off a cliff, embracing each other all the way down. This is why Russia (along with other countries) is now busy accumulating gold.

The end of money

Financial wizards will tell you that they have models that allow them to quantify risk, allowing them to structure complex financial instruments that are virtually risk-free. Take Myron Scholes, the Nobel Prize–winning co-author of the Black-Scholes method of pricing derivatives and the man behind the crash of Long Term Capital Management, as well as the inspiration behind much of the current financial debacle. Subsequent to the Lehman Brothers disaster, he said, "Most of the time, your risk management works. With a systemic event such as the recent shocks following the collapse of Lehman Brothers, obviously the risk-management system of any one bank appears, after the fact, to be incomplete." But such systemic events are now regular occurrences—LTCM, Lehman Brothers, AIG, MF Global, PFG.... They used a variety of models to quantify risk, and these models all fail to take into account the increasing probability and severity of such "systemic events." Thus, there is no reason to continue to assume that when economists or financial wizards use the term "risk" they know what they are talking about. They may be able to tell you a thing or two about risks to your portfolio, but they are unable to tell you anything about the systemic risks to the system which makes your portfolio worth anything at all.

Money that has been conjured into existence on a century-long tide of economic growth has nowhere to go once that growth is over, and there are plenty of indications that economic growth is at an end. Looking at the last century or so, we can observe an exponential explosion in several important parameters, all of them related. The first of these is the increase in the use of fossil fuels, most significantly the use of oil for transportation and in a wide variety of industrial applications. The second is the increase in global population. The third is the increase in debt, or, more specifically, money loaned into existence. Some economists like to think that money makes the world go 'round, but they can disabuse themselves of this notion by trying a simple experiment: stuffing some dollar bills into their gas tanks and seeing how far that gets them. A far more likely reason for economic growth is a sustained increase in the availability of natural resources, most importantly of energy. In the case of our present industrial civilization, that energy comes from fossil fuels; renewables add up to significantly less than one percent of the total. Looking at the three exponentials—energy, population and debt—it is difficult not to come to the conclusion that the three are related in a certain obvious way: energy drives economic growth, a larger economy sustains a larger population and the increase in debt follows along because of hope for a future... of even more growth.

Not too far into the first decade of the twenty-first century one of these trends came to an end: global oil use first slowed down in its upward trajectory, and more recently has stopped growing altogether. The reasons for this have to do with geology: most of the cheap, easy-to-get-at oil reserves have already been depleted. There is still plenty of oil left in the ground, but it can only be brought to market at prices guaranteed to inflict economic damage: history shows that if over six percent of GDP is spent on oil, the result is a recession. There are good reasons to think that the decline in the availability of oil is terminal: the world has been using it much faster than the petroleum geologists have been able to find new sources. There are probably no more supergiant fields—like the ones that still produce a quarter of all the oil—left to find, and these days the discovery of a field that might provide just a few days' worth of global oil consumption is a major cause for celebration.

As oil use stops growing and then declines, the economy also stops growing and then shrinks, and the pool of money that has been loaned into existence based on an optimistic outlook dries up as well. Population will eventually start to spiral downward too; my guess is that this will happen not through lower birth rates but through much higher death rates. Although we tend to think that we are very special, and indeed some of us are, humans as a species are not a special case when it comes to experiencing population explosions and die-offs. The idea that human population should increase forever is just as unfounded as the idea that it is possible to have endless economic growth on a finite planet. The exponential growth of the human population has tracked the exponential rise in the use of fossil fuels. Fossil fuel use is now declining: why shouldn't the population?

If you find this perspective distressing, let me assure you that your distress will be relieved once you stop dwelling on it. Stories told by survivors of epidemics, world wars, waves of emigration, periods of starvation and the like show that most societies are able to absorb sudden losses without much fuss at all. There was a huge spike in mortality in Russia following the Soviet collapse, but it was not directly observable by anyone outside of the morgues and the crematoria. After a few years people would look at an old school photograph and realize that half the people were gone! The most painful part of living through a die-off is realizing what is happening. But those who survive quickly put this experience behind them and are back to having children in no time.

Population, fossil fuel use and economic activity can contract gradually, but not money. This is because, unlike energy, economy or population, money is a mere concept, and once it fails, it fails catastrophically.

Banks lend money in expectation of future economic growth. Borrowers (companies and governments alike) try to survive temporary recessions and setbacks by cutting back spending and taking on even more debt. If the recession turns out to be part of a long-term trend, debt defaults become inevitable, causing a deflationary slide. Banks are designed to finance economic growth, and can survive temporary recessions, but a sustained global economic contraction is fatal to all of them. In a deflationary slide caused by their loan portfolios going bad, they go bankrupt. Their retained earnings and shareholder capital only amount to a tiny fraction of their loan portfolio, and so it doesn't take much of a loss to put them under. In a contracting economy all banks fail, but this process has been contained so far by governments and central banks that have been propping them up. This process cannot go on forever: "In the end the only backstop a central bank has is the ability to print infinite money, and if it has to go that far, it has failed because it will have destroyed confidence in the money," writes David Korowicz in *Trade-Off*.[9] The central banker's console has just one panic button on it, and it is labeled "print."

What central banks try to do is slowly erode the value of the currency they control without destroying confidence in it. In this, they have been quite successful. Before 1971, the last year a US dollar could be redeemed for gold, one US dollar was worth one-twentieth of an ounce of gold; four decades later it is worth one sixteen-hundredth of an ounce of gold, just over one percent of its 1971 value. But this is just garden-variety inflation—how fiat currencies normally behave in good times. In fact, central banks tend to have an inflation target and consider a small amount of inflation healthy. For example the Maastricht Treaty, the basis for the monetary union that created the euro, set forth an inflation target of up to three percent a year. But in bad times confidence in a fiat currency tends to get destroyed altogether, with sudden and spectacular results. In the second half of 1923 prices in Germany doubled on average every three days. Tax receipts dwindled to zero, and the state supported itself solely through printing money. A more recent bout of hyperinflation in Zimbabwe was even more spectacular, and broke all previous records. But the previous record-holder was not Germany but Hungary, where in 1946 one gold penge of 1931 came to be valued at 130 quintillion ($1.3 \cdot 10^{20}$) paper penge. Hyperinflation is not just a bad case of inflation, because it changes the definition of money;

it continues to serve as a medium of exchange (grudgingly and only for a time) but ceases to be a store of value.

There is an opposing process: deflation is the process by which the amount of money in circulation goes down relative to the amount of goods and services that are available; things get cheaper. As a practical matter this may not be a bad thing at all, and it happens all the time, for instance in high technology. Any computer you might buy today is far more powerful, and much cheaper, than any of the ones that were available twenty years ago, and few people complain about that. In fact, they've come to expect it. Nor is this limited to high-tech toys: thinking of a toy tropical island economy where cowrie shells are traded for coconuts, the ratio between the two may fluctuate based on how many cowrie shells or coconuts are produced in any given year. Before the advent of fiat currencies, when money consisted of precious metal coins, the ratio of money to goods fluctuated based on how much precious metal was mined and put into circulation relative to how good the harvests were or how much product manufacturers were able to produce. Deflation was considered perfectly normal in the nineteenth century, when the economy expanded while the amount of gold and silver stayed relatively constant. But whenever gold mining outpaced growth in other areas, as happened repeatedly during gold rushes, the ratio of money to goods and services changed in the opposite, inflationary direction. All this meant was that holders of precious metals became slightly wealthier or slightly poorer over time relative to holders of other types of assets. But these were small, gradual shifts that were not particularly disruptive. But a gold-induced deflationary collapse is not possible, while the only instance of gold-induced hyperinflation occurred during the pilgrimage to Mecca of emperor Musa I of Mali in 1324, on which he was escorted by a retinue of sixty thousand men and twelve thousand slaves carrying over a million and a half Trojan ounces of gold in bars plus eighty camels carrying many thousands of pounds of gold dust. He moved, endowing cities and commissioning mosques along the way, and leaving economic devastation in his wake.

An entirely different sort of deflation occurs in an economy where most participants carry a very large debt burden. When you lend, you risk a loss on inflation; when you borrow, you risk a loss on deflation. But the critical difference is that deflationary losses can make it impossible to continue servicing debt. As prices drop, so do business and tax revenues, and if revenues drop below the level needed to continue making payments on the debt, default rates soar and deflation turns into deflationary collapse, or hyperdeflation, in which much of the money that had been lent into existence simply disappears. This is qualitatively quite different from gradual, moderate, nineteenth-century deflation: instead of the value of money going up, it simply vanishes, because the financial system locks up and can no longer issue new credit. Without new credit, commerce comes to a standstill because most goods are shipped on credit. In turn, incomes decline precipitously and, shortly thereafter, tax revenues drop to zero. With financial institutions wiped out, governments have no ability to continue borrowing to finance deficits, which now run at close to 100 percent. Their only recourse is to turn on the printing presses, triggering hyperinflation, which tends to run its course in a few months. Once that happens we are in a brave new world: there is plenty of paper money, but it is only worth its own weight as recycled paper, finance is gone, commerce is at a standstill and government is paralyzed.

This is why the stages of collapse should be expected to occur roughly in this order: financial collapse, then commercial collapse, then political collapse. Once these first three stages have run their course, everyone's energies should be redirected toward preserving as much of society and culture as they can by rebooting into an entirely new mode: clandestine financial arrangements and transactions within exclusive circles of trust, informal face-to-face commerce largely based on tribute, barter and gift, and spontaneous self-governance at the local level.

It would be pointless to attempt to reconstitute global finance, commerce or state-legal relations to anything even vaguely resembling their pre-collapse state: these are all systems that co-evolved during the exponential growth phase of the fossil fuel era, and will have collapsed shortly after the conclusion of this growth phase. By then, the material basis for reconstituting them would no longer exist. Fossil fuels were a one-time material endowment which humanity has been using up faster and faster, along with metal ores, fresh water aquifers, fisheries and arable land. What comes next is bound to be an effort to return to life in balance with nature—or what remains of it.

Nor would there be any point in attempting to restart the global fossil fuel industry, container, tanker and bulk shipping, the US interstate highway system or the electric grid: the infrastructure supporting all of these activities was designed to operate as part of a very large, global economy, and will exhibit severe *negative* economies of scale once the economy becomes small, local and poor. It is not a reasonable proposition to maintain a fleet of container ships and a network of container ports if the ships only sail once every few years, and even then lightly loaded. Nor is it reasonable to maintain an oil refinery if it only operates a few weeks out of the year. It may be possible to operate parts of the electric grid, for a time, for a few hours a day, but much of the benefit of having an electric grid goes away once the electricity supply is no longer reliable. It may also be possible to make use of certain sections of existing railroad track and rolling stock. But the main use of the old, industrial-era infrastructure will be as a plentiful source of scrap, which is sure to be reused in entirely new, improvised ways.

Options for cashing out

And there we have it: a global financial system founded on interest-based lending and the assumption of endless growth, and it is starting to look to many people like that endless growth is already failing to materialize. It would seem logical to think that the financial system is becoming a dangerous place for investors to keep their money, would it not? Suppose that you have some money—be it cash in a bank account, bonds, stocks or gold in a bank vault. And suppose that you do not want that money to evaporate in a puff of smoke—because you think you might need it later, or simply because you are fond of it. And suppose that you have been following along and see reasons to think that this financial system is rigged to blow. Well, then, aren't you being a tiny bit irrational, keeping all your eggs in a basket labeled "finance," which happens to be in free-fall? Some of the eggs have already cracked, just from the turbulence: LTCM, Lehman Brothers, AIG, MF Global, PFG and, as I write this, Knight Capital.

Those of us who still have some savings face difficult choices, most of them unsatisfactory. We can continue to entrust our money to financial institutions, even though the results of doing so already tend to be poor, and are likely to become progressively worse, all the way to total loss of one's savings. Many people who have entrusted their retirement savings to financial institutions are finding out that they can no longer afford to retire. Others find that they lose access to their money altogether: those who entrusted it to the now defunct MF Global have seen their money confiscated, to pay for what are essentially private gambling debts incurred by MF Global's head, Jon Corzine, former senator and governor of New Jersey. Although dipping into the till to cover your private bets remains illegal, he remains at large, along with an entire wolf pack of elite financial managers who now feel empowered to do more of the same. They have been able to pay off politicians with political campaign funds and have been granted informal and unspoken yet complete immunity from prosecution, setting the scene for even bigger confiscations of investor capital. With the risk of legal repercussions so small and the temptation to steal so large, why would any of them not take advantage? What do they have to do to stop people from entrusting them with their savings? Put up a neon sign that says "We steal your money"? It could even be argued that, at this point, they are duty-bound to follow the instinctive drive to steal from those who still trust them, as predators are evolutionarily duty-bound to cull the slow and the weak from the herd to keep it healthy.

Once we rub the sleep out of our eyes and realize that we are risking total loss, we can attempt to take matters into our own hands and invest our money in some part of the global economy that we think is still destined for rapid growth. For example, shale gas seemed like a good investment just a little while back; not so much any more, now that Chesapeake Energy, the biggest player in the field, has decided to cut its losses and stop drilling for gas. (You'd have to have a high tolerance for contributing to environmental devastation that accompanies shale gas drilling. You'd also have to be a bit daft to invest in producing gas that can only be sold at a loss.) Given the overall economic landscape, even where there is growth, it is likely to run its course rather quickly. These are not so much investments as "plays" — that play out just as quickly as shale gas wells. Another economic sector that is experiencing growth is firearms; after each shooting spree, firearm sales go up. (After the recent school massacre in Newtown, Connecticut, stores quickly sold out of the Bushmaster assault rifle which that murderer of children happened to like.) There are probably profits to be made in firearms, but again, profiting from (potential) murder may not be everyone's cup of tea, and it is hard to argue that there are not enough guns, in the US especially. Survival goods is another growth industry that is less reprehensible than any of the above, although these are mostly purchased and stockpiled out of fear, and profiting from people's fears still doesn't qualify as good works. In any case, at the end of each of these risky "plays," if you are lucky, you will be left with a bit more money than you started out with, that you won't know what to do with next.

If your tolerance for profiting from fear and environmental mayhem is low, you could also invest in green technologies. Market research shows that there is a great reservoir of pent-up eco-guilt out in the general population for marketers and advertisers to exploit. But you would be using up nonrenewable resources, used to make and sell "green" consumer products, to help people feel less guilty about ruining the environment, all the while topping up the landfills with "green" trash, and this, again, poses something of a moral dilemma: if you want to help save the environment and prepare yourself for a life without access to consumer goods, then you probably shouldn't try to do so by selling, or buying, consumer goods. A much better plan is to buy as little as possible, but it doesn't solve the problem of what to do with large sums of money. And the greenest technology of all is not embedded in consumer products; it is used by green living things called trees, and relies on certain magical properties of a green substance called chlorophyll. You could plant some trees, I suppose, just to be "green" and to feel good about yourself, but trees don't need us. Trees plant themselves (with some help from squirrels, birds and other animals). Plus they are not much of a financial investment.

And so, there is a case to be made for "cashing out": pulling your money out of the economy altogether and buying up objects that hold their value over time. In a deflationary environment everything loses value and everyone becomes poorer, but holding onto objects of value may allow you to become poor more slowly, and end up less poor than those who allowed their savings to evaporate entirely by entrusting them to a financial institution or holding on to cash. Yes, you'd lose your savings too, but not all of them, and not all at once.

You should hold on to some cash, for purely didactic purposes. I remember my great-grandmother, who passed away when I was seven, and I remember playing with her little hoard of *kerenki*—ruble notes in ridiculously high yet worthless denominations that had been issued by the Russian Provisional Government, under the leadership of Prime Minister Alexander Kerensky, whose tenure lasted from July to November 1917, and who then fled the country dressed either as a sailor or as a woman (reports vary). I was quite taken with the ten-thousand-ruble note, which seemed like a lot of money to me at the time, and was very surprised to hear that it was completely worthless and that I could take one and use it as a bookmark (which I did). It was not until the 1990s that Russia again issued a note in that denomination, which likewise became worthless soon after it was printed.

And so, you too should hold on to a few dollar, or euro, or ruble or yuan notes, in the highest denominations available at the time they all become worthless, as a keepsake. Then you will be able to show them to your great-grandchildren and say, "Can you imagine, this ugly piece of paper was once a prized possession!" And your great-grandchildren will no doubt think that you are a little bit senile, but then they will probably think that anyway, because by then you probably will be. But it certainly won't be helpful to hold on to multiple shoeboxes full of old currency, because then your great-grandchildren will think that you are in fact insane, because no sane person would be hoarding such trash. It is important that they don't think that, because the lesson is an important one: chances are that during their lifetimes some tin-pot pseudo-nationalist leader will print up ugly slips of paper with pictures of dead people, Masonic symbols and big numbers, and attempt to charge people for using them as a medium of exchange in all transactions, and your great-grandchildren need to know, from an early age, that it is a scam. It is an official scam, backed up by the threat of violence, but it is still just a scam.

They also need to know how to work around that scam. The main trick is to refuse to hold on to the slips of paper or entrust them to an institution. While they still have value, they should be used to buy objects that do not lose value over time. The most obvious ones that we often hear propagandized as the correct investment for our times are gold and silver bullion (one-ounce coins) and bars. (Here I mean physical metal held by you, not metal held by a financial institution, and not notional metal that only exists on a piece of paper issued by a financial institution.)

But there are several problems with hoarding gold and silver. First, these things are actual money—not the fake paper money printed by governments, but a perpetual store of wealth, based on their relative scarcity in the Earth's crust and the advanced state of depletion of gold and silver ores as global resources (gold is now mined in concentrations of as little as three parts per million of crushed rock; silver is concomitant to copper and other metal mining, and is also becoming quite diffuse). The material in ancient Persian or Byzantine coins is the same as the material in a Maple Leaf or a Krugerrand. Its value, in weight of metal, never varies, plus it can accrue numismatic value over time. Being actual money, gold and silver compete with the fake paper money printed by governments, and governments don't like that. One of the prerogatives of being a government is seigniorage, which is the ability to profit by controlling the currency, and precious metals erode this ability. Most of the time governments remain unconcerned about this, since the overall volume of gold is not high enough to significantly impact their operations, but when they find their paper currency undergoing rapid devaluation, or find themselves in a solvency trap, or run into other financial dire straits, they are apt to confiscate all the gold held by their citizens, as President Roosevelt did in April of 1933, using Executive Order 1602. Those who wished to access their safety deposit boxes could only do so in the presence of a government agent, who promptly removed any gold found therein.

Precious metal coins and bars are also highly susceptible to theft: they are a very concentrated, portable store of value. While not exactly ugly, they are rarely exhibited, being far too gaudy to put on show, and are usually hoarded in secret. They are relatively uncommon, and it is often difficult to find buyers or sellers for them among people one trusts, forcing one to conduct rather sensitive business with strangers. They are also liable to prove useless: in a socially disrupted situation people often lose the ability to do anything at all with their hoard of coins, leaving them buried someplace cryptic, such as in the garden under a statue. To this day pots of late-Roman gold are periodically dug up in England during excavations of Roman villas; the residents of these villas were unable to derive any benefit from their hoards as their empire collapsed and the Dark Age closed in on them.

That said, gold coins are uniquely useful in a number of unusual situations: paying a ransom, buying a passage on a ship directly from the captain, and other transactions where their compactness, undisputed value and untraceable nature make them the tool of choice. But they are just that: a tool, lacking in any aesthetic or cultural value, deriving all their perceived value from the relative scarcity of the metal of which they are made. They have to be kept hidden, because they inspire theft. Putting them on display is both risky and in poor taste. As with paper currency, their generic, impersonal nature makes them a thoughtless gift. In short, gold coins are tacky.

There are many other objects that can and do serve as concentrated stores of value, which can be pressed into service as a medium of exchange if the need arises, and which can be practically useful, aesthetically pleasing, culturally significant and even highly personal. They derive their value from their beauty or rarity or uniqueness, their quality of fine craftsmanship or their usefulness in skilled hands. Objects made of precious metals and precious or semiprecious stones, such as jewelry, bracelets, cigarette cases and snuff boxes, are closest to a form of currency and often function as money, but they can derive a large part of their value from their rarity, quality of craftsmanship or unusual provenance. Silver plate, paintings, statuettes, vases, rare books, musical instruments, weapons, antiques and collectibles of all kind and objects of historical significance all hold significant value over long periods of time. Although such objects can be stolen, confiscated or looted, as often happens in times of political upheaval, occupation or civil war, unlike gold coins, they tend to be unique or distinctive, and can sometimes be later identified and restored to their rightful owner. Their distinctiveness and uniqueness also make them good, thoughtful gifts.

There are many other, more diffuse stores of value. At this point, it seems well and truly uncontroversial to say that we have every reason to expect that concentrated forms of energy will become scarcer and increase in price over time. This would indicate that energy itself is a good store of value over time, though there are few options for storing it directly. Crude oil keeps for millions of years (obviously) but is quite useless unless you happen to own an oil refinery. Gunpowder is certainly energetic, and it keeps forever if kept dry, but since it cannot be used (safely) for cooking, heating or illumination, it is of limited use economically. The fuels that keep forever are solids and nonvolatile liquids, and these are few in number: coal and charcoal, alcohol in glass containers, firewood, paraffin wax and butane. Diesel and kerosene biodegrade, gasoline and higher distillates are too volatile, gases such as methane and propane are expensive to store in large quantities and leak out over time. Energy carriers in solid or nonvolatile, nonbiodegradable form can be stockpiled and used as a store of value, and it is possible to imagine an austere time when a brick of paraffin is more valuable than a gold brick, which has no use value.

There are many other objects which require a lot of energy to make and which will, over time, increase in value as energy itself increases in value. Examples of standardized, generic products that can be stockpiled in bulk include aluminum and copper sheet, galvanized chain and wire rope, fasteners and rigging supplies. Sometimes such stockpiles already exist, but people don't realize their value. I was once hauled out and doing repairs on my boat at a boatyard that had seen better times. There were piles of hurricane wreckage hastily bulldozed together. The rest of it was crowded with derelict hulls of long-abandoned yachts, with trees growing through some of them. Other, slightly more intact hulls were inhabited by people who sometimes worked at the boatyard, but only enough to afford rent and beer, and who mostly just sat around on lawn chairs and drank beer. The boatyard was across the street from a ghetto and was guarded by fierce junkyard dogs. When the boatyard's owner started lamenting the sorry state of his finances, I asked him whether he counted in the value of the lead ballast in the keels of all the derelict sailboat hulls he was storing (lead prices happened to be spiking at the time). I did some back-of-the-envelope calculations for him, and his eyes lit up. He was sitting on a goldmine (lead mine) and didn't even know it! I didn't get charged for too many incidentals from that point on.

Beyond such generally useful items, it is possible to think of more strategic ways of pre-deploying capital by creating useful stockpiles. For example, in an area with good soil and dependable rainfall it may make sense to stockpile tools used in farming—spades, pitchforks, hoes, scythes and so on—and wait for the day when people once again take to growing their own food the old-fashioned way, without mechanical assistance. Or you might bet on the rebirth of sail transport and stockpile the industrial products needed for building and outfitting cargo sailing vessels for coastal trade (my particular area of interest).

These and many other stores of value are even today much better than ephemeral, notional value held by digits inside computers at banks and finance companies. They are physical, tangible resources rather than hypothetical ones whose putative value is predicated on the continuation of a status quo which we know to be precarious and unsustainable. Once fiat currencies fail, physical possession of such stores of value makes it possible for a community to create an internal medium of exchange out of thin air. I will discuss this in detail later.

Alternatives to money

For a community to be able to maintain its own independent store of value and its own medium of exchange based on trust, that community first has to exist. Furthermore, it has to be a strong, cohesive community that shares a common a sense of identity and has compelling mutual interests, mutual respect and trust. This is by no means a given. For such a community to take shape, it must first be made up of strong families. This is, likewise, by no means a given. Strong families, in turn, require strong family ties: what God hath joined together let no banker, investment advisor, accountant, estate attorney or probate judge rent asunder. Before we discuss the specific ways in which families and communities can survive the demise of financial institutions and fiat currency, we must discuss what such families and communities must be like in order to even try.

In the social order that prevails in the economically developed countries, economic relationships within the family have been under-emphasized. Most of the services that families formerly provided for themselves and their neighbors, on an informal basis, have been professionalized: everything from child care to elderly care is done by underpaid strangers at great private and public expense. Nothing has been spared in the dismantlement of the extended family: each individual or, at most, each married couple has a separate bank account and little, if any, property is held in common. The ideal toward which we all strive forces each person to function as a lonely, helpless individual at the mercy of an impersonal system. The trend is to have a financial mediator inserted into every transaction. No matter how intimate or personal or innate the behavior—be it sleeping with your spouse or breast-feeding your infant—we now have a wide range of professionals to advise us, but only after charging your credit card.

Let us try to put finance in its place. It is understandable if a bank is involved in shifting real estate or another large transaction requiring vast sums to be held in escrow, although even this is only necessary when dealing with strangers. But the trend is toward a financial "tax" on every single transaction, no matter how small: when you pay with a plastic card, or via one of the many kinds of e-money, you are feeding a system that provides convenience but at a cost. If you always cash your entire paycheck and proceed to pay everyone with cash, you run the risk of getting robbed, once in a great while, and losing a large sum all at once; when you leave your money in the bank and pay with plastic, you don't run the risk of being robbed—it's a dead certainty that you are being robbed every time you swipe that card, to the tune of 2.5 percent, which is the equivalent of being robbed of your entire weekly paycheck once a year. In order to accept credit cards, merchants are forced to raise their prices by the corresponding amount; however, they rarely offer cash discounts (less than ten percent of gas stations still do so). Note, however, how it doesn't take much of a financial disruption to cause "Cash only" signs, hastily drawn on sheets of cardboard, to go up everywhere; cash becomes king overnight, and those who are credit-rich but cash-poor tend to get left out.

But an even bigger chunk is taken out of your hide by the creeping tendency to finance everything. If you buy a house with 20 percent down and pay off the rest over many years, you will have paid more than double the purchase price—the equivalent of having your every other mortgage check stolen. Alternatively, if you rent a smaller place than the house you eventually wish to buy, save the difference between the rent and the mortgage, and, when you are ready, use it to buy the house with cash, then you will come to own the house free and clear at least twice as fast. Once there is a house within the family that is owned free and clear, whether it was bought the right way (with savings) or the wrong way (with a mortgage), one would think that people would do their best to avoid going into debt again, keeping the house within the family for many generations: with each generation, the parents would pass the house on to their grown children and downsize in place, taking up just one room or, if the house gets too crowded, renting a room nearby. But that is not the pattern we normally see. Instead, the grown children move out and get mortgages of their own, then the parents get a reverse mortgage to finance their retirement, or sell the house and buy a condo, and all of this continues until they have all been bled dry, foreclosed and bankrupted. All the while, chances are that they have also been financing the purchases of cars, making financed, monthly payments on annual insurance policies, revolving credit card debt and making payments on all sorts of installment loans. Oh, and let's not forget, the parents probably held on to their soon-to-be-worthless private retirement funds while letting their children go into debt on cars, houses and college tuition. They have been paying interest with every breath they take! You have to be a saint to *not* want to rob such people! The madness!

I hope that this makes me sound hopelessly old-fashioned—to most of you, because some of us were lucky enough to have had grandparents or great-grandparents who tried (most likely unsuccessfully) to instill in us the ethos of saving before spending, of paying everything forward, of never going into debt (unless it's a real emergency, and even then only if you are certain of your ability to extinguish the debt quickly) and of never doing business with people you don't know personally. Such people, in former times, and to this day in older, more traditional cultures, are called the elders. In societies with local, informal systems of self-governance, the elders are often the only form of authority, both within and outside the family. To a society that worships at the altar of youth such a practice may smack of reverse age discrimination: a leadership requirement of being old? But old people often make better candidates for positions of authority than the young. They are less self-interested and less easily corrupted, because opportunities for self-gratification and wicked temptations become fewer and farther between as we age. Old people are cautious, by virtue of the fact that they are still alive (the incautious tend to die young). They care more about the future (their grandchildren) and their legacy (what their grandchildren stand to inherit) than about anything else. They may also be wise, but wisdom is entirely optional; what is important is that they lack certain youthful qualities that can make leadership lethal: drive and ambition, reckless abandon, impulsiveness, competitive zeal and an illusion of personal immortality. When it comes to leadership qualities, the best teacher is not experience; it is attrition. Ninety percent of leadership is showing up—once you have survived long enough to become an elder, with your health and your reputation intact. Of course, in a society that worships youth, where old people try to "keep up" with the young and almost everyone survives, randomly, through no merit or fault of their own, and gets to try and try again even after they fail decisively, death and failure lose their didactic value. There is no fool like an old fool, and old fools don't make good elders.

What I am laying out here may be starting to seem hopelessly idealistic. After all, strong, extended families that pool all their resources and are presided over by elders, of the sort that could band together, form a community and achieve self-governance via a council of elders, may seem like something from a century long gone. But they aren't; there are plenty of communities of this sort still to be found around the world. They just happen to be those families and communities that have not become addicted to economic growth, either because of their conservatism or their adverse circumstances, or both. They will be around following the collapse. But families and communities of this sort may be rather difficult to reconstitute within a Western European or a North American context of atomic families, parents who can hardly wait until their children grow up and "become independent," alienated children who yearn to grow up and abandon their parents, elders not worthy of the name who only care about preserving their "independence" for which they have neither the savings nor the mental fortitude—an anonymous crowd of pseudo-rugged individualists abjectly dependent on the consumer economy and government services for survival. This gaping chasm between what should exist and what does exist is going to be very difficult to bridge. Those people whose only experience is of surfing a bubble economy, abandoning their relatives and their communities and throwing themselves on the mercy of global finance, are like millions of kittens up tall trees, with no fire brigade available to rescue them and no ability to climb back down on their own. Because, you see, they have been taught that these are magic trees that always grow faster than they can climb them.

Far from sketching out some sort of financial utopia, I am describing a successful human cultural universal: a family is three generations at a minimum, living together, pooling resources and allocating them in the best interests of the whole. A community is a band of such families capable of self-governance. The traditional form of self-governance, for the reasons outlined above, is a council of elders. I will present much more material on the operation of such families and communities in the chapters on social and cultural collapse, including detailed case studies. Here my goal is to describe how they handle financial matters in the absence of banks, investment companies or legal access to an official medium of exchange. In doing so, I wish to avoid appearing fanciful or idealistic and begging the inevitable question: "Where on earth would people trust each other enough to do this?" Because here's the answer: in a world where the simple words "I knew your grandmother" carry more weight than any VIP pass, college degree or famous surname.

This is a world that exists all around us, unnoticed, but it is not the one most of us have been taught to see or know how to enter.

How we did it

My family left the USSR early in 1976. We were allowed to leave because Moscow wished to comply with Washington's Jackson–Vanik amendment to Title IV of the 1974 Trade Act (repealed in 2012 and replaced with the far more obnoxious Magnitsky Act). This amendment denied most favored nation status to certain countries with non-market economies that restricted emigration. Moscow used this as an opportunity to open a safety valve, allowing for a relatively amicable departure of certain undesirables and dissidents; Washington used it to incite brain drain, attracting Soviet specialists to come and work in the US with the largely empty promise of secure professional employment. We received an uncharacteristically cordial phone call to inform us that our exit papers were ready from Sergeant Boreiko of the Interior Ministry, on Christmas Eve, 1975; such details are impossible to forget. The emigration was ostensibly justified as facilitating the reunification of families, but this was largely faked: a service existed that manufactured fake invitations from fake Israeli grandmothers. These the Soviet authorities accepted unquestioningly, even from people who were not the tiniest bit Jewish.

My parents had not been able to save much, but our family as a whole had substantial savings, in Soviet rubles, some of which we wanted to take with us. But there was no official mechanism for transferring money abroad. Soviet citizens were not allowed to own foreign currency, and rubles were a closed currency that could not be exchanged or even transported outside the USSR. But the transfers took place anyway, using a variety of methods.

The first method was to use the rubles to buy jewelry, cameras and watches, which we sold off as needed once we arrived in the West. Soviet 35mm SLR cameras, with their rugged mechanics and superb Carl Zeiss lenses (the Zeiss Jena factory having been relocated from East Germany to Kiev after World War II), were particularly valued in the West. Another method of money transfer came into use later, once our wave of emigration had settled in the West in considerable numbers. Some of us wanted to send money to our relatives in Russia; others wanted to receive money from their relatives in Russia. The solution was simple: transfer dollars between the two parties on the US end and rubles, in the opposite direction, between the same two parties, on the USSR end. The sum of the transfer was the lesser of the two sums made available by the two parties. This sort of barter-transfer was available only sporadically, because it relied on coincident wants, and the wants didn't often coincide in timing or in amount. The fallback was to continue exporting objects of value by placing them in the baggage of new immigrants, and importing objects of value via foreign visitors bringing lavish gifts.

Once the émigrés were able to obtain citizenship in the West, another possibility opened up for transferring money out of Russia—by tricking the Soviet government into disgorging its dollars. A sum of money would be "airdropped" into the USSR using one of the techniques described above. A Soviet citizen would then will that sum of money to a close relative living in a foreign country. Once the Soviet citizen had passed away, the Soviet government was compelled, under international law, to assist with expatriation of the inheritance. What made this trick particularly useful was that the Soviets applied a ridiculously high "vanity" exchange rate—close to one dollar to one ruble—which grossly overvalued the ruble. This exchange rate was not normally used for financial transactions and existed only to boast about the strong Soviet currency in the press and make the Soviet economy look bigger on paper.

Keep in mind that all of these transactions were not just informal but illegal under Soviet law, and took place under the watchful eye of the KGB. All international telephone conversations were listened in on; all letters were steamed open and read. Everyone had to be very careful to avoid getting caught. It was a badge of honor to be sent to a prison colony as a political prisoner. It was quite another to go there as a common (economic) criminal. (It was still a badge of honor, but only among professional criminals.) Thus, none of these transactions could be arranged in clear text, and, with the participants stuck on the opposite sides of the Iron Curtain (émigrés were not allowed to travel back to the Soviet Union until 1988, and few Soviet citizens were allowed to travel abroad), face-to-face negotiations were impossible.

I am sure that certain readers will at this point recollect schlocky American Cold War novels they wasted their time reading, or automatically conjure up secret codes and communications technologies used to play a spy vs. spy cat-and-mouse game with the KGB, while others will want to think that the KGB was sufficiently incompetent and/or demoralized to just let all that secret communication slip by (I assure you that it was not). Well, having seen how it all works in practice, I am happy to disabuse you of all such notions. The only technologies involved were spoken word and pen and paper; the good results were achieved thanks to mental fortitude and solidarity.

The technique I saw used was an instance of steganography, which "is the art and science of writing hidden messages in such a way that no one, apart from the sender and intended recipient, suspects the existence of the message, a form of security through obscurity. The word is of Greek origin and means 'concealed writing' from the Greek words *steganos* (στεγανός), meaning 'covered or protected', and *graphei* (γραφή), meaning 'writing.'"[10] There is the outer, public message, which is innocuous or insipid or annoyingly redundant (except for a few easily overlooked details); then there is the inner, private message, which can only be discerned by the intended recipient, who has prior knowledge. The key security feature is that the recipient needs to know that the message is a message at all, never mind decipher it.

My mother and my grandmother kept up a voluminous correspondence augmented by regular telephone conversations. They discussed everything from the weather to their reading to what they ate for breakfast. They also seemed to be curiously obsessed with pieces of porcelain: which tea set was a present from whom, who would have liked it, who had owned a similar one at one time or another, from whom they may have purchased it and how much they may have paid for it, how many cups were cracked or broken, whether they could be repaired, who was the clumsy one and broke a cup, who had been particularly skillful at gluing together a broken cup so that it is now as good as new and so on and so forth, all seemingly innocent prattle between two dotty women reminiscing about sentimental bits of bric-à-brac—but for someone in the know, laden with secret meanings. Cups were thousands of dollars. Tea sets were tens of thousands. Cracked cups were expenses incurred. Broken cups were deals that had fallen through. Any persons mentioned were not referred to by full name but by informal diminutives and endearments and referenced not to actual places and times but to private, shared memories. But there were also passages of general interest, such as soup or cake recipes, sometimes supplied with a passing comment addressed directly to the KGB censor, such as "Others who are reading this might find this interesting as well." Who could possibly suspect secret, nefarious, conspiratorial intent in someone so seemingly guileless? Not even the KGB!

Chits, specie and stock-in-trade

How does one trade when there is no bank and no currency? Carrying around bulky bits of metal is both inconvenient and risky, plus there usually isn't enough metal to go around, to represent all of the objects that need to be traded. Printing a local paper currency backed by precious metals is sometimes a possibility, but what if there is no authority that is sufficiently powerful and trusted to carry out such a task? And what if there isn't enough precious metal on hand to back such a currency at 100 percent? What is needed is an improvised, ad hoc scheme that is independent of any central authority and is based on limited trust between trading partners.

James Clavell describes such a scheme in his 1993 novel *Gai-Jin* (Japanese for "foreigner"), set in Japan of the 1860s. The story is set shortly after Commodore Perry used the threat of naval bombardment to force Japan to open itself up to international trade. Most of the action takes place in a small trading outpost populated by American, British, French, Dutch and Russian traders trying to import and sell their wares to the Japanese. The traders mistrusted each other but, living close together within a single makeshift community, they were also forced to cooperate. With their home ports many months away by sea and with communications delayed and sometimes unreliable, they could not rely on having up-to-date knowledge of financial markets or commodities prices. They were also loathe to use each other's national coinage, since that would give an unfair advantage to the most populous group (at the time, the British).

Instead of using a currency, they used chits (slips of paper), backed by specie (gold and silver) and stock-in-trade (all sorts of valuables and commodities). Chits are slips of paper bearing a date, from whom, to whom, amount (usually stated in weight of silver or gold) and a signature. At the end of each month, accountants would net out all the chits and, as needed, arrange a transfer of specie between vaults, under armed guard. If there wasn't enough specie (as was often the case), stock-in-trade was pressed into service to settle debts at the end of each month; if there wasn't enough stock-in-trade, the debt could be carried forward, or certain other property could be exchanged or liquidated to make up the shortfall. Thus, a medium of exchange can be summoned instantaneously ex nihilo, the necessary and sufficient ingredients being pens and slips of paper, gold and silver coins, and various other things that have a recognized value.

In this scheme, there is no currency in circulation, no need for an intaglio press, or armored cars to drive bags of currency around, or bank branches or ATM machines to dispense it or police to fight counterfeiting. There are no bankers to feed, and not even accountants if everyone nets out their own chits at the end of the month. Chits can be stolen, but this hardly ever happens, since they are of no value to the thief. All chits are netted out at the end of each month, so there is no currency in circulation and no debt that can be carried over automatically. But people can also agree to hold one or more chits over a month's time, if there is no urgency in settling, or if some circumstance makes settling that month inconvenient. They can also agree to tear up a chit if a certain trade went badly, for the sake of saving the relationship. There is no concept of legal tender backed by the "full faith and credit of the government"—and this is quite useful during times when the government has neither faith nor credit, does not provide any useful services or does not exist. There is just a promise between two individuals, one of whom trusts the other enough to extend a bit of interest-free credit until the end of the month. This system is secure because none of the participants carries anything valuable or negotiable on their person. And it scales up to arbitrarily large transactions, because numbers on chits can be arbitrarily large.

Similar systems are used within criminal groups, by black market operators and in other cases where the use of an official currency or a banking institution is either inconvenient or risky. In these cases, the system is modified in two ways. First, there are no chits. Second, there is no monthly (or any other regularly scheduled) settlement cycle. The chits are a risk because they create a paper trail; it is far safer for people to hold the transactions and the tallies in their heads, and to rely on their word of honor (there is enforced honor among thieves, because the alternative to an amicable settlement is a violent one). The monthly settlement cycle is a risk because then everyone knows when stores of value are going to be changing hands, and can schedule their heists accordingly. In critical cases, the exchange can even be staged as a mock robbery (to make property officially disappear from public records) or a casual lose-find operation ("Darling, look what I found wandering in the woods today!") or any number of other ploys that allow the two parties to deny that they had any knowledge of or dealings with each other. The indications are that such a system is quite resilient, insensitive to being driven underground and can prevent governments, mafia and other violent actors from muscling in on the action.

A likely endgame

Here is a likely endgame for the finance and import-driven global economy. Supposing global finance suffers another "whoopsie" à la 2008: a "credit event," money markets lock up and so on.... This scenario has been rehearsed once already, and nothing has been done to prevent it from happening again except for some temporary stopgaps consisting of national governments sopping up all the bad debt. What is different now is that all the governments have already shot all of their magic bailout bullets. The guilty parties are still at large, richer than they were before this crisis and probably thinking that the next crisis will make them even richer. The last time it happened, President Bush the younger famously declared: "If money isn't loosened up, this sucker could go down," and money was indeed loosened up, and is getting looser all the time. But how loose is too loose? At some point we are bound to hear, from across two oceans, the shocking words "Your money is no good here."

Fast forward to a week later: banks are closed, ATMs are out of cash, supermarket shelves are bare and gas stations are starting to run out of fuel. Nothing useful happens when people swipe their credit cards at the few stores that remain open (not that anyone is shopping, except for food and ammo). And then something happens: the government announces that they have formed a crisis task force, and will nationalize, recapitalize and reopen the banks, restoring confidence. In short, the government will attempt to single-handedly operate their corner of the global economy by other means. The banks reopen, under heavy guard, and thousands of people get arrested for attempting to withdraw their savings. Banks close, riots begin. Next, the government decides that, to jump-start commerce, it will honor deposit guarantees and simply hand out cash. They print and arrange for the cash to be handed out. Now everyone has plenty of cash, but there is still no food in the supermarkets or gasoline at the gas stations because by now the international supply chains have broken down and the delivery pipelines are empty. Restarting them requires international credit, which requires commercial banks to start operating normally, and that in turn requires functioning supply chains and retail.

Cold-starting instructions

Supposing you knew that this was going to happen, and moved yourself and your extended family to a place where you know and trust some people. You have invested your time and savings in creating a resilient network of friends with whom you can cooperate and barter, to survive the shutdown of the global economy in relative comfort and style. The national currency is plentiful but only worth its weight in recycled paper, making it a bit bulky for transacting business. You can survive through barter, but this is often less than optimal; you really want some sort of private medium of exchange.

You would like to create a system of the sort described above: a closed, one-to-one trading system based on chits and specie, except that you are quite short of specie. Well, to jump-start the system you can pledge anything of value: jewelry, collectibles, antiques, taxidermy, curios, weapons, boxes of ammo, tools, shrunken heads, baseball cards, bottles of wine, celebrity autographs, whale penis bones...the possibilities are virtually endless. The value of any one piece may vary depending on the person with whom you are trading: a grandfather's medals are more valuable to someone who knew him; Mack the Knife's knife holds memories precious to one of Mackie's former business associates. With each person, you agree to trade by pledging certain items for settling whatever trade imbalances occur from time to time, as needed. You appraise them at the time they are pledged. And then you write each other chits as needed. Other people can be included, until the trading system encompasses an entire group; others can be temporarily excluded while they are unable to settle. But the act of exclusion is up to each person: each person decides, in the case of each transaction, whether to accept a chit or not.

One of the benefits of this system is that it avoids the otherwise inevitable devaluing of one's possessions. When money is in short supply, by default people resort to bartering their possessions for what they need, driving down their value. With this approach, items of value are kept off the market for as long as possible, and then exchanged rather than sold between people who have agreed on their fair value when they were initially pledged.

Once such a trading system becomes sufficiently large, it starts to make sense to create a community vault to store and safeguard the more concentrated stores of value. Then, to settle at the end of the month, nothing has to be physically moved. When communities decide to trade with each other, they may enter into an agreement to store valuables in each other's vaults. Then the two communities can trade using chits, and settle without moving anything. If a significant trade imbalance develops between the two communities, then a single trans-fer between the two vaults, under heavy guard, suffices to correct it.

If this system seems medieval to you, that's because it is. And then came Western imperialism, and imperial nation-states grew rich on in-dustrialization driven by fossil fuels, plantation economies to produce commodities and captive markets to absorb manufactured products. Eventually there came along the global economy, with globalized fi-nance, tangled supply chains spanning the entire planet and labor ar-bitrage that moves production to lowest-cost countries. Transnational financial institutions and corporations supplanted national govern-ments as the ultimate centers of power. Huge trade imbalances became expressed in piles of paper representing sovereign debt, which derives its value from the sovereign's ability to continue taking on more debt faster and faster; this, in turn, is only possible as long as there is sus-tained economic growth.

And so, a reversion to baseline should not seem too unexpected. That baseline is the rich and ancient tradition of trade and finance that predates all of these modern developments. It only works at a smaller scale, but that is exactly what is needed to bring a local economy back to life amid the wreckage of the global economy. It does require a very different skill set than what universities and business schools teach, and a very different mindset to go with it. But that is, I hope, why you are reading this book.

Beware financial despotism

The use of objects of value in trade predates all of the social institutions that have evolved around money and the use of money by many thousands of years. The earliest examples of what we could consider money, in the form of "coin of the realm" bearing an image of the sovereign, were introduced to streamline the process of extracting tribute from the population, by levying taxes denominated in the coin of the realm. This, in turn, forced the population to either work for wages paid in money or to trade goods in exchange for money, in order to be able to pay the taxes. The sovereign usually tried to maintain a monopoly on coinage, using to his advantage the ability to coin as much or as little as the situation required. In more recent years, the prerogative of seigniorage—of coining or printing money—has been severely eroded by the financial markets: now governments in need of money to finance their fiscal deficits are forced to attract private capital with promises to pay as much interest as that private capital demands. However, the creation of money remains a state monopoly to this day, as one Bernard Von NotHaus, the architect behind Liberty Dollars, has recently discovered. He was sentenced to fifteen years. His transgression—minting and circulating a currency designed to compete with the US dollar—was likened to domestic terrorism.

But the urge to create an alternative currency is always present, given the profligate use of the printing press by virtually all governments. Many people like money, but dislike the fact that the system is rigged in favor of governments and against savers. The US dollar has lost 8000 percent of its value over the last 41 years since the US abandoned the gold standard. Those who save and do not wish to see their savings evaporate are forced to gamble in the financial markets. What many people want is honest money—money that doesn't lose value over time and isn't controlled by corrupt, greedy government officials. To this end, the classical liberalist economist and philosopher Friedrich Hayek proposed to denationalize currency and to undermine the state monopoly of money by introducing a currency managed by a transnational entity dedicated to its long-term stability. This proposal remains hopelessly utopian; given a temptation and an opportunity, people will undermine any system, even if it was crafted at the outset to serve as the paragon of honesty. Worse, by setting up nongovernmental, transnational entities to govern an activity that easily lends itself to monopolistic practices, one risks the unintended consequence of creating a sort of international despotic financial regime that is the opposite of what is intended. As Franklin D. Roosevelt said in a speech on

October 31, 1936, "government by organized money is just as dangerous as government by organized mob."

It can be said that financial despotism is a natural byproduct of unfettered financial markets allowed to operate without political meddling. The main unintended consequence of having relatively stable, almost universally recognized currencies such as the US dollar and the euro is that they amplify disparities, allowing wealth to be efficiently drained from the periphery and toward the center, continuously impoverishing the former and enriching the latter, until the periphery finally collapses. A long series of debt crises in Latin America and Africa attests to this fact. More recently, as financial collapse looms closer, the action has moved from the periphery toward the center, encompassing countries such as Ireland, Spain, Portugal and Greece. Greece is now a post-collapse country in many ways: the unemployment rate there is heading toward 30 percent, and the vast majority of the population would like to emigrate but can't afford to do so. Spain is drifting in the same direction, with Italy not far behind. It is becoming clear to all that the euro is flawed beyond repair, but Europe's politicians, like so many sorcerer's apprentices, do not know how to undo the damage.

Just how flawed is the euro? The Maastricht Treaty obligated Eurozone member states to keep inflation under 3 percent a year, budget deficits also below 3 percent a year and government debt to under 60 percent of GDP. Of these, only the inflation target has been met, because this is the only bit of policy that is under the control of the European Central Bank. The other two are affected by the policies pursued by national governments; consequently, Greece's debt is now 160 percent of GDP and Italy's is 120 percent. But perhaps the greatest flaw designed into the euro is the so-called "social chapter" of the Maastricht Treaty, which obligated member states to guarantee such things as equitable renumeration for workers and guaranteed retirement benefits, but which was dead on arrival. Without it, the unstated but self-evident purpose of the euro becomes the enrichment of Germany.

Perhaps the quest for perfect money is at its heart a misguided one, for the very concept of money is deeply flawed. It is said that "money does not smell," meaning that it operates the same way regardless of how it was obtained. But to think this way is to deny reality, for money does very much smell: it smells of greed and of fear, of the sweat that earned it and the blood that was spilt for it. Disagreements over money have ruined more friendships and marriages than any other kind. Crime follows money like a shadow. The more money there is within a society, the greater are its social inequalities. Financialization dehumanizes human relationships by reducing them to a question of numbers printed on pieces of paper, and a blind calculus for manipulating these numbers mechanically; those who take part in this abstract dance of numbers dehumanize others and, in turn, lose their own humanity, and can go on to perform other dehumanizing acts. Money is, in short, a socially toxic substance. And it is, of course, addictive. Attempting to further purify and refine money is like turning cocaine into crack or codeine into desomorphine—unlikely to take you in a direction that's helpful.

Quite a few books have been written devoted to discussing ways to change the way money works, so that it can serve local needs instead of being one of the main tools for extracting wealth from local economies. Michael Shuman's *Local Dollars, Local Sense*[11] is a good example of the genre. But there is hardly any discussion of why it is that money is even necessary. That is simply assumed. But there are vibrant, thriving communities around the world that have little or no money, where there may be a pot of coin buried in the yard somewhere, for special occasions, but hardly any money in daily use. Thus, while the economic crisis is ravaging Athens and other Greek cities, there are small Greek islands in the Aegean where life goes on, fresh produce is still plentiful and many of the people remain blissfully unaware that there *is* a financial crisis. Similarly, the *disembancados* of México lived through the collapse of the peso in 1994 without giving it much notice. They get along without using much money at all, by growing and catching their own food and bartering with their neighbors.

Lack of money makes certain things very difficult. Examples include gambling, loan sharking, extortion, bribery and fraud. It also makes it more difficult to hoard wealth, or to extract it from a community and ship it somewhere else in a conveniently compact form. When we use money, we cede power to those who create money (by creating debt) and who destroy money (by canceling debt). We also empower the ranks of people whose expertise lies in the manipulation of arbitrary rules and arithmetic abstractions rather than in engaging directly with the physical world. This veil of metaphor allows them to hide appalling levels of violence, representing it symbolically as a mere paper-shuffling exercise. People, animals, entire ecosystems become mere numbers on a piece of paper. On the other hand, this ability to represent dissimilar objects using identical symbols causes a great deal of confusion. For instance, I have heard rather intelligent people declare that government funds that had been allocated to making failed financial institutions look solvent could have been so much better spent feeding widows and orphans. There is no understanding that astronomical quantities of digits willed into existence and transferred between computers do not directly nourish anyone, because food cannot be willed into existence by a central banker or anyone else and because nature, with its frosts, heat waves, droughts and floods, does not respond to price signals.

To the extent that money is necessary, it is more effective when pooled and wielded by a group than by a lone individual. When an entire extended family or clan pools their financial resources, put the most competent person in charge of managing the kitty and make negotiated, wholesale purchases, their money goes a lot farther than if each person spends their own money buying what they need at retail prices. Thus, a group of individuals and nuclear families requires many times the financial resources as the same-sized group organized as an extended family or clan and coordinating their purchases using a common fund. Providing unpaid services within the family or clan can reduce the need for money even further. These can include cooking, cleaning, auto repair, security, construction, legal services, accounting, storage and transportation, sewing, landscaping, childcare, education, medical care... to name just a few. Oh, and let's not forget money-lending—at zero percent interest, of course! Taking each of these activities in-house destroys a financial dependency, and liberates the not insignificant share of labor that was formerly expended on feeding the financial system.

Monetary mysticism

The main tools of modern finance are mystification, obfuscation and hypnosis. The great mystery of money, to most people, is the sacrament of money creation. The high priest pushes a button and, ex nihilo and seemingly effortlessly, generates more of that which we all want to have more of. This is indeed an impressive trick: what we struggle to earn by the sweat of our brow the high priest blithely summons into existence with the help of a cryptic incantation. It is more advanced than a shaman's rain dance and far more reliable—to a point. Obfuscation comes from the use of mathematical formulae that few people understand. Even fewer understand their implications and how they (persistently fail to) map onto the physical world. The key formula of finance—debt raised to the power of time—is the ticking time bomb inside all of our modern financial arrangements.

Beyond the formulae of finance lie the models of economics that are used to provide rationales for economic decisions and to dictate policy. That it is even possible to adequately characterize the economy using mathematics is an empty conceit on two separate levels. On the more superficial level, the financier and philanthropist George Soros defined this as the *reflexive principle*: in financial markets especially, the markets respond to the perceptions of the market-watchers, in turn affecting the outcomes, invalidating supposedly objective measurements. Economic models make assumptions about the rational preferences of market participants, but according to Soros reflexivity causes markets to not have rational preferences and to behave unpredictably and even perversely. The broader implication of this is that when it comes to characterizing society (and finance is but one facet of society), the opportunities to be objective are rather circumscribed and, in truth, there can be no such category as non-fiction. Any observation that becomes known to the observed, even indirectly and through hearsay, is tainted by reflexivity and is therefore subjective and, to a certain extent, a work of fiction. The reflexive principle undermines pretensions to objectivity in social "sciences" such as economics. Better understanding is often achieved through works of drama and literature, which have no pretensions to objectivity and can synthesize new knowledge directly out of the wealth of individual sensory perception and emotion, without being restricted by what is quantifiable or measurable or objectively observable. It seems self-defeating to wear the straitjacket of rationalism while studying social phenomena which themselves exhibit no such rational traits.

On a deeper level, there is a logical flaw in attempting to use finite mathematics (in the very straightforward sense of having to use models that contain a finite number of symbols) to accurately characterize an infinitely complex system such as the economy. This flaw is addressed in Reed Burkhart's forthcoming article "The Limits to Maths: Correcting Some Erroneous Foundations" (which I expect to be unpopular with both economists and mathematicians). Mathematical models can still be useful, even when applied to social phenomena, but only in characterizing a carefully defined subset of the system, in its state at the time it was observed. This rather explains why the economists' strenuous efforts to "do math" have not increased their ability to make accurate predictions, instead giving rise to a joke: "What do you call an economist who makes predictions? Wrong!" Why economists remain undeterred by the almost complete inability of their "science" to make predictions is a question worth pondering. Could it be that their "science" is not descriptive but prescriptive? After all, their clients in government do not seem at all dismayed by their lack of predictive ability. What if their "science" is not driven by data but by the assumptions—or should we say the dogma?—of free market liberalism: that free markets allocate resources optimally, that political meddling in markets causes distortions and so on. What if this is just capitalist central planning masquerading as science?

The very idea that there is a "free market" that is automatically, in and of itself, efficient and optimal and, when unmolested by meddlesome politicians, spontaneously produces prosperity—this very idea is mired in politics. In fact, the free market is completely reliant on a system of property law, a legal system that is able to enforce contracts and a law enforcement system that can deter economic crime. As I will describe in detail in the case study following Chapter 2, the Russian experience in the 1990s showed that without these vital ingredients a free market quickly becomes a criminal market, where debts can be settled for pennies on the dollar simply by shooting one's creditors. In the end, the free market turns out to be a clever government scheme by which to benefit from a sustained period of economic growth. But it becomes collapse-prone during a sustained period of contraction, and at such times a government, should it still have the capacity to do so, would do well to institute a centrally planned resource allocation scheme that disregards market mechanisms and ensures poor but predictable economic performance at a level that can still be sustained. Wartime gasoline rationing is but one example of such a scheme being successful in the US.

If mystification and obfuscation were not enough, modern finance has yet one more method to effect docility and compliance in the populations it holds in thrall: hypnosis. It is a type of hypnosis produced by superimposing suggestive but irrelevant signals on noise. It is a property of our overdeveloped brains that they spontaneously attempt to formulate explanations for events that have no explanations and try to extract messages out of noise. The sound of the surf is basically white noise with some rhythmic structure added, but anyone who listens to it long enough starts to hallucinate, hearing music and voices. The financial markets achieve the same effect by superimposing a layer of interpretation on the fractal noise that they spontaneously generate. Every day millions of people check their charts for signs of meaning, which simply isn't there, but remains forever enticing, forever elusive. Looking at the inane gyrations of the markets the way ancient oracles regarded sheep's entrails, they try to pull meaning from meaninglessness, possessed of a mystical faith that something is there beyond just noise. Financial web sites and cable news channels indulge them by juxtaposing reports of market movements with financial news headlines.

And there we have it: the crumbling edifice of modern finance rests on three pillars: magic money creation rites, mathematized politics masquerading as science and a population in thrall to the fractal noise of the marketplace.

The untrustworthy and the trustful

Within a modern, highly financialized economy, most interactions are impersonal, based on purchase and sale within a market system. If you are the loser in any one transaction, it is your fault, because you chose to deal with people you had no particular reason to trust, and therefore it is your mistake. If the swindle is not illegal, you have no legal recourse. You can, of course, complain to a few friends, perhaps even blog or tweet about it, but then, in a market economy, more of a stigma attaches to being swindled than to swindling, and most people are reticent when it comes to telling the whole world that they let someone take advantage of them.

Once the financial sector goes through its inevitable deflationary collapse followed by a bout of hyperinflation, financial arrangements unravel precisely due to mistrust: nobody, from the largest banks to the humblest private individuals, knows who to trust—who is still "good for it." Whatever transactions are still possible tend to be conducted in a furtive, suspicious, streetwise manner: "Show me the goods!"—"Show me the money!" Whatever business reputations people had in the financialized economy are either ruined or simply fade away. New reputations are established based on readiness to resort to violence or ability to oppose violence. For an individual who is not backed by a criminal organization, the chances of getting robbed go up appreciably. Instead of advertising, businessmen hide, afraid to expose either their product inventory or their wealth. For many, dealing with strangers becomes simply too dangerous.

A cultural flip is needed to change from impersonal, commercial relationships to personal relationships based on trust, and the first hurdle, for many people, is in understanding what trust actually is, because there is no innate human quality called trustworthiness, possessed by some people, lacking in others. Rather, it is more along the lines of a generalization concerning a given individual's behavior over time, within a given relationship. Trust is transactional: a person needs a reason to trust you, and you need a reason to trust that person. There is, however, such a quality as trustfulness: this is the property of small children, tame animals and, most unfortunately for them, many regular, salt-of-the-earth, mainstream Americans. It is of negative survival value in the context of financial collapse. It is being exhibited for all to see by some of the people who recently lost money when MF Global stole it to cover some private bets it had made. They licked their wounds, complained bitterly, and then...went looking for another financial company—to be taken advantage of again. Since the head of MF Global wasn't punished, why wouldn't another company do the same to them, knowing that it can do so with impunity?

There also seems to be a certain set of traits possessed in abundance by a category of highly effective American financial operators that makes it easy for them to prey on trustful people. It may be the suits they wear, or the English they speak or their general demeanor—let us call it "trustiness," to go along with the "truthiness" of their financial disclosures. Deep down, trustful people feel privileged to be robbed by such superior specimens. The predator-prey relationship has been honed to the fine point of a pen: told to sign their life away on the dotted line, the besotted, trustful American gulps quietly—and signs.

Clearly, whenever there is an asymmetry between trustfulness and trustworthiness, the trustful party loses. Trust is not the property of one individual but the property of the relationship between individuals, and it must be balanced. There are roughly three types of trust. The first and best kind is trust borne of friendship, sympathy and love.

People simply do not want to lose the trust of those they care about, and will do anything they can to make good on their promises. The second type of trust is based on reputation. It is not quite as solid, because someone's reputation can be ruined without you knowing it. People who realize that their reputation has been ruined tend to stop being trustworthy rather suddenly, because they see that they have nothing left to lose in the trust game. Rather, they try to salvage whatever residual value their formerly trustworthy reputation still holds by taking full advantage of anyone who is still trustful through force of habit, lack of up-to-date information, inattention or sheer inertia. The last category of trust, the worst kind, is coerced: it is a matter of making it too expensive or too unpleasant for someone to break your trust. If you are forced to do business with someone you don't trust at all, trade hostages for the duration of the transaction or come to some other arrangement that compels good behavior from both sides.

The people most deserving of trust are usually one's own relatives—provided the family is a close-knit one and that it has an internal reputation for being trustworthy, which it values. This is especially the case in societies where putting a stain on the family honor is considered to be a cardinal sin. The next tier of trust is generally reserved for one's close neighbors, if the neighborhood is a relatively static, close-knit and mutually supportive one; if it is not, then neighbors can make the worst sorts of strangers—ones you can't avoid dealing with even though you don't trust them. The last tier of trust consists of complete and total strangers. Here, trust has to be tested before it can be established, by taking small risks: offering small but thoughtful gifts and seeing whether there is reciprocation; putting oneself temporarily in a weakened position (perhaps even on purpose) and seeing whether the other person offers help freely, refuses to come to your aid or attempts to take advantage. At the end of the process, either the stranger ceases to be a stranger, or he is excluded.

Obviously, it is never smart to signal your lack of trust, except in confidence. But for social interactions based on trust to work well, society as a whole must have a way of excluding those who are found to be untrustworthy. In a healthy community in which people normally cooperate or trust each other, there may be a few episodes where someone breaks the trust and is expelled or shunned. In a sick community where neighbors are alienated, combative and mistrustful of each other, you are better off shunning the entire community—by relocating. Sick communities of this sort—and I have seen a few—become sick quickly and take a long time to heal, if they ever do. A certain network effect makes a degenerate condition far more durable than a healthy one. In a friendly, cooperative community, the trust is between each individual and the community as a whole: n individuals—n relationships of trust. In a broken, mistrustful community, each individual mistrusts every other individual: that's $n(n\text{-}1)$. A healthy community of ten individuals has ten healthy, trustful relationships. A sick community of ten individuals has 90 broken, mistrustful relationships. It seems like a better idea to try to establish and maintain the former rather than attempting to fix the latter.

It may be helpful to put the concept of normal, cooperative human relationships based on trust into a wider context. Humans are a social species, and thrive through cooperation. Opposing groups of humans often fight: the bigger the group, the bigger the war, all the way to world war and, if we ever achieve a unified world government, perhaps to spontaneous self-annihilation. But within smaller groups—small enough to avoid the pitfall of self-annihilation through major conflict—cooperation prevails. The great Russian scientist and anarchist revolutionary Peter Kropotkin, in his 1902 book *Mutual Aid: A Factor in Evolution*, argued that it was cooperation rather than competition that made advanced species, including humans, successful. An emphasis on competition, on setting people against each other, on forcing them to struggle against each other economically, may benefit the community if it is viewed as a machine of expansion and domination, but only for short periods of time, and to the detriment of most of its members. An inevitable holdover from this bout of over-competitiveness is that the mindset of social Darwinism and a Hobbesian "war of all against all" remains prevalent, with people deriving their sense of self-worth from their individual, personal achievements and superiority rather than from their often unstated and informal membership in various groups without which they would have surely failed. This mindset is diseased and contagious, and there may not be time to cure it. When time is short and resources scarce, a better response to someone who favors competition over cooperation is to give them more of their own medicine: no cooperation at all.

Götterdämmerung

There are people who really do think that what they are worth as individuals can be defined as their "net worth," which is a number written on a piece of paper, denominated in US dollars or euros. It is as if the only thing that is real to them is money. For such people financial collapse results in a radical loss of meaning, as if all the words in the only language they speak no longer refer to anything they can identify within their surroundings. In such people financial collapse produces a dangerous sense of unreality, an *anomie*.

The term, used by the father of sociology Émile Durkheim, in his 1897 book *Suicide*, indicates a loss of social norms and bounds, a breakdown of the bonds that tie an individual to the community and an inability to regulate or control one's own behavior. People who have previously lived relatively humble lives within rigid financially and socially defined limits simultaneously lose their appetite (not knowing what their new status determines it proper for them to desire) and become insatiable (not knowing how much their new status determines their proper allotment to be relative to those of higher or lower status). In some of these people, once they are severed from the system of financial inducements and constraints to which they had previously been conditioned and which had regulated their social behavior, this sense of unreality resolves into a masochistic drive—a Freudian death wish—to dissolve in a whirlpool of fraudulent financial abstractions. If the financial crisis of 2008 is viewed as a botched suicide attempt by the financial elite, then it seems likely that they will try again.

Viewed as a religious cult, modern finance revolves around the miracle of the spontaneous generation of money in a set of rituals performed by the high priests of central banking. People hang on the high priests' every word, attempting to divine the secret meaning behind their cryptic utterances. Their interventions before the unknowable deity of global finance assure them of economic recovery and continued prosperity, just as a shaman's rain dance guarantees rain or a ritual sacrifice atop a Mayan pyramid once promised a bountiful harvest of maize. All such rituals derive their effectiveness from one key requirement: that the thing they promise to deliver happens in any case, and does so regularly enough to make the oracles' failure to deliver the exception rather than the rule. But when the monsoon fails year after year, when the Nile does not flood and irrigate the fields, when the earth is parched and crops wither and when, in spite of the actions of the Federal Reserve, the European Central Bank and the IMF, the economy goes from bad to worse, the result is *Götterdämmerung*—twilight of the gods. This is the name of Richard Wagner's *Der Ring des Nibelungen*—*The Ring Cycle*, a suite of four very long operas. According to Old Norse mythology, *Götterdämmerung* is a time when the gods battle each other to the death while the world is (almost) destroyed in a flood (perhaps allowing for a rebirth later on). Many cultures have similar apocalyptic myths. The plot is always the same: people have put their trust in their gods; their gods have forsaken them; everyone perishes.

The odd thing with the financial *Götterdämmerung* (laughably, there is actually a book called *Financial Apocalypse*, with the four horsemen on the cover) is that there is only one place where it can actually happen: in each person's head. It is an apocalypse that you have to put your reading glasses on to see: an apocalypse of numbers printed on pieces of paper and displayed on computer screens. In waging their Armageddon, the gods of finance could not possibly do much worse than give each other paper cuts or carpal tunnel syndrome, and the flood is a flood of waste paper, meaningless figures and other nonsense. But our predicament is such that we cannot ignore financial "Apocalypse," for all of its manifest silliness. We have painted ourselves into a corner where, unless the global financial racket keeps going, commerce will come to a grinding halt. But life without global, or even national, finance is possible. In many ways it is even desirable. It has happened before, and it will happen again. We have the technology! The tricky part is surviving the transition, when the collapse of finance causes the collapse of commerce, which then cascades into the collapse of national politics. It is that tricky transitional bit that we will take up next.

Case Study: Iceland

In September of 2008 the Icelandic economy blew up spectacularly. As a result of a crisis affecting that country's three major banks—the ones that carried out operations overseas—the country was brought to the brink of bankruptcy. There was a 90 percent plunge in the stock market, 60 percent of which consisted of shares of the three banks that were going bankrupt. There was a ninefold rise in unemployment. Inflation shot up to 18 percent, with the Icelandic currency eventually falling 50 percent against the US dollar. The three banks were declared insolvent and taken over by the country's financial regulators. Since then, Iceland has paid off the depositors of the failed banks, and was early in repaying emergency rescue loans to the International Monetary Fund. In February 2012 Iceland's credit rating was restored to investment grade, and GDP growth in 2012 is expected to be in the neighborhood of 2.2 percent—better than most of the Eurozone. Relative to the size of the Icelandic economy, the crisis of 2008–2009 was the largest financial crisis ever to afflict a country: the debts of Iceland's three largest banks amounted to $61 billion, which is twelve times the country's GDP.

Financial crises are a dominant feature of our contemporary landscape. There is no shortage of countries whose fiscal position is untenable and of banks and financial companies whose speculative positions and practices lead to spectacular implosions. But it is always risky to predict when a particular situation that does not inspire confidence will precipitate an event in which confidence is lost and a catastrophic unwinding of the country's financial schemes ensues. The list of countries that are poised on the brink is long. Perhaps the sickest patient is Japan, followed by the United States, but, having started out from a position of relative strength, both countries have managed to push their undoing further out on the timeline. Smaller, weaker countries such as Greece, Ireland, Spain and Portugal were quicker to lurch over the brink. Relatively tiny Iceland, with a population of just 320,000—the size of a middling-sized town—was the canary in the financial coalmine. But unlike these other countries, where the only questions we might reasonably ask are "What went wrong?" and "What might be done about it?", in the case of Iceland we can also ask "What went right?" because there, quite unlike all these other financially sick countries, something clearly has gone right.

It wasn't about finance

Perhaps the largest advantage that Iceland had over its rivals was that its people understood immediately that what was happening was not strictly a financial problem—one that could be solved through strictly financial means. According to Iceland's four-term President Ólafur Ragnar Grímsson, "...we were fortunate to realize early on...that the collapse of the banks was not just an economic or financial crisis, but also...a very profound political, social, and even judicial crisis."[12] Grímmson is a very popular democratic leader whose attempt to retire after his fourth term was thwarted by a petition signed by 15 percent of the electorate urging him to run again. Grímsson is an impressive figure who knows a lot more about Iceland than I do or ever will, and I am happy to defer to his opinions.

That the crisis was not strictly financial was driven home by the decision taken by Gordon Brown's UK government to invoke anti-terrorism legislation against Iceland in order to freeze the assets of Kaupthing, Iceland's biggest bank, forcing it to suspend operations. Grímsson again: "...the Gordon Brown government decided to put Iceland under the terrorism legislation, which is something that did enormous damage to the Icelandic economy, and was a great offense to the Icelandic people...." Iceland, "one of the most peace-loving countries in the world, a founding member of NATO, a strong ally of Britain during the Second World War—was put together with the al-Qaeda and the Taliban on the official list of terrorist organizations." It turns out that the financial part of the problem was rather circumscribed. Of the three Icelandic banks that operated outside Iceland, Glitnir and Kaupthing have paid back their depositors in full and Landsbanki would have been able to do the same were it not for this rather shameful maneuver by the Gordon Brown government.

The popular anger against the invocation of anti-terrorist legislation against Iceland on October 8, 2008 was one of the factors that precipitated the popular protests that shook Reykjavik on November 23. Three days later Geir Haarde, Iceland's prime minister, dismissed the government. Much of the political battle that followed focused on whether it was fair for Iceland's tiny population to be held financially responsible for the overseas losses incurred by the country's privately owned banks.

On February 3, 2010 the Alþingi, Iceland's Parliament, voted to repay depositors in the UK and the Netherlands US$3.5 billion. In response, Grímsson exercised his authority under the constitution and vetoed the legislation. On March 6th the question of repayment was put to a national referendum, and 90 percent of Icelanders voted against it. On February 17th the Alþingi voted to authorize repayment of funds owed by Icesave, but Grímsson refused to sign the agreement with the UK and the Netherlands; another referendum was held in which 57.5 percent of Icelanders voted against repayment. Grímmson's rationale:

What the British and the Dutch were arguing was that somehow the European banking system was such that a private bank would operate anywhere in Europe, and if it succeeded, the bankers got extraordinary benefits, the shareholders got big profits. But if it failed, the bill would simply be sent to ordinary people back home: farmers and fishermen, nurses and teachers, young people and old. And that, I maintain, is a very unhealthy formula for the future of the European banking system. If you sent a signal to the bankers that you can be as irresponsible and daring as you want to be, and if you are lucky, you become very rich, but if you fail, other people will pay. I don't think that is a wise journey to enter if you want to build a healthy European financial system in the future.

This, I would contend, is by no means a problem that is specific to the British and the Dutch. The same approach is being promoted everywhere by politicians who are beholden to bankers for their livelihood and the continuation of their political careers. And this, unfortunately, describes a great many of them. Unlike them, Grímsson had the freedom to act. He was also a brave man:

> ... [E]very government in Europe was against me. Every big financial institution, both in Europe and in my own country, was against me, and there were powerful forces, both in Iceland and in Europe, that thought my decision was absolutely crazy. And to some extent, of course, it was a complicated issue. But once I had analyzed every aspect of it, it boiled to the fundamental choice of the interest of the financial market on one hand, and the democratic will of the people on the other, and rarely in history—but it does happen—do we come to such crossroads that we are forced to choose.
>
> And my answer was clearly, not only with respect to the democratic structure of Iceland, but also with respect to Europe's contribution to the world. What is our primary legacy to countries and nations in modern times? Is the European democracy the right of the people? Capitalistic financial markets can exist in many other parts of the world, even without democracy. So in my opinion, Europe is and should be more about democracy than about financial markets. Based with this choice, it was, in the end, clear that I had to choose democracy.

Perhaps you sense a certain incongruity in this line of reasoning? Here we have the president of a country—albeit a country the size of a smallish provincial town—standing up to the leaders of over a dozen countries, disregarding their opinions, then going on to lecture them on the virtues of democracy and the importance of the popular will. Is Grímsson the mouse that roared? Not quite, it seems; he did rise to the occasion, but with the support of his people: scoring 90 percent in a national referendum on a contentious issue is not something that any politician anywhere can safely ignore.

It is important to point out two aspects of the Icelandic financial saga: the failure of representative democracy and the success of direct democracy. When the Alþingi voted to hold the Icelanders financially responsible for the losses incurred by private banks, representative democracy failed. This is not surprising: once an individual rises above the crowd and becomes its democratically elected representative, a chasm opens up, and the individual becomes very easily corrupted and swayed by moneyed interests. Elected officials soon form a class separate from the classes they represent, and the only force that can constrain them, and those who curry favor with them, is the popular will, expressed preferably through direct democracy or, failing that, open revolt. Another option, and the only one left if democracy does not exist or has been completely discredited, is some sort of enlightened despotism or benevolent dictatorship. Even a putsch that installs a military junta can be viewed as a positive development once a representative democracy becomes so utterly corrupt as to threaten the life of the population.

But Iceland is blessed with a very ancient, mature and stable form of democracy that goes back to the direct tribal democracy of the Norse, who settled Iceland between 874 and 930 AD, the year they founded the Alþingi. A thousand years of uninterrupted democratic rule seems like a good round number; on the other hand, anything less than a century is definitely insufficient. Of the other patients in the financial intensive care unit, Spain and Portugal have a recent history of dictatorship, Greece of rule by a junta, while Ireland is the victim of five hundred years of British colonial rule, in the course of which it had been forcibly acculturated to the British system of governance through hypocrisy, which excels at making sure that democratic procedures produce non-democratic results. Case in point: on October 27, 2011 Ireland held a referendum and voted against a constitutional amendment to allow their parliament to investigate bank fraud. Unsurprisingly, the Irish public has been successfully saddled by foreign banking interests to repay their private losses. Compare that to Iceland's response to bank fraud: "On the judicial side, we appointed a special commission headed by a Supreme Court judge that issued a report in 9 volumes, we appointed the office of special prosecutors, we have enacted various legislation and laws that relate to the judicial and legal system."

Iceland is also blessed with a population small enough to make direct democracy work. The world's oldest and most stable democracies are all small and local. There is Iceland with its three hundred thousand inhabitants. There is the Isle of Man with a population of eighty-five thousand, whose parliament, the Tynwald, is likewise of Norse origin, and likewise over a thousand years old. There is Switzerland, which has eight million inhabitants but is a confederation of twenty-six cantons, the largest of which, Bern, has a population of under a million, so that no one canton can dominate the rest. Beyond a certain size it becomes impossible to get anything done without acting through representatives, and that is where the rot sets in. To work as a direct democracy, each citizen has to have a sizable share of sovereignty. A 1/500,000 share is definitely effective; perhaps ten times that can be made to work reliably. But at the parts-per-billion level the probability of the individual's sovereign will percolating all the way to the national level becomes miniscule. Thus the Icelander is a sovereign giant compared to the Chinese or the Indian sovereign dwarf. And while the larger countries can assert their will by standing up to others, middling countries that are too big for direct democracy but too small to stand up to the rest end up in the weakest position of all.

There are many lessons to be learned from this. One of them is that if your country is too large to be effective as a democracy, breaking it up into smaller pieces joined into a confederacy may be a good idea. The recent moves toward holding a referendum on Catalonia's independence from Spain is one example of a move in this direction. At a bigger scale, the European Union may yet regret Germany's reunification. A better, more Swiss-like and more democratic confederate balance would have been achieved if Germany's participation in the EU were not as Bundesrepublik but as autonomous *Länder*. But then France, which is even more highly centralized, would have needed to be dismantled as well.

Aside from such general musings on the failings of democracy, one observation from the Icelandic financial saga that is worth examining as a candidate for a general principle is this: above some minimum threshold for social viability, a democracy's effectiveness for its people is inversely proportional to their number.

A bout of madness

How does a small, ancient society that based its economy on the North Sea fishery get plunged into the murky world of international finance, and then surface with debts twelve times the size of its economy? Iceland first diversified into energy and aluminum production. Then, thanks to the neoliberal market reforms of the former premier David Oddsson, who drew his inspiration from the ideology of Margaret Thatcher, it liberalized its financial sector. Its privatized banks went through a period of rapid growth through foreign borrowing and expansion into foreign markets. As its financial system grew to many times its capital base, Iceland began to resemble a hedge fund.

The groundwork for Iceland's financial collapse was laid in 1999, when the Alþingi enacted legislation concerning international trading companies, which set tax rates and regulations for foreign companies registering in Iceland. According to this law, the revenues of foreign companies registering in Iceland were taxed at a very low rate of 5 percent, making Iceland competitive with offshore tax havens. These companies were also freed from having to pay property taxes or customs duties, all for the very reasonable registration fee of $1,400 a year. This set up Iceland as an offshore tax haven and business center. But foreign companies registering in Iceland received the status of normal Icelandic international businesses, and Iceland's status as a European nation and a member of NATO allowed them to escape the scrutiny of central banks. In addition, Iceland's Kaupthing bank acquired an interest in an actual offshore, the Isle of Man, and used the Manx operation to provide a wide variety of services such as private banking and investment management, including the setting up of shell companies.

When, in the wake of the collapse of Lehman Brothers in the US, Kaupthing's finances soured, the international trading companies that had been set up under its auspices felt the pinch. Some of these were connected with high-ranking Russian officials such as Vladimir Putin, Dmitry Medvedev and Boris Gryzlov and, rumor has it, were used by Russia's state-owned oil company, Rosneft, to move large sums. Others were connected with Russian oligarchs, including Roman Abramovich and Oleg Deripaska; one, Alisher Usmanov, used the services of Kaupthing to buy up shares of Norilsk Nickel. Several Icelanders became fabulously rich in the process, but when Kaupthing failed the Russian interests are estimated to have lost some $20 billion. In October of 2008 there was talk of Russia offering $5.4 billion to bail out Iceland. This deal did not go through, and in the end Russia participated in a package of emergency loans administered by the International Monetary Fund. But the initial impetus behind Moscow's seemingly odd desire to jump in and stabilize Iceland no doubt came from the desire to minimize its own losses.

The right approach

Iceland's approach was to let financial companies go bankrupt rather than prop them up with public funds. As Grímsson put it, "I have never really understood the argument: why a private bank or financial fund is somehow holier for the wellbeing and future of the economy than the industrial sector, the IT sector, the creative sector, or the manufacturing sector." The Icelanders had other priorities: "[W]e have, in our economic measures, tried to protect the lowest income sectors…some of the elementary social and health services…." Indeed, if Russian oligarchs or British and Dutch investors park their money where it isn't guaranteed, why shouldn't they be the ones to absorb the risk? Of course, the bankers *would* want the citizens to bail them out, but if the country is sufficiently democratic, they can't insist.

But a further case can be made that the failure of financial institutions can be a good thing, because it frees up resources for productive activities that benefit the entire society rather than just the rentier class and the über-rich. According to Grímsson: "…[p]aradoxically, what we are seeing in the last two years is that many sectors in Iceland—the energy sector, the tourism sector, the IT sector, the manufacturing sector, and the fishing sector—are doing better…than they did prior to the banking crisis." What Iceland accidentally discovered is that having a large banking and finance sector imposes a brain drain on the economy: the talent that would otherwise be employed in creating value for the country as a whole is instead employed in (ultimately unsuccessfully) managing and manipulating financial risk, in what in the final analysis amounts to a negative-sum game. Grímsson again:

> The Icelandic banks, like all modern big banks in Europe and America and all the other parts of the world, are no longer banks in the old-fashioned way. They have become high-tech companies. [They employ] high-ranked engineers, mathematicians, computer scientists, programmers and so on and so forth. And their success depends largely on how successful they are in hiring people with this education and capability, not necessarily those trained in business schools or finance, but in engineering, mathematics, computer science and so on.
>
> And when the Icelandic banks collapsed, what we saw was that a great number of companies in these creative sectors, IT,

high-tech, and all of those, who had the large growth potential in the previous years, but had not been able to realize it because they couldn't get the people, due to the fact that the banks were buying up all the best engineers and mathematicians and computer scientists, suddenly had the pool of talent available to them. And within six months, all these people who came out of the banks with these qualifications had been hired. So since then you have seen a great growth period in the Icelandic IT sector, the high-tech sector, the manufacturing sector, because they could suddenly get the engineers, the mathematicians, the computer scientists.

So the lesson from this is: if you want your economy to excel in the 21st century, for the IT, information-based high-tech sectors, a big banking sector, even a very successful banking system, is bad news for your economy. You could even argue based on this that the bigger the banking sector is, the worse is the news for your economy, because their magnetic attraction of taking engineers and technically qualified people and computer scientists into the banking sector is due to high bonuses and higher salaries prevents these creative growth sectors from realizing their full potential.... If you want to excel in the 21st century economy, it's more important to give high priority to your creative sectors, and IT companies and high-tech companies, and not building up big banks, because if you need money you can always get it somewhere in the world in the globalized financial system. But if you lose the most valuable manpower in your creative sector, there is nothing you can do to repair that damage.

So this, then, is perhaps the most important lesson we can draw from Iceland's success in recovering from the biggest financial crisis ever to afflict a country. Perhaps it can be summed up in just four words (plus a footnote):

Let The Banks Fail*

---

* But pay off the depositors, eventually.

CHAPTER 2

Commercial Collapse

STAGE 2: Commercial collapse. Faith that "the market shall provide" is lost. Money is devalued and/or becomes scarce, commodities are hoarded, import and retail chains break down and widespread shortages of survival necessities become the norm.

For those of us living in the economically developed countries of the world, our relationship to commerce is one of abject dependence. In order to procure food, clothing, housing or medical care—or just about everything else—we are forced to deal, not directly with farmers, tailors, cobblers, builders or doctors, but with middlemen who produce nothing and only add expense. In the process of erecting this elaborate commercialized, financialized structure we have lost sight of what it means to trade, which is to offer services or create objects of value and offer them in exchange to other service providers or producers of objects of value. This definition excludes those who make money simply by moving it from pocket to pocket.

This is by no means a new idea, nor is it the least bit radical; it is deeply conservative and highly traditional. It was Aristotle who first defined the economy as the exchange of goods and services for money, commerce as a parasite on the economy (where those who create nothing extract a share by trading) and finance a parasite on commerce (which extracts a share by switching money from hand to hand—a parasite on a parasite). A typical US politician, such as the president, who counts financial companies such as Goldman Sachs among his top campaign donors, could be characterized as a parasite on a parasite on a parasite—a worm infesting the gut of a tick that is sucking blood from a vampire bat, if you like.

It is rather unusual for a steady-state economy based on trade to suddenly sprout a gigantic, superfluous superstructure of commerce and finance. In circumstances we might consider normal the flow of goods and services is in balance with what nature can sustainably provide. There may in addition be some mining and manufacturing operations that slowly deplete nonrenewable resources, but these are in general so labor-intensive as to be self-limiting at a fairly low level. If such a steady-state, ecologically neutral economy were to become afflicted by a legion of parasitic traders and financiers who produce nothing but nevertheless manage to extract a share, be it through violence or guile, then the economy would be driven into depression and collapse, starving out the parasites in the process.

It is rather less unusual for this to happen when a particular society gets a great new idea and sets off in wild abandon in pursuit of it. This is not an infrequent occurrence: madness is rare in individuals, but strikes quite regularly in societies. The new idea might be the construction of gleaming white temples surfaced with plaster (deforesting the countryside in the process, to make the plaster) or the smelting of weapons out of bronze or iron to slay one's enemies (deforesting again, to make charcoal) or the construction of ocean-going navies to set off on voyages of conquest (again deforesting, for timber) or any other such pursuit. In all these cases, no matter the pursuit, the eventual results seem to be deforestation, soil erosion, environmental calamity and collapse.

But things really take off if a new, concentrated, easily produced source of energy is discovered in time. The Dutch turned to peat moss as fuel (turning much of their farmland to swampland in the process), then switched to coal, then added oil and gas. The English went straight from wood to coal, poisoning the Thames with coal tar and coming close to asphyxiating themselves with the infamous London fog. Everywhere the progression was much the same: wood, then coal, then oil and gas and, in some cases, nuclear. Transportation, both on sea and on land, went from wind and muscle power to coal-fired steam to oil-fired steam and then to diesel (and nuclear). And now that most of the easy, cheap, plentiful reservoirs of these fossil fuels have been used up and what remains is difficult, risky, expensive to extract and rather small in size, we are due for another collapse. The difference is that this collapse will be on a completely unprecedented scale, and global in scope.

Cascaded failure

The process by which the collapse of the financial house of cards triggers commercial collapse, which then triggers political collapse, can be characterized as cascaded failure, in which the first failure (which happens when the assumptions underlying contemporary financial arrangements suddenly come to be regarded as untenable) has a knock-on effect on commerce (due to a lack of commercial credit), which, in turn, has a knock-on effect on government finances (through a rapidly shrinking tax base).

At this point virtually all of the highly developed economies are very highly indebted and are either shrinking or not growing. Such a situation cannot be considered stable: whenever exorbitant levels of debt exist, credit must expand continuously in order to service previously issued debt, but in order for money that has been lent into existence to retain its value relative to the goods and services available in the economy, economic growth must keep pace with credit expansion. If economic growth cannot be restored, the end result is national default.

The fact that Greece is in some stage of national default is no longer controversial. Nor does it appear likely that Spain, Italy or Ireland will sort out their problems, or that growth will resume. First, there is the problem with natural resources, oil foremost among them. Oil is now too expensive to fuel further growth, and it is not likely to become any cheaper because the remaining resources—such as deep water, tar sands, shale oil, Arctic oil and other dregs that were previously passed over as unpromising—are expensive to produce. Second, there is a problem with levels of debt: too high a level of debt is known to choke off economic growth even without any of the other impediments. Third, we are at a point now where it no longer appears to be possible to stimulate growth: recent figures show that it takes a 2.3 units of new debt to produce one unit of GDP growth. Based on the available data, we have achieved diminishing returns with regard to debt-fueled growth.

There are some who entertain the romantic notion that national default can be seen as a positive development: bad debt is wiped out, new, sound money is printed and put into circulation, and the economy recovers. In fact, this has been observed in Argentina, Russia and a few other countries. Could similarly positive things happen for larger pieces of the global economy? Couldn't some forceful and concerted action by governments and central banks suddenly restore banks to solvency and make commercial credit available once again? One key observation is that this would have to happen rather quickly, almost instantly, and require a level of international coordination that would be completely unprecedented. In theory this is possible, but as a practical matter, why should anyone think that those same people who haven't yet understood the root causes behind the financial collapse of 2008 will suddenly be able to grasp all of the key details of an intricately interconnected, global system of staggering complexity, and not only grasp them but use this newfound understanding to quickly work out a solution to its numerous problems?

Still, national defaults have happened before, and global finance has recovered, so why wouldn't it now? Well, there is the question of size. The significance of a national default varies in accordance with the size of the nation's economy relative to the size of the global economy. Argentina's default was a non-event at the global scale. Russia's default almost took the entire financial system with it when Long-Term Capital Management suddenly failed as a result, and the US Federal Reserve had to step in and coordinate a bailout. The US subprime mortgage crisis and the failure of Lehman Brothers brought global finance even closer to the brink, and required much bigger bailouts. And now, with Greece, Spain and Italy on the rocks, bailouts are coming fast and furious, but each one seems to restore confidence for a shorter and shorter period of time. All of these shocks add together, and at some point one of them will force the global financial system across a tipping point and result in cascaded failure that will cause global commerce to lock up.

The effect of each shock is to make the system as a whole less resilient. After each localized national default (Argentina, Russia, Iceland), recovery was critically dependent on access to a relatively healthy world economy and financial system. As we move from one financial crisis to the next, we continue to assume that each one will produce a proportional reaction. But any one of them can move the global system out of its linear range, and cause a crash from which there is no recovery because the process turns out to be irreversible: the complex global financial system cannot be recreated once the global economy that gave rise to it no longer exists.

In turn, the financial system does not exist in isolation from the rest of the economy, and the process by which financial failure causes an instant breakdown in commerce is rather crisply defined. All cargoes have to be financed. This is done by banks on opposite sides of the planet that are willing to grant and honor letters of credit, issuing loans which are paid off once the cargo is landed. If these loans cannot be obtained, cargo does not move. Within days, missing shipments mean empty supermarket shelves, idled production at factories due to missing components, standstills at construction sites and maintenance operations, hospitals running out of drugs and supplies and so on. Within a week, local fuel inventories are depleted and transportation is disrupted. Modern manufacturing and distribution networks rely on a global supply chain and very thin, just-in-time inventories. High-tech manufacturing is most easily disrupted, because key components have just one or two suppliers and little or no possibility for substitution. Experience of various disruptions (the Japanese tsunami of 2011, the Eyjafjallajökull volcano eruption of 2010) shows that their impact does not scale linearly with their duration but accelerates—and recovery takes disproportionately longer. Within a month or so the electric grid collapses due to lack of supplies and maintenance; it is probably at this point that recovery becomes impossible.

But even before then the contagion will start to feed on itself. The global aspect of the global economy would be perhaps the fastest to disappear because trust between strangers builds up slowly but is lost rapidly. In a rapidly shrinking economy "taking care of one's own" becomes more important than maintaining a trust relationship with strangers on another continent. What does this bode for societies that are dependent on infrastructure that cannot be maintained without globally sourced, imported components that can only be purchased on credit?

Widespread sovereign default is not some sort of spring shower that passes and then the sun comes out again. At some point what is now still a gradual process will lead to a sudden, irreversible, catastrophic disruption of daily life.

Liar word: efficiency

Although traders and money-lenders find a steady-state economy a hard and rocky place on which they can barely gain a purchase, their fortunes change for the better as soon as there comes into view some new source of energy, raw materials or gainful purpose on which to squander the remaining living trees or their fossilized remains. If the future looks to be bigger, fatter and busier than the present, then those who are willing to bet that it will be can help make it happen even faster. In effect, they borrow from the future and assume that the future will be able to make the payments; if it can't, they lose, and everyone loses with them. The converse does not hold, for it is not the least bit true that while the parasites are winning, everyone wins with them. They tend to make everyone work harder than necessary and ignore the ecological and social consequences of their actions. But in the context of a booming economy that is flush with cheap energy, plentiful raw materials and restless, underemployed labor, their charms become irresistible. They can conjure up capital simply by snapping their fingers, and they can deploy that capital to make the economy more efficient—at burning through these plentiful resources until they are all gone. And if you decline their services, then you, in effect, make yourself less efficient, in the sense of being less competitive; then you fall behind, and they either buy you out or put you out of business.

Efficiency is an odd sort of word that can have many different meanings. A steady-state economy is resource-constrained by what nature makes available by capturing and processing energy from sunlight, and consequently it is also needs-constrained, because those whose needs exceed what is available quickly perish. Thus, all activities in a steady-state economy are moderated by your needs; to meet them, you try to expend as little energy as possible, and once they are met, you again try to expend as little energy as possible. If a fisherman needs to catch three fish a week to remain fed and to barter for the other things he needs, he can catch them all on warm, dry days when he feels like fishing. Once he has caught his three fish, he can rest, nap and entertain himself, but he certainly would not exert himself trying to catch even more fish when it is cold, dark and rainy. And this is highly efficient of him.

If, however, his needs have outgrown the steady-state economy and he now catches fish for a multinational conglomerate so that he can afford to make payments on a trawler, a house and a car, then he has no choice but to try to catch as many fish as possible, rain or shine, because if he doesn't then the trawler will get repossessed, and instead of the three fish a week he actually needs to survive, he will have zero fish. And this, you see, would be because he was not as efficient as his competitors.

Thus, efficiency is a liar word: it means different things to different people at different times. For example, it is more efficient to offshore industrial production and assembly work to low-wage countries. International wage arbitrage lowers production costs, so that consumers pay lower prices for products and consumption increases, driving growth. It is more efficient to replace local specialty shops with big box stores that sell cheap imports. Big box stores are more efficient because they can negotiate more effectively with their suppliers, and can pass the savings on to their customers. Advanced logistics and the "warehouse on wheels" model of just-in-time delivery takes advantage of efficient economies of scale which are, again, unavailable to small shops. But once their customers are mostly broke—because their jobs have been offshored—it becomes more efficient for big box stores to cut their losses and close than to stay open for the sake of a few remaining customers. And once commerce is dead, it is then more efficient to evict, foreclose and demolish towns than to try to save them, and more efficient yet to build new big box stores in China where people still have some money, and offshore Chinese production to countries where wages are even lower. This cycle can repeat as long as there are poor people left to exploit anywhere in the world, and as long as oil is cheap enough to make transportation costs negligible compared to labor costs. And although the world is not running out of poor people—quite the contrary!—it has already run out of cheap oil, so the days of this model of exploitation are counted.

A ready retort is that this problem can be addressed by improving the energy efficiency of transportation, by the application of new
and exciting technology. But even energy efficiency is not without its
share of problems. In recent years, shipping companies have resorted to
something they call slow steaming—lowering the speed of big ships by
partially dismantling their giant diesel engines and changing the gear-
ing. They are now at the limits of slow steaming: the ships cannot move
any slower. The other adaptation to high oil prices was to increase the
size of ships, hoping to realize ever greater economies of scale, but this
process has also now run its course. Freight rates are still low, but this is
due to the lingering effects of previous massive overinvestment in ship-
building, in which the lag-time between order and delivery is several
years. By the time shipping companies took delivery of the vessels, there
was no longer enough cargo to fill them, so they are operating at a loss
and will be forced to consolidate, at which point freight rates will begin
to climb upward, becoming a major limiting factor for global trade.

This will render globalized consumerism inefficient, but then perhaps efficiency will be improved again by "on-shoring"—instead of shipping in products from overseas, shipping in the sweatshop labor that
makes these products, and setting up domestic labor camps. We don't
yet know how far people are willing to go, and what principles they are
willing to sacrifice, in the name of efficiency. Lost in all of these considerations of efficiency is the key question: *Cui bono?* Who benefits from
increased efficiency? Is it you and me, or is it someone else? Efficiency
is often an opaque, abstract game played by self-assured specialists who
hold up their conclusions as some sort of absolute measure of technical
virtue, but to cut through all of that it is often enough to establish who
gets to walk away with the savings. And then we can decide, from our
personal perspective, whether it would be efficient for us to allow that
to happen.

Tangential to the confused and arbitrary notion of efficiency is the
somewhat less self-contradictory concept of resiliency. Efficient systems tend to be more highly optimized for a given set of uses or conditions, making them more fragile and less resilient. Every step in an
optimization process makes a system more highly adapted to its specific
circumstances, in turn making it not just less efficient but altogether
not functional once these circumstances change. Resilient systems operate nowhere near their maximum capacity, are insensitive to quality

and quantity of inputs and are not highly specialized. A good example is a house cat, which sleeps some eighteen hours a day and can eat just about any kind of an animal. If food runs low it will sleep one hour a day less and hunt one hour a day more. It is very well adapted to just about anything. Cats are very good hunters that do not have to hunt very much. That is their secret, and that is why they have taken over the world. A good example of an optimized, efficient system is a hummingbird, which starves within a day when deprived of nectar or sugar-water. Efficient systems are highly specialized, fine-tuned to process specific inputs and operate close to their point of failure.

In our relentless pursuit of efficiency we make our world more fragile. By prizing all that is optimal, advanced and specialized, we sink our resources into evolutionary dead ends. For example, we value purebred horses (which are finicky eaters and require grass, hay or grain) over donkeys (which will eat straw, seaweed and even newspaper) and when we can no longer afford to feed the horses we sell them to a slaughterhouse or abandon them. Examples of this sort can be seen all around us, because efficiency and specialization convey status while resiliency, universality, simplicity and robustness are seen as unfashionable and ignored.

Technology evolves in the same direction. In computers, we have moved away from clunky desktop systems with many interchangeable parts, which could be nursed along for decades, and toward slim and fashionable mobile devices which have just about zero interchangeable or user-maintainable parts, last just one or two years and become all but useless once any one thing goes wrong with them, or even once the company that made them decides to no longer issue software updates. With cars, we have moved from models that could be endlessly repaired using remanufactured or junkyard parts to models that have nothing user-serviceable under the hood—not even an oil plug—and are designed to be crushed and melted down once the useful lifetime for which they are designed has been exceeded. New cars are computerized and use electronic fuel injection, which is more efficient than using a carburetor. But just one little earthquake and tsunami in Japan managed to knock out production of a third of the microcontrollers needed to manufacture electronic fuel-injected cars, in turn shutting down a third of the car production around the world. And so it turns out that simple, inefficient, outdated carbureted engines that can be overhauled using simple hand tools are more resilient than high-tech, efficient ones. Their fuel efficiency may be lower but their overall efficiency, especially in the face of economic disruption, is higher, because they will continue to work when more advanced engines will grind to a halt due to a lack of high-tech replacement parts.

Certain circumstances are virtual crucibles for the concepts of efficiency and resilience. Single-handed ocean racers—people who cross oceans alone in small sailboats to win prizes—have to be both efficient and resilient. Their boats have to be efficient, in terms of being fast enough to win races. But they also have to be resilient, because it is hard to invite mechanics on board or order replacement parts while in the middle of the ocean. Ideally, the only systems on board are either so rugged that their chance of failure is minimal or so simple that the sailor can repair them using tools and supplies she carries on board. One such system that went through quite a process of evolution is the autopilot. It is impossible to stand continuously at the helm for the several weeks it takes to complete a transatlantic race, and in a single-handed race there is no other crew on board to take over. After many bad experiences with complicated electrical and hydraulic systems, the standard that emerged is a deceptively simple but actually very clever wind vane which, through a simple mechanical coupling, keeps the boat's course constant relative to the apparent wind. A bit of cleaning is all that this system ever needs.

Efficiency and resilience need not be mutually contradictory, but we must be mindful of how the terms are used. Measures of economic efficiency, such as labor productivity, are all but useless because they do not take account of the replacement value of energy inputs in terms of human labor. A lumberjack operating a chainsaw is considered more productive than the same lumberjack operating an axe, neglecting the fact that the energy contained in each gallon of gasoline used to power the chainsaw is equivalent to some five hundred hours of human labor. A farmer driving a four-wheel-drive tractor with a tiller attachment while sitting in its air-conditioned cab, monitoring a computer console and pushing buttons, is far more labor efficient than a farmer walking behind two oxen hitched to a plow, but far less energy efficient and far less resilient.

A better way to evaluate efficiency is as personal efficiency, in terms of the amount of personal energy unamplified by external energy inputs needed to complete any given task. Eating hand to mouth—literally, by picking an apple from a tree and eating it—is by far the most efficient way to procure food: there is no harvesting, transportation, sorting, washing, packaging, distribution or sale involved. The more steps we can eliminate from a process, the more efficient we become. Common measures of efficiency neglect the efficiency of *not* doing something. Take the example of a single mother who drives to work, pays for day-care for her children, has no time to cook and so has to buy more expensive and less healthy pre-cooked food, develops stress-related medical problems that cost her even more money and, as a result, goes bankrupt. Or she could stay at home, take in a boarder, take in some wash and some ironing, participate in the local informal economy in a few different ways and save on transportation, food, day care and medical expenses and, as a result, still go bankrupt. One of these is the more efficient way to go bankrupt; which is it?

Life upside down

Before the sixth century BC most people believed in the archaic notion that the Earth is a flat plate or disk covered by the inverted bowl of the firmament. When the idea of Earth being round was first floated, because it gave much better agreement with astronomical observations, some people thought it impossible—because those on the other side of the Earth would fall off. Others thought that people living on the other side of the Earth (the antipodes) would have to be standing on their heads to remain right side up. It took people a long time to realize that gravity works in a certain mysterious way that obviates such problems. The people who entertained such archaic notions also adhered to an archaic, tribal lifestyle that seems hopelessly quaint to us now, for their interactions with each other were dominated by gift, followed in importance by tribute and barter, with trade reserved for certain high-status and luxury items. People depended the most on those nearest to them—family, clan, tribe—and depended the least on strangers in faraway lands. Commerce—the process of buying and selling without actually producing anything—had no part in their world.

The idea of Earth being flat was relegated to the status of myth in much of the world by the time Columbus set sail toward the sunset, hoping to discover a shortcut to India. Thanks to his efforts, and to those of other sailors, discoverers, conquerers and colonizers, much of the planet was eventually subjugated to the needs of its best-organized, best-armed representatives, whose power was concentrated at a few imperial centers. Over time, the archaic, tribal economies were destroyed and supplanted by their mirror image, to the point that it is commerce that now dominates economic interactions, followed far behind by trade, tribute and barter, with gifts being relegated to a ceremonial, vestigial role. We are now much less economically dependent on (extended) family, the terms "clan" and "tribe" seem hopelessly antiquated and all of us are abjectly dependent for our survival on strangers halfway across the world who provide for most of our material needs. Furthermore, we are unable to trade with these strangers directly without the services of commercial middlemen. The current economic paradigm of most of the developed world is the upside-down version of what we humans have been doing throughout much of our three million-odd years on the planet—the universal human cultural norm stood neatly on its head. It is we who are well and truly the antipodeans now: people who have to stand on their heads in order to remain upright.

The progression from local to global was fueled by slave labor during its early stages, and later by fossil fuel energy. While global trade relied on sailing ships, shipping costs limited the cargoes that could be transported economically to high-value, compact, lightweight, exotic or energy-dense products such as spices, sugar, rum, cloth and fiber, indigo, salted meat and fish and manufactured goods. Once sail was supplanted by fossil-fuel-burning steamships, and later by modern diesel-powered tankers and container ships, transportation costs came to be considered negligible and global trade grew to include items such as plastic orange Halloween pumpkins, Christmas lights and a myriad of other cheap, short-lived, disposable plastic products. This state of affairs can only persist as long as transportation costs can be considered negligible—which, with oil prices hovering around a hundred dollars a barrel, they no longer are. There are ways to improve energy efficiency, such as the slow steaming approach described earlier, in which very large ships move very slowly, but this has also reached its limits. The result of these pressures is a long-term decline in the volumes of global freight.

Thus the antipodal episode, during which the normal economic pattern is stood on its head, promises to be rather short. It is a fundamentally flawed idea that could only work for a short period of time while nonrenewable resource use could continually increase. Once it no longer can, it can be extended for an even shorter period of time while it is still possible to endlessly expand debt. But that runs its course rather quickly too and, again, leads to collapse. The whole process is, in fact, a strategy for collapse; there are no other possible outcomes. Now that it is collapsing, our task becomes to flip the economic pattern right side up again, in order to give ourselves another chance.

Numerous national and international public health organizations, including the World Health Organization and the United States Department of Agriculture, have published various food guide pyramids that seek to define, in general terms, a diet that provides for good health. At the base of the pyramid are basic carbohydrates from cereal crops, such as bread, rice and pasta. Right above, a slightly smaller slice of the pyramid is made up of fruits and vegetables; above those an even smaller slice contains dairy, animal protein (meat, poultry, fish) and vegetable protein (beans and nuts). And above those are fats, oils and sweets, which are labeled "Use sparingly." Of these, only the fats and oils are truly necessary to maintain health.

None of these organizations publish a human relationship guide pyramid, which would indicate what types of human relationships, and in what proportion by the amount of interaction, are required in order for us to remain socially healthy and maintain a healthy society. This is most unfortunate, because a sick society made up of physically healthy individuals is no better than a healthy society made up of physically sick individuals. To make up for this glaring oversight on their part, I have endeavored to present one here.

The base of my pyramid, representing a royal share of a healthy human interaction diet, is made up of family, extended family, clan or tribe—those people who are closest to you, and whom you have known all your life (or all of their life if they are younger). These are your people—those before whom you have irrevocable obligations, who you can trust completely and will support, defend and protect unconditionally as a matter of family honor. This is the context in which all of the most important social interactions, such as nurturing, social grooming, teaching and learning, take place. Next, a somewhat smaller slice is made up by friends and allies—those people with whom you are united by bonds of friendship or solemn promise, but who are not your people. Next, an even smaller sliver is made up of strangers: those with whom you are drawn together, not through blood relations or personal allegiance but through accident or necessity or fleeting circumstance. While accident and necessity are to be avoided, a fleeting circumstance such as hosting a performance by an itinerant musician may be pleasant, but it cannot be prioritized above the needs of those who are not strangers. This, I submit to you, is the pattern of human interaction that stands the best chance of producing a healthy, happy, carefree society in most circumstances.

Note that the amount of social interaction is inversely proportional to the number of people involved in that type of interaction. Family, extended family, clan and tribe are small but get most of the attention; friends and allies make up a larger group but they get less time, and the universe of strangers is arbitrarily large and is largely ignored. This pattern has to do with our evolved traits: we are physiologically evolved to have about a dozen people who are closest to us. Beyond that group may lie a hundred or so friends, acquaintances and allies—people we know and trust somewhat. This is how humans normally relate to each other; most of our interactions are with those closest to us. Beyond a small set of individuals lies the universe of people about whom we care very little, no matter what we say to ourselves, because this is how we have been programmed over three million years' worth of evolution.

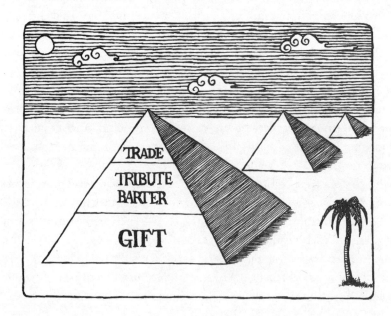

People pay lip service to the billions and billions of people alive in the world today that they superficially care about. That is like the billions and billions of stars in our galaxy, all of them light years away from us. We can never get to know more than a tiny sampling of these people, and we would be foolish to trust them. Here is how people are meant to treat each other, and if they do not, then strange things begin to happen to their characters and to their societies.

This is how people have lived and worked together for most of human history. The very bottom, the foundation of the economic relationship hierarchy, which includes just about everything we need to survive, is mostly made up of gifts, especially when we are young; when we are young and helpless, everything that people give us is a gift. We are not expected to reciprocate until we have at least learned to walk and talk, at which point we might be asked to do some chores. We accumulate gifts during our first two decades of life, and then we are expected to recompense for everything we have been given later on.

Tribute and barter form a layer above gift and involve people who are not in a gift relationship with us. With barter, we expect the compensation to be more immediate and the terms to be to some extent negotiated, but not necessarily involve the operation of anything we might call the free market. Both tribute and barter are still based on personal relationships rather than some kind of impersonal, public scheme. And at the very top of the pyramid is trade, which has normally been reserved for various specialty items, not everyday necessities: luxury goods, weapons, objects that convey social status, exotic collectibles, artwork and the like. None of these is necessary for day-to-day survival. If any of these imports were to be cut off suddenly, people might feel poorer, but would not be put in any sort of immediate danger.

Interestingly, none of these types of exchange are specifically human—examples of them occur among higher and lower animals alike. Gifts, from feeding the young to sharing the kill with the entire pack to gifts presented to the mate as part of the mating ritual, are ubiquitous among animals. Tribute is represented by predator-prey and host-pathogen relationships, where the predator/pathogen keeps the prey population healthy and in balance by eliminating the weak. Another example of tribute is parasitism; often cast in an entirely negative light, host-parasite relationships sometimes benefit the host. Examples include the hookworm, which cures its host of allergies. Even

Plasmodium malariae, the nefarious protozoan that causes malaria in humans, has sometimes played a positive cameo role, such as keeping out malaria-susceptible invaders from malaria-infested coastal zones of Borneo. How different is this from peasants paying tribute to a local aristocratic thug who keeps other thugs at bay? The principle of barter is reflected by the sometimes rather inflexible hierarchies that exist among some of the higher mammals; those who have a lot to offer also claim the right to demand more in return. Trade is commonly represented as theft; I once had some magpies steal my bar of soap and shaving mirror while I had my back turned. What the magpies offered me in trade was the right to be in their territory without having them defecate on my head, so these objects were a sort of rent. Adélie penguins have a set ritual for stealing each other's rocks to make nests; if they look at a rock, then look at you quizzically and you don't return their stare, then the rock is considered rightfully theirs. Some people may be scandalized to hear that trade and theft form a continuum, but they do; if they did not, then the government departments that break up monopolies and fight consumer fraud would have nothing to do. In fact, the most straightforward and general way to define trade is as a process by which property passes between strangers. Whether both benefit, just one or none at all depends on how many of the strangers within a given situation happen to be suckers. And although some might think that some Darwinian process is responsible for eliminating suckers from the system, there is no reason to think so. There is nothing to prevent suckers from being taken advantage of from generation to generation, until they can be said to be purpose-bred to play suckers, and they can continue to thrive in this role provided they do not depend on trade for survival; or, to put it another way, as long as they are not robbed of their livelihoods.

But fascinating though they are, let us leave analogies with the animal kingdom behind and concentrate on human universals instead. Here, some more specific definitions are in order. Let us assume that trade is where goods or services are exchanged for abstract monetary units. Creating a system in which all participants are willing to trade generally involves forming a monopoly. This is not a theoretical requirement, and although theoreticians such as Hayek have proposed privatizing money (to no avail), as a practical matter money tends to be a monopoly wherever it exists, be it in the form of coin of the realm or of paper fiat money, and making your own money is called counterfeiting and is considered a crime. Social status tends to be based on one's possession of these abstract monetary units.

Trade also presupposes the existence of a public market mechanism—a commons in which trade is conducted in full public view and where market prices are established by observing a large number of transactions and averaging across them over time, and in which none of the participants holds the upper hand or has the ability to distort prices for their private benefit. Markets do not function well in situations where a large volume of business is transacted in secret.

To summarize, trade works best when everyone is plugged into a monopolistic system for issuing and regulating the use of money, which has a public process of price discovery and negotiation and where social status depends on how much money one manages to accumulate through trade.

Tribute describes various contributions and donations based on allegiance, religion, tradition, charity and so on. Social status is not based on how much you have but on how much you can give away to support some local institution or tradition. One common form of tribute is as a recurring payment demanded by the winning side in a military conflict. It is a contract entered into to make peace: instead of continuing to wage war one opts to make payments. The conquered often decide that being reconquered endlessly is a bad idea and, having no better options available to them, willingly agree to pay their conquerers not to conquer them again. This, for a lot of nations, has turned out to be a very successful scheme. Once they become enshrined in tradition, such payments can go on for centuries. One example of a surprisingly long-lived tribute arrangement is the tribute the Russian empire paid to the Crimean Tatars all the way up to the Russian Revolution; the tribute was initially established in 1274, right after the Mongol invasion. The payments spanned 643 years, during most of which the Tatars no longer posed a threat.

Barter describes exchanges in kind, which can take place either inside or outside of a market system based on coincident wants: A wants something that B has, and B wants something that A has. There is a large grey area where A wants something specific from B while B is willing to accept any number of valuable items (that are not money) that A happens to have. This arrangement may be a precursor to a private trading system, where people barter use goods (that are consumed) for trade goods (that serve as a store of value and are pressed into service as a private medium of exchange). Thus, as I described in detail in the chapter on financial collapse, barter can evolve into a clandestine system for avoiding the use of money in cases where money is scarce or its use risky, inconvenient or onerous. It is helpful in repressive circumstances where unsanctioned use of money invites persecution, or in conditions of lawlessness where the use of money invites official or criminal predation.

Social status is based on one's usefulness to those with whom one chooses to barter. Although it is commonly thought that barter is just a less evolved and inconvenient precursor to trade, in reality it can be an entirely different kind of system, in which one takes into account somebody else's needs in addition to one's own, as well as the market price. If you choose to exchange your surplus of onions for your neighbor's surplus of potatoes, you will likely take into account the local need for onions and potatoes—among the people you are bartering with rather than in some abstract market that exists outside your local community. You and your neighbor may know the market price of onions and potatoes, but since you are bartering specifically because neither of you wants to pay money for what you are short of, and since neither of you can be bothered to take your surplus to market and try to sell it for money, that is a moot point. What is not a moot point is how much these onions and potatoes are worth to you and your neighbor. And it often turns out that one's taste for onions is, shall we say, circumscribed, whereas potatoes happen to be quite popular with the family and very much missed when they run out. And then the basis of the barter arrangement becomes "Take as many onions as you need, and give me as many potatoes as you can spare." This makes a far better and fairer barter arrangement than one that blindly accepts the dictates of the market in potatoes and onions, in which neither you nor your neighbor particularly wish to participate.

The many advantages of gift

While barter involves some amount of friendly confrontation, or haggling, and an explicit quid pro quo even when practiced among good friends, no such explicit dividing line exists when it comes to exchanging gifts. In fact, with gifts it is taboo to even allude to there being any expectation of a quid pro quo, and doing so can be the gravest of insults.

While barter involves an external conflict between two conflicting sets of interests that is resolved through negotiation, gift internalizes this conflict in each person. Explicitly and publicly one never gives gifts expecting to get something back. But gift also presupposes a debt of gratitude that is discharged through reciprocity. Nevertheless, with gifts one's social status is based on one's generosity and is destroyed by any explicit expectation of reciprocation.

Gratitude is an amazing, very highly evolved human cultural universal; every society understands what it means. Even animals understand gratitude: take good care of a cat and it will periodically bring you the gift of a mouse. Such symbolic gifts play a role even among humans; but to give a gift that is meaningful, one must first gain a good understanding of somebody else's personal needs relative to your own. This process involves a balance, which is an amazing thing; it is one of the few human virtues that involves the notion of a balance as a core principle. Honesty, compassion and fairness can be practiced without limit, but one must not be either overly generous or not generous enough when discharging a debt of gratitude.

According to sociological research conducted by Marcel Mauss, author of the groundbreaking book *The Gift* (1950), gift economies existed in just about every culture and on every continent and predate market economies, which only emerged a few thousand years ago. Crucially, he found that practices of reciprocal gift-giving formed the foundation of public life in archaic societies, and that in these societies gift-giving was a collective rather than an individual activity. Although his findings can be readily extrapolated to politics, leading to the conclusion that market economics is a degenerate form of human contact, and perhaps coming to view socialism as a way of reintroducing morality into social relations, a far less controversial and more defensible conclusion to draw from his work is that gifts predate and therefore exist outside of any ideology, invalidating any ideological claims to restoring morality through gift because gift is self-regulating, being based on an innate system of ethics.

The advantages of gift are numerous. A gift-based economy is well suited to surviving hard times. Severe economic downturns and collapses invalidate many of the promises with which people bind themselves within a market economy by signing contracts. Since gifts are voluntary, there are no contracts to breach and nothing to litigate. A gift-based economy is self-governing through custom and taboo and requires no regulatory regime, making it resilient in circumstances where the government is corrupt, predatory or defunct. Gifts tend to preserve diversity of culture, since gifts are valued more highly when they are unique; a handcrafted, artistic gift is vastly superior to a mass-produced one.

Gifts tend to create or restore cooperation, solidarity and social harmony: when participating in a market economy, individuals are motivated by greed and fear and compete in pursuing their own advantage; but when participating in a gift economy, individuals are motivated by generosity and compete in their ability to respond to each others' needs. Whereas market interactions can be coercive (you must buy health and car insurance, pay privatized utility companies and so on) gifts, to be valid, must be voluntary, and so gift economies preserve and defend freedom. Gifts are passed between people who know each other personally, so a gift-based economy tends to be local rather than global and exclude risky dealings with strangers across the world.

A gift-based economy tends to conserve resources by limiting production, since generosity and recognition of mutual needs have natural, recognizable limits, whereas a market economy tends to squander resources by maximizing production as market participants vie with each other to achieve dominance through increased market share, economies of scale and monopoly pricing, even if this involves going into debt and risking a loss. Gift economies distribute wealth, resulting in a more egalitarian, and therefore more unified and less conflicted, society, whereas market economies tend to concentrate wealth in fewer and fewer hands until, inevitably, the revolution comes, perhaps bringing with it some guillotines or death squads, and the wealth is expropriated; then the process of wealth concentration begins anew.

Market economies are driven by suspicion and mistrust, and *caveat emptor* ("buyer beware") always remains the watchword, while gift economies create trust between individuals and groups of people. The pernicious nature of market relationships is plainly visible in the commonly held view that friends and family should not have business dealings with each other, because if they do they risk ruining their relationships and friendships. It is perhaps possible to go even further and to say that the free market, with its unfettered pursuit of gain motivated by fear and greed, is corrosive to the human spirit, and should be avoided whenever possible, but to be pragmatic we have to concede that the free market has a role to play—but that it is best kept to a cameo role that does not affect the plot.

It is important to keep a lookout for degenerate cases of gifts that are not really gifts. Charitable donations, endowments and other forms of largesse are gifts that cannot be reciprocated and are thus not gifts at all; they are handouts designed to please the benefactor. They do not give rise to gratitude or a desire to reciprocate. They do give rise to resentment, dependency and unjustified feelings of entitlement. Charity, grift and extortion form a single continuum of perversely motivated exchange, and where you find yourself on that continuum depends on who wields the information and the power in a given relationship. A gift that can never be reciprocated is naturally taken as a form of abuse or an insult, and the inability to express these feelings causes feelings of inferiority and psychological stress. Charity is really a sort of imposed hypocrisy—a system of domination by those who have the upper hand financially, and who first put one in need of help and then turn around and offer help in the most humiliating way possible. "Crumbs from the master's table," even if accepted gladly, create hostility and alienation. A natural response is to try to gain the upper hand in the relationship by subverting the purpose of charity, for instance, by clamoring for more than you need and selling off the surplus.

But such problems are generally avoidable. Because gifts are a cultural universal, most people already know the rules that must be followed when giving or receiving them. As I already mentioned, any allusion to quid pro quo is an automatic disqualification. While money is the thoughtless gift par excellence, standardized gifts, where everyone receives the same thing, are almost equally thoughtless. Re-gifting is possible but its desirability varies. On the one hand, it is embarrassing when the same Christmas present passes from hand to hand on consecutive Christmases. On the other hand, intergenerational re-gifting is quite acceptable and even admirable. (There are certain books that have been in my family for generations, passed by one generation to the next several times, each time with a carefully penned dedication on the title page.) Selling a gift is best done in secret, and complaining about a gift you have received marks you as an ungrateful person. Boasting about a gift you gave is quite rude, because gratitude cannot be assumed or forced. Giving too generous a gift is thoughtless because it results in an unreasonable onus of reciprocation. To keep a gift a secret is a strange thing to want to do: generosity is a public virtue, and those who give gifts anonymously or in secret appear sinister. Trivial gifts are insulting, as is making a gift of something you dislike or find useless; such items can be passed off, but never as gifts. While giving or receiving gifts, most people abandon the utilitarian ethic and automatically assume roles that accord with a subtle etiquette. In short, gifts bring out the best in us.

Money corrupts

A gift-based economy neatly avoids the use of money. To start with, money makes a poor, thoughtless gift. A gift of money sends the message "I can't be bothered to think about your needs, figure them out yourself." It should be viewed not as a proper gift but as a bribe given to overlook the obligation to give a gift. A reasonable and polite response to somebody proffering money in lieu of a gift is to say something like "Thank you, but I really don't need your money." Next, money is a tacky or ugly gift: gold and silver coins are gaudy, shiny bits of metal; paper money is an ugly, useless bit of paper with the picture of a dead person on it that makes good kindling, has limited usefulness as a bookmark and does not work too well as toilet paper. Eventually all paper currency comes to be worth its own weight in recycled paper. The use of money increases social inequality over time by inevitably concentrating power in fewer and fewer hands (until the revolution comes).

It is not often recognized that it is exceedingly difficult to do good by spending money. It is often thought that however a fortune is made— be it by exploiting sweatshop and child labor, by robbing widows and orphans, by accelerating environmental destruction or by robbing the elderly by devaluing their savings—the fortunate person can redeem himself by setting up a foundation to do good and lavishing funds on it. But the hypocrisy of this approach is plain to see; it is like un-raping a girl by sending her flowers. The damage done by making money cannot be undone by spending some of it. But this may not even be the true goal, for often the object of philanthropy is simply to indulge the vanity of the philanthropist. Add to this the fact that charity is a degenerate form of gift, a gift that cannot be reciprocated and therefore demeans its recipient.

Frequent and regular use of money tends to warp the mind in a particular direction, where one starts to treat money as a yardstick for all sorts of things that should never be assigned a monetary value. This is manifested in vulgar, low-class expressions such as "He looks like a million bucks!" as well as in the often unsaid undercurrents of thought in the wealthy, who—the poor things—are forced to constantly reappraise their self-worth in view of the fluctuating fortunes of others within their class. The endless, joyless banter in Jane Austen's *Pride and Prejudice* over the size of this or that person's estate would be quite comic if it were not also quite sad.

In turn, the use of money as a universal yardstick inspires mediocrity. By the nature of its universality, money has the widest possible appeal, cutting across all strata of society. But society is a sea of mediocrity punctuated by a few flashes of brilliance, most of which are only recognized at the time by a few connoisseurs, if at all. A case in point: in societies where literature is commercialized, most of the authors whose names live on forever languish in obscurity during their lifetimes, while the widely read authors of any given era remain of interest only to literary historians of a subsequent era, if that. The use of money as a measure of quality cheapens the efforts of the connoisseurs to distinguish the excellent from the run of the mill while encouraging artists, authors, craftsmen and other creative people to cater to the lowest common denominator. In short, money corrupts culture.

Use of money concentrates trust in a single central authority—the central bank—and, over extended periods of time, central banks always tend to misbehave. Eventually the "print" button on the central banker's emergency console becomes stuck in the depressed position, flooding the world with worthless notes. People trust that money will remain a store of value, and once that trust is violated a gigantic black hole appears at the very center of society, sucking in peoples' savings and aspirations along with their sense of self-worth. When those who have become psychologically dependent on money as a yardstick, to be applied to everything and everyone, suddenly find themselves in a world where money means nothing, it is as if they have gone blind; they see shapes but can no longer resolve them into objects. The result is anomie—a sense of unreality—accompanied by deep depression. Money is an addiction—substanceless abuse, one might call it—and a society that binges on money in turn becomes hollow, substanceless and unreal, and sets itself up for a severe and lengthy withdrawal.

Opportunities for gift-giving

It may at first glance appear difficult to expand the role of gift as long as the consumer economy continues to offer a large selection of shoddily made, short-lived, extremely cheap items for sale, but the pressure to do so increases steadily as the number of those still employed continues to decline, their wages remain stagnant, and almost everyone's purchasing power gradually dwindles. It will remain challenging to substitute homemade, hand-made gifts for purchased consumer items as long as these remain available. But there are many other areas where gifts already offer major advantages.

One such area is community labor. There is nothing (except social inertia and lack of initiative) to prevent a neighborhood that already happens to have a good selection of unemployed or underemployed tradesmen (a plumber, an electrician, a carpenter, a roofer, a stone-mason, a few landscapers and a whole lot of watchmen, caretakers and gardeners) from setting up an informal labor exchange. In an area where shopping involves a long drive, there is nothing to preclude neighbors from setting up a shopping cooperative, where a single truck, with more cargo capacity than an entire fleet of passenger cars, makes a weekly trip to stock up on behalf of the entire neighborhood, taking advantage of wholesale prices in the process.

Opportunities of this sort already abound, but the most effective—and most traditional—ways of getting people together revolve around construction (barn-raising is a typical example, but other types of construction work are also best done in large teams) and, of course, planting and harvesting. Some of these tasks can involve children, especially harvesting, which offers a chance to give children a productive social role to play from a very young age while keeping the line between work and play purposely blurred. When such tasks are treated as jobs they are tedious and often unpleasant, but when they are recast as opportunities to socialize and play with children, with much banter, singing and laughter, their nature changes and the work goes quickly. The impetus switches from working hard to making the work easy—which it often is if done right. Of course, there are certain tasks that no amount of creative thinking can turn into a party—dredging ditches comes to mind—but most tasks can be livened up considerably if there are a few children playing nearby, a picnic table with cold lemonade and a few people to talk to during breaks.

Although community labor in all its forms can be seen in purely utilitarian terms—as a way of getting things done without spending money—there is a larger and quite possibly more important reason for promoting it: community labor offers an opportunity to deemphasize, and perhaps eventually supplant entirely, the industrial model of work. To put it in very precise terms, community labor offers a way to *deproletarianize* society. The industrial definition of work is the exchange of time for money. During this time, people are not free to do as they see fit but are expected to follow orders. Work time is different from the rest of the time, separates one from one's family and follows a different set of rules. The industrial model of labor attempts to fashion people into commodities whose value is defined by their education and training. It was considered optimal and efficient (according to yet another self-contradictory definition of efficiency) in the context of an endlessly expanding industrial economy powered by cheap fossil fuels. But in the context of an eroding industrial economy with an endlessly contracting demand for industrial labor, each unemployed or underemployed worker becomes, in one way or another, a burden on the system, causing the economy to erode even faster. In this context, an entrepreneurial attitude toward work becomes far more effective as people, of their own free will and initiative, come together to perform work for the benefit of those around them—their families and neighbors. The end state of this process is a society that refuses to be proletarianized and where working for wages is considered disgraceful and taboo—a sort of desexualized prostitution. As we shall see, there are societies of this kind, and they do quite well. Their members can be engaged to do work, usually as entire families or informal work groups, but they cannot be made to serve.

Community labor is an excellent way to bring people together by having them share their time; community facilities are an equally excellent way to do this by having people share a space. This is best done as informally as possible—the best-equipped, largest kitchen becomes the community kitchen; the best and largest workshop becomes the community workshop. Having it be owned by one person or, better yet, one family keeps organizational overhead down to almost nothing while making sure that someone is in charge. The benefits of community facilities are numerous: they provide a place for people to meet, to work and to learn from each other; they minimize the amount of underutilized space and equipment; and, by achieving community-level economies of scale, they reduce the amount of labor required to achieve a given level of community self-sufficiency.

Meanwhile in Soviet Russia

Some of my perspective on all this comes from growing up in the USSR, which never had much of a market economy. In Soviet Russia, goods were not so much sold as distributed. The foodstuffs that were always in stock were the most bland and boring ones: a few types of grains, pasta, bread, some canned goods and vodka. When something more desirable appeared for sale (bananas, for instance) the news would spread through the neighborhood like wildfire and people would queue up to snap up all that was offered. When something was made available for sale, it was said that something was being "thrown out," and people showed up not so much to buy it as to pick it up. Whether you had money to pay for it was not all that important, because if you happened to be short of cash a relative or a friend might give you some. Since there was often a limit on how much one person could buy, entire families would queue up. This made it possible to get three times as many bananas as you needed and then sell off two-thirds of them, provided you charged exactly the same price; if you started marking them up the authorities would haul you off to jail for "profiteering," which was illegal. Buying and selling for profit was called "speculation" and was considered immoral. The Soviet economy wasn't about money, it was about access, and social status was based not on possession but on access. Certain people were respected for their ability to find things; they were called *dostavály* (procurers). This state of affairs inevitably gave rise to widespread reliance on personal favors. Nobody really benefitted from selling you the extra bananas; they were just doing it out of the goodness of their hearts. And then you were expected to compensate them by doing them personal favors. Attempting to pay for favors was considered an insult. And because all access was based on personal favors, gaining access was often quite tricky.

There were many occasions when what was nominally a gift strayed into barter territory, where people would give gifts to each other expecting to get something specific in return. For example, my father was a professor, and some new graduate students, hoping to claim him as their advisor, would lavish presents on him upon their arrival; bottles of cognac were the usual, but one student came up with a whole set of silver cutlery. This was rather extreme, and my father turned him down, because if that were to be the starting present, the compensation would perhaps involve writing the student's entire dissertation!

It was generally expected that family members would help each other out. If a well-off family member refused to help a relative in need, he or she would lose face. This help was not necessarily provided happily, resulting in quite a lot of tension, and was sometimes accompanied by constant jibes at one's no-good son-in-law or brother-in-law who failed to provide. But the help would flow regardless, because helping that person was less painful, overall, than not helping.

That system was doomed, but in some of its backwardness it retained many traces of an earlier, much more humane way of doing things, and some elements of earlier forms of social organization. I would never suggest that we should go back to the Soviet way of doing things, because it was quite terrible in many ways, although there are still some older people in Russia who think of the Soviet era as the good old days and detest the harsh new social reality that was forced upon them by the introduction of the market economy. I mention it here not as an invitation to wallow in nostalgia but as an opportunity to learn, because the Soviet economy, in spite of its many imperfections, left more room for certain positive cultural universals that the market economy has effectively walled off and consigned to oblivion, leaving us far less prepared for its inevitable demise.

The new normal

No survey of doomed systems would be complete without a discussion of the status quo in developed market economies. The antipodal "new normal" is a topsy-turvy version of how humans normally live and behave toward each other. In the current way of doing things, trade holds the dominant position at the top of the antipodal relationship pyramid; we can get most of the things we need only by giving money to strangers, many of whom live in faraway lands. Tribute remains; the biggest form of tribute is taxes, but other forms are also present, such as enforced contributions to retirement and health insurance schemes (most of which are, by this point in time, either insolvent or nearing insolvency). Barter is quite marginalized, continuing to exist as an exchange of minor favors (helping someone move is a typical example). Most interactions are impersonal, based on purchase and sale within a market system. Although legal systems offer some protection against

outright fraud, many kinds of swindles are considered perfectly legal, and if you lose and somebody else wins, that is considered perfectly fair and nothing personal. If you neglect to read the fine print in every lengthy legal document you sign, then it is your fault when you lose out as a result, because it was your choice to deal with people whom you have no reason to trust and therefore your mistake. You cannot turn around and say, "You were unfair to me," because here "fairness" is interpreted as abiding by an abstract set of rules that are interpreted quite technically, and "unfairness" has lost its previous meaning of neglecting someone else's needs in favor of your own.

Although for most people tribute is limited to taxes and other non-negotiable, imposed expenditures, the well-to-do practice another form of tribute in the form of charitable donations and other impersonal status-seeking behaviors. Those who have an excess of capital from their commercial transactions can devote some of it to things that raise their status, in an impersonal way, because very rarely, if ever, do they have a personal relationship of mutual dependency and trust with whoever benefits. Gifts remain as vestigial cultural forms reserved for ceremonial uses, such as the engagement ring, wedding and anniversary presents and, that most vestigial of all vestiges, the retirement watch (for those lucky few that manage to keep their jobs until retirement). The marginal, degenerate nature of these examples of tribute, barter and gift underscore a central point: everyone is completely dependent on financialized, commercialized, impersonal systems. When these systems fail, as they do repeatedly, there is nothing for people to fall back on.

Worse yet, this sort of topsy-turvy living appears to provide a direct path to national bankruptcy, because, with the global economy in its current, now permanent climate-disrupted and resource-strapped state, and with further economic growth largely impossible, the only way to keep the topsy-turvy arrangement running is by constantly taking on more debt. In turn, since individuals, municipalities and other entities are already highly indebted and bad credit risks, that debt is, by default, assigned to national governments. Central banks become black holes that constantly inhale public debt while issuing credit at zero percent interest. Everyone is living in fear that the magic of credit creation will fail (which it eventually will) and that the financialized, commercialized, impersonal global economy will disappear, leaving behind towering piles of plastic debris and a gradually dissipating pall of smog.

But there is a fallback: the normal human relationship pyramid, based on personal, tribal and familial relationships and dominated by gifts, barter and tribute, can provide a solid basis for a local economy. In such an economy, just about everything circulates nearby, and even if there are some items that have to be acquired through long-distance trade, they are just the very tip of the pyramid, reserved for luxury goods and some key necessities that are not available locally. Imports remain naturally restricted in scope because a localized economy is geared to serving local needs rather than providing a large surplus of trade goods. Most people find that they are able to get what they need by calling in favors or receiving gifts, see no reason to struggle and work long hours in order to accumulate abstract wealth with which to impress strangers, and get to quietly enjoy their self-sufficiency, uniqueness and independence from the whims of faraway people in the big, hostile outside world.

A cultural flip

Although many people find it pleasing to think it possible to introduce half-measures such as local currencies, some amount of local production, more emphasis on locally provided services and so on, in reality such a transition may be hard to effect. This is because while the global economy is still functioning, on credit, it is very difficult to compete with it by any means other than its own: by taking on endless debt and shifting production to where it is cheapest. But competing with it becomes utterly irrelevant once it has failed, so any effort expended on doing so now is wasted effort. On the other hand, the moment your credit lapses or you can no longer expand it, you go bankrupt, you lose your access to imports, and then all you have left is the tiny little frustrum labeled "gift" that sits at the very bottom of the upside-down pyramid, and you must suddenly depend on it to provide you with everything you need to survive.

The idea of effecting a transition to a self-sustaining, deglobalized economy while clinging steadfastly to the commercial paradigm is fundamentally flawed; it is akin to attempting to cure one disease by catching a different one with fewer or more benign symptoms. Instead, a change in perspective is required, a cultural flip. Gradually at first, but faster and faster, all economic relationships need to be deproletarianized and rehumanized—by dealing with people you actually know, and dealing with them face to face; by avoiding the use of money and documents while emphasizing verbal agreements as a way of cultivating trust and knowing who to shun should they break your trust; by giving preference to family, relations (even distant ones), then old friends and neighbors, then new friends and neighbors while doing your best to cut out everyone else, be they representatives of transnational corporations, squinty-eyed people with bulging moneybags or royally pedigreed nincompoops with posh accents.

Before even starting in this direction, false gods must be exorcised: these are the faulty ideas that have penetrated and polluted people's minds. One such idea is that the "free market" is efficient and optimal, and that it spontaneously produces prosperity if unhindered. In fact, the free market is completely reliant on a system of property law, a legal system that is able to enforce contracts and a law enforcement system that can deter economic crime. The Russian experience in the 1990s showed that without these vital ingredients a free market quickly becomes a criminal market, where debts are settled for pennies on the dollar by having creditors murdered. In the end, the free market turns out to be a government scheme and fails when the government fails through national bankruptcy.

An inferior alternative to the free market government scheme is a planned economy government scheme, Soviet-style. Government-instituted market systems are marginally better at chewing through non-renewable resources than centrally planned government systems. Both collapse shortly after they become resource-constrained and find that they are unable to grow any further. The Soviet Union was less efficient, in the particularly bizarre sense of efficiency defined as the ability to squander natural resources down to the last drop—be it a drop of biofuel, fracked shale oil or synth oil from tar sands—and so was the first to collapse, but then this gave Russia time to recover. Inefficiency really pays sometimes!

It is sometimes very difficult to see through the fog generated by the antipodal authorities whom we have been taught to trust and respect. But most of what we have been and are being told about economics has to do with a specific special case—the growth economy—that now is all but over. Nevertheless, people keep going on about an economic system that no longer exists and is irrelevant, because it is all that they are able to discuss. Nobody within the economics profession seems to want to look at how the economy collapses once growth stops, which is about the only relevant topic left for them to ponder.

Antipodal society relies on some crisp functional delineations. In order to function within antipodal society, you must first classify your role. You can be a customer or a client; this is by far the easiest role to play, since it primarily involves spending money (and when you run out of money, credit). If you are not a customer/client, you can be a business owner, an employee, a contractor or self-employed; an investor, an official or a professional. If you cannot be any of these, then your remaining choices are to be juvenile, indigent, retired, disabled or deceased. But what if you are none of the above? As far as antipodal society is concerned, you are a delinquent, a loiterer and a nuisance.

In the meantime, the fastest-growing categories of people are not on this list. They are: recent college graduates with no prospects of employment; unemployed people whose unemployment benefits have run out; retirees with insufficient retirement benefits or savings who are unable to work; servicemen discharged from the military who are unable to find civilian employment; and young people who are not entering the labor market for lack of prospects. It is autumn in the global economy, and the squirrels are falling out of the trees and getting run over. Few people find it advantageous to classify themselves as dropouts, a classification that receives little recognition and provides few benefits. As we get ready to bid adieu to the antipodes, we must remain careful to avoid being classified into a category that is not to our advantage. To do this, we can create categories that are neither too much of this nor too much of that. Categories such as researcher, freelancer, hobbyist and volunteer work well; they are all flexible and difficult to pin down. I, for instance, am a writer; if you want proof, I can show you my pen.

While we learn to be creative and take clandestine liberties with the ways antipodal society attempts to classify us, we must also learn to be creative in numerous other ways. You can look for ways to use your residual money to reduce and for periods of time even eliminate the need for a continued cash flow. You can learn both general and specialized skills, eliminating the need for most specialists. You can learn how to find the lowest-tech, cheapest, most robust and most maintainable solution that works in any given situation, opting out of the world of consumer gadgets. You can create closed-cycle systems for food production, shelter maintenance, transportation, entertainment and so on.

Most importantly, you can work on reducing your dependence on impersonal relationships and institutions. You can learn to avoid relying on money and monetary equivalents, and instead learn to rely on gifts and the various extensions and generalizations of gifts. You can create new custom and ritual, laying the foundation for a new culture that is right side up.

Case Study: The Russian Mafia

Modern societies rely on the government to defend property rights, enforce contracts and regulate commerce. As the economy expands, so do the functions of government, along with its bureaucratic structures, laws, rules and procedures and—what expands fastest of all—its cost. All of these official arrangements show an accretion of complexity over time. Each time a new problem needs to be solved, something is added to the structure, but nothing is ever taken away, because previous arrangements are often grandfathered in, and because simplifying a complex arrangement is always more difficult and initially more expensive than complicating it further. But socioeconomic complexity is never without cost, and once the economy crests and begins to contract, this cost becomes prohibitive. In the context of a shrinking economy buffeted by waves of escalating crises, an outsized officialdom comes to exhibit ever greater *negative* economies of scale, while the arduous task of reforming it so as to scale it down and simplify it cannot receive priority due to a lack of resources. In the best case, after a more or less chaotic transitional period, new, simplified and scaled-down official structures do eventually arise.

The government, at least in its nonfunctional, purely symbolic form, may not be abandoned outright. A few of its key functions may come to be served by unofficial groups. An almost completely lawless envi-. ronment may prevail in certain particularly distressed areas for a time, after the government loses all ability to act due to lack of resources, and before local forms of unofficial self-governance spontaneously arise. It must be remembered that governments exist mainly through taxation. In a declining economy, the tax base shrinks while the government's expenditures on social spending and crisis mitigation only go up, but the population cannot afford to pay a higher tax rate. In this situation, most governments nevertheless try to raise taxes, with the effect of driving economic activity underground. As the population is forced to resort to illegal forms of commerce, to informal arrangements, barter, gift and subsistence economies in order to survive in conditions of increasing poverty and joblessness, this vicious cycle feeds on itself and the government withers away, turns to criminal activities to survive, or both.

As the process of governmental disintegration runs its course, alternative, unofficial forms of governance take its place rather quickly. It is neither accurate nor helpful to imagine a spontaneous descent into some sort of Hobbesian state of nature, which, given what we now know, is best regarded as a ridiculous fable, a work of whimsy and a projection of ignorance, for where there is no law, there is custom and taboo that have the force of law and are upheld through judicious use of violence. Where there are no official authorities, unofficial ones spontaneously arise. Trade and commerce go on, but without government involvement or protection.

What's more, in a transitional, crisis-wracked environment such unofficial forms of governance often turn out to be far more cost-effective. The government, with its predictable, impersonal, rule-governed, procedure-oriented set of evolved behaviors, is only able to function effectively in a stable, predictable environment. A collapsing economy is not such an environment. Here, all judgements and actions have to be based on the local, immediate situation, all solutions have to be improvised and ones that involve going through official channels and gaining official approval become noncompetitive. Illegal ways of doing business easily outcompete legal ones.

The focus on illegality is in some sense inevitable, but it is also not entirely helpful, because it tends to paint all activities as black or white. It is far more helpful to view them as grayscale, or as distributed over a two-dimensional map. In one corner, we have public institutions functioning legally—or perhaps not functioning at all: the police, the courts, code enforcement, inspectional services and so on. In the opposite corner we have private institutions functioning illegally: organized criminal groups. But there are two more corners. We also have public institutions functioning illegally—police and security forces acting privately, either for hire or on their own behalf. There can also be private organizations legally providing services that the government can no longer provide: private security and protection companies. There are numerous gray areas, such as officials randomly enforcing laws to settle scores with certain individuals or groups, or to provide a credible basis for later demanding bribes in exchange for agreeing to look the other way.

A large increase in illegal activity is often the direct fault of the government. A government that makes many essential activities illegal but lacks the ability to enforce the ban succeeds in only one thing: creating a large field of action for illegal enterprises. This, in turn, creates demand for their private protection. It is this key function of offering private protection for illegal enterprises that provides the initial basis for an entire new mode of governance. In this context, organized crime should be regarded not just as a form of social organization but as a form of alternative governance, which succeeds or fails based on personal and group reputation for honest dealing, and on its ability to use violence when it is justified and suppress it when it is not.

In many ways a weak government, which can impose a ban but not enforce it, is far worse than a largely defunct government, whose officials perform a few ceremonial duties and rarely set foot outside the heavily guarded official compound in the capital city. A weak government with some residual capacity for law enforcement produces a far more violent environment than a defunct one, by disrupting the work of organizations that offer private protection to illegal enterprises. Once the government has given up on law enforcement and become purely ceremonial, private protection organizations can begin to provide services to both legal and illegal enterprises, and indeed to the government itself. Ties between such organizations can then be worked out and territories and spheres of influence divided up, minimizing the level of violence. In this sense, a weak government's efforts at law enforcement further weaken the economy by making it difficult for organizations that provide private protection to do their work, while their services are in demand precisely because of the government's inefficiency in providing protection. Of course, this only further undermines the government.

The concept of deviant or criminal behavior "becomes less relevant in the case of a transitional society when social and legal norms are in flux"[13] writes Vadim Volkov in *Violent Entrepreneurs: The Use of Force in the Making of Russian Capitalism*. According to Volkov, the transition in question should not be regarded as one that begins with the rule of law and ends with something else, but as a transition from badly-organized crime to well-organized crime. Examples of this sort of succession can be found throughout history and in many parts of the world. Be it the Sicilian Mafia, Al Capone's Chicago in the 1920s or Russia in the 1990s, there are numerous parallels in how such a transition occurs. If allowed to run its course, it eventually supplants the government and forms a system of self-governance and private protection whose legality is no longer in dispute.

Nor is this a recent phenomenon: during the Middle Ages, and even into modern times, protection rents were the largest source of fortunes made in commerce, playing a larger role in generating profits than production technology or industrial organization. Protection rents offer a means of stimulating an economic recovery (subject to natural resource constraints). This is because an organization that offers protection forms a natural monopoly within its territory, allowing it to raise the price of protection above its costs and generate a monopoly profit, which it is then able to invest in productive resources. In the absence of a government, it is the only actor that can create temporary austerity but produce greater prosperity down the road by reallocating resources from consumption to capital goods. If more competitive institutional frameworks are allowed to evolve, formerly criminal groups can become legitimate shareholders in the businesses from which they had previously extorted payments.

Such a scheme does not spontaneously arise everywhere. The demand for protection services is a matter of scale; it does not exist in societies where people deal only with those they know personally, face to face, and where disputes are mediated by family and clan. It is a by-product of economic specialization, impersonal relations and the need for long-distance trade. In societies where interpersonal trust is high, no one needs enforcers, and where there is sufficient solidarity, people can unite and defeat the common threat of gangsterism. Like weeds that opportunistically colonize areas of disturbed soil, criminal groups sprout up in disturbed societies. Small-scale enterprises in large-scale societies are the most susceptible; kiosk owners and street vendors are traditional targets for racketeers. Next are corrupt public officials, who spontaneously give rise to private protection, because they create a market niche for those who broker bribes and guarantee the transactions of bribery, protecting both sides: the briber from non-performance and the bribed from non-payment.

The need for protection, be it private or government, is everywhere born of mistrust: "The business of private protection consists of producing a substitute for trust in a market economy where the state justice system is ignored."[14] It is therefore necessary, as we start to explore this topic, to set aside our negative reactions to terms such as thief, racket, mafia, gangster and so forth and concentrate on the circumstances that create a need for their services, and on how the racketeers and the gangsters can evolve in a positive direction because, strangely enough, they often do.

Thieves, and proud of it

Most people hear in the word "thief" either an accusation of theft or a term of abuse. If you are one of them, then it may surprise you to learn that in Russian the word *vor* (thief) is an honorific, at least among other *vory* (thieves). One does not automatically become a *vor* by stealing; a mere criminal is not a fellow-*vor* but a lowly *blatnóy* (thug)—someone who inhabits a twilight zone between the loathsome government-imposed reality and the criminal underworld which they lovingly call *mat' rodnáya* (the mother who bore me). A *vor* is someone who stands proudly apart from all that filth and rot, and is recognized as a *vor* only after a lengthy and arduous apprenticeship, sponsorship and formal acceptance into the fraternity. Above the rank-and-file *vory* towers the supreme *vor*, or a *vor*-in-chief, called *vor v zakóne* (lawful thief): an individual who has accrued sufficient status among *vory* and has exhibited great purity of character. A *vor v zakóne* is crowned with the title in a solemn ceremony, although, given the recent decay in morals, the title is now sometimes purchased, for upwards of a quarter of a million dollars.

Criminal fraternities and guilds have existed in Czarist Russia since time immemorial, but they found their fullest development and expression in response to the great challenge faced by the criminal underworld in surviving the Gulag. They emerged around 1920, dominated life in the Gulag until 1950 or so, then reemerged again in 1970s. Their challenge was in constructing a survivable existence while upholding the principles of the fraternity when most of its membership was serving out lengthy terms in the labor camps. This they did by constructing an alternative governance structure and economy within the camps, separate from the camp authorities, and maintaining tight control over other inmates. A crackdown by prison and labor camp authorities between 1948 and 1953, dubbed *súchya voyná* (bitches' war), decimated the fraternity, but it bounced back. The *vory* were well positioned to take advantage of the collapse of the USSR and the ensuing chaos. But then things did not go quite according to plan.

Russia's *vory* speak their own language, called Fenya, which has the same grammatical structure as Russian but its own vocabulary. The fraternity is not specifically Russian but cross-ethnic, and had a presence in most parts of the USSR. As part of the initiation ritual, each *vor* is given a *klíchka* (nickname or handle) in a symbolic, identity-altering rechristening. This new identity demands adherence to a set of rules of behavior, customs and taboos. A *vor* is required to be honest, truthful and helpful to other *vory* (but not to the general population). He is forbidden to work and must live on what he steals (although gambling winnings are also considered honorable). A *vor* must never cooperate with any government official, must never plead guilty and must never acknowledge the existence of official law. He is forbidden to serve in the army or to testify in court, and must collect tribute from non-*vory* for the *obshchák* (communal fund), which is managed by the local *vor v zakóne*. When imprisoned, a *vor* should use the threat of prison revolt to defend his way of life. He is expected to exercise control over *blatnýe* (thugs). A *vor* is forbidden from engaging in unsanctioned violence and may not commit murder except in self-defense, in defense of his honor or to carry out an execution when the verdict has been pronounced by a *skhódka* (council). Professional murderers are never accepted into the fraternity. To become a *vor*, one must sever all familial ties, and may never marry or start a family. A *vor* may own a prostitute, who is called *zhená* (wife) but is not quite the same thing. A *vor*'s wife is expected to cohabit with a colleague while he is imprisoned, but there is always one lawful owner, and there are never any ménages à trois. Active homosexuality is allowed, but passive homosexuality is forbidden; thus, a *vor* may sodomize a *blatnóy* but never another *vor*, and never the other way around.

A Russian city or town is presided over by a single *vor v zakóne*, who is responsible for pooling together tribute and maintaining the *obschchák* (communal fund). The purpose of the *obshchák* is to provide a comfortable living for members who are in prison by procuring and smuggling in supplies, and to help them get established in business upon release. The term used for this support is *gret' zónu* (to warm the zone). The cold climate makes warmth a precious commodity associated with every kind of goodness. At the opposite extreme, a thoroughly despicable person is referred to as *ótmorozok* (frostbitten). The term *zóna* (zone) referred to the entire Gulag archipelago—all of the real estate inhabited by the prison population. In contrast, the rest of the USSR was called *bol'sháya zóna* (the big zone)—making it clear that the difference between life on the inside and life on the outside was one of degree of imprisonment.

The ruling body of the fraternity of *vory* is the *skhódka*—a convention in which everyone has a voice, although that of a *vor v zakóne* carries more weight. Major, national-level *skhódki* were held in Moscow in 1947, in Kazan in 1955, in Krasnodar in 1956 and in Kislovodsk in 1979. Each was attended by hundreds of *vory*. In addition to a wide variety of policy decisions, a *skhódka* can be used to decide whether to induct or expel members or to bring sanctions against anyone—not just *vory*. These sanctions may include a ban against boasting (which is unbelievably painful for a proud and boastful thief), a public slap in the face, fifty strokes with a stick and even death. Death sentences were carried out in accordance with a fixed ritual: the condemned man was to rip his shirt open and exclaim "Take my soul!" whereupon several people would stab him with knives. A death sentence passed at a *skhódka* in one prison colony or labor camp could be carried out at another one in the opposite corner of the country, eleven time zones away; there was no way to hide, and officials found it almost impossible to protect those who had been sentenced to death by any *skhódka* anywhere.

While living outside in the "big zone," *vory* lived in communes, which varied in size depending on the environment, from *sháika* (two to five individuals) to *malína* (ten to fifteen) to *kódla* (twenty to thirty), all engaged in gathering tribute to the best of their ability. Each commune combined an assortment of skill sets—pickpockets, burglars, forgers and so on. Over time, extortion became responsible for a bigger and bigger share of tribute going into the *obshchák*. Russian patterns of institutionalized corruption started under Stalin. Forged production reports made it possible to survive the Gulag, as Solzhenitsyn described in Part III of his opus. Later, the same tactics were used not for survival but for self-enrichment. The first large-scale illegal enterprises appeared in the 1970s, and people who made millions in them were preyed upon by amnestied *vory*.

Then came Gorbachev's anti-alcoholism campaign, which lasted from 1985 to 1990. Mikhail Sergeevich Gorbachev, the last General Secretary of the CPSU, is a respected figure and the recipient of the Nobel Peace Prize. But do you think that the anti-alcoholism campaign was an intelligent move on his part? Rationing vodka...in Russia....What could have possibly gone wrong? As vodka production and distribution went underground, gigantic criminal fortunes were amassed, setting the scene for what happened in the 1990s. For Russia's underground millionaires, it was far better to deal with the extortionists than with the authorities, because their riches had been illegally obtained. The extortionists would only take away their riches; the authorities, their riches *and* their freedom. At the *skhódka* in Kislovodsk in 1979 the nation's *vory v zakóne* decreed that 10 percent of all revenue from illegal enterprises should go directly into the *obshchák*, establishing an official criminal tithe. Then came the collapse of the USSR and market liberalization. The Russian reform program was designed to please two sides: on the one side were the former Soviet apparatchiks, who still had power, in one form or another, but were broke and wanted money; on the other side were the black market entrepreneurs, who had plenty of money but no power, and were beset by *vory*. Each wanted what the other had, and market liberalization was supposed to give them a way to get it. Rapid market liberalization...in a country lacking any recent experience with market economics...or any regulatory framework for market economics...beset by a nationwide, battle-hardened, organized, professional, proud, rich confederacy of thieves....Again, what could have possibly gone wrong?

Market liberalization as racketeering

The first wave of market liberalization occurred even while Gorbachev was still general secretary. New rules permitted small private businesses, called *kooperatívy* (cooperatives), to be started, but it was never clear who or what they were supposed to cooperate with, other than racketeers, who started preying on them the day after they were founded. Between 1989 and 1992 the prevalence of racketeering and extortion increased 20 to 25 percent per year, keeping pace with the establishment of private enterprises. The new Russian entrepreneurs were marginalized as a class, since their activity was only recently considered illegal and had little, if any, official protection. The new *chástniki* (privateers) were considered self-serving, dishonest and even criminal, and had little to lose in consorting with criminals. Little was done to combat this new wave of organized crime; initially, very few racketeers went to jail, and then only for a maximum of three years—perhaps just long enough for a young racketeer to graduate from *blatnóy* to *vor*. In 1994 the maximum sentence was increased to fifteen years, but, as private protection companies were granted legal status two years earlier, the horse was very much out of the barn by then.

The new crop of criminals was quite different from Soviet-era organized crime. Most of the early racketeers were young athletes—wrestlers, weightlifters, boxers, predominantly between eighteen and twenty-four years of age—who branched out into racketeering after state funding for sports was withdrawn. They initially learned their trade by watching Western films about the Mafia, from which they picked up such charming tricks as torture with a soldering iron, handcuffing to a radiator and making the victim dig his own grave. The appeal was obvious; physically impressive young men found racketeering to be less work than actual work. Furthermore, with the state security apparatus atrophying, their services were in high demand. Karate schools, which were officially banned between 1981 and 1995 but operated anyway, giving them a certain underworld cachet, provided trained cadres for racketeering organizations. There was much friction between the old *vory* and the new *sportsmény* (athletes), the latter being much more violent and willing to resort to murder. These young men in tracksuits were to be seen everywhere, as symbols of the new economic reality which focused on "the gym as a symbol of organized force and the street market as an elementary form of free economic exchange."[15] Many Russian criminal groups, not just the ones composed of former athletes, cultivate a healthy lifestyle, strict discipline and maintain physical fitness through regular attendance at private gyms, which serve as their meeting places. This trend toward clean living has even caught on with some *vory*, who have traditionally had nothing against the use of alcohol and drugs; now some of them meet at juice bars and toast each other with orange juice!

In all, the old *vory* did not fare well, although quite a lot of their traditions and vocabulary live on among the new criminal class. Many of the new *vory* have spent little or no time in prison, which was previously considered an essential badge of honor. (Years served were recorded as church onion domes in prison tattoos.) Some new criminals purchased the title of *vor*, for as little as $150,000. These lowered barriers to entry eroded the authority and status that came with being a *vor*, and, in due course, having the title stopped being essential in the new Russian underworld. Nevertheless, there was much cross-pollination between the two groups: a *vor* might set himself up as new criminal *avtoritét* (criminal authority, Mafia capo), and an *avtoritét* might be ordained as a *vor*. Many of the *vory* became embroiled in intra-group conflicts and killed, allowing the new criminals to take over. The major difference was that the new criminals were much more violent; the major similarity was that both groups cultivated an aristocratic spirit of entitlement and insisted that they do not, under any circumstances, do any work. The businessmen and the population at large owed them tribute "by definition." They saw themselves as a leisure class; their calling was not to do but to simply be. Their common ideal was to make a lot of money by remaining perfectly idle.

But another major difference lay in the fact that whereas the *vory* refused to serve in the military (or cooperate with any part of the government), many of the new criminals—the ones who were not former athletes—came out of the military. The end of the Afghan war in 1989 created a large pool of potential new racketeers. The combat veterans who returned home soon found that they did not have any legal role to play in the new economic reality. They were full of bitterness over the senseless sacrifice of the war, and this caused them to withdraw into closed circles and only interact with each other. Those who had developed post-traumatic stress disorder had certain advantages when confronting or doling out violence: a reduced sense of danger, a willingness to die and identification with a certain combat brotherhood to which they remained loyal. The conflict in Chechnya in 1994–96 was similarly senseless and bloody, but fully 75 percent of those who fought in it wanted a return to war once that conflict was over, perhaps because for them Russian society during those years was just as senseless and bloody as the war, but without the sense of solidarity and structure they found in the army. In any case, many of them did continue fighting, back home rather than in Chechnya: "Combat experience gives one vital physical and psychological advantages in a business where violent conflicts are routine...." [16] Faced with competitors who had such training and firepower, the old-style *vory* did not stand a chance.

Yet another group that swelled the ranks of racketeers was the Chechen mafia. The Chechens' success in forming criminal organizations had much to do with their tribal structure and practice. In Chechnya, land has always passed from the father to the eldest son, forcing other sons to leave home and become raiders. While they were at home, they had to pay absolute obedience to the tribal elders, but while away their freedom of action was absolute. When they brought home the loot, they were received as heroes and the most famous (or infamous) ones came to be celebrated in song and legend. Thus, in Chechen society, predation on their neighbors evolved into a high-status occupation. It was not seen as morally reprehensible on any level, because according to sharia law enrichment at the expense of the infidels is an honorable activity. The Chechens were never known for loving their neighbors, but the Russian conquest of the region under Alexander II was by far the most humiliating event in Chechen history and gave rise to an eternal and implacable hatred toward the Russians. These sentiments were only further deepened when Stalin exiled four hundred thousand Chechens to Kazakhstan after World War II, as punishment for their dalliance with Hitler. All of these factors made the appearance of a Chechen criminal class eager to heroically settle scores almost inevitable.

The Chechen mafia started preying on the *kooperatívy* during the *perestroïka* years, eventually becoming the largest and best-organized criminal organization in Moscow. They survived several rounds of violent conflict with local Slavic criminal groups, but most of their original members are now either dead or in jail. Nevertheless, over the course of the 1990s they not only ran Moscow's largest racket but also ran illegal, underground banks and traded precious metals, oil and weapons. Eventually the Chechen mafia moved away from racketeering and diversified into hotels, banking, shell companies and money laundering. It now operates a large number of diversified trading companies in commodities such as oil, lumber, gold and rare earth minerals. On paper these companies feature Russian figureheads, making them difficult to spot. During Chechnya's separatist rebellion, the vast sums they amassed were used to finance the separatist regime of Dzokhar Dudayev.

The ideal bandit

Russia's new criminal class—people liked to call them *bandity* (bandits)—gained its power due to its willingness and ability to use violence. This has set it apart from all other types of organizations, criminal or otherwise, for violence is not just a method but a specialization. A business that deals in violence is different from any other kind of business, be it legal or illegal. First, we must distinguish institutional services from all other goods and services. Second, we must distinguish violent institutional services from all other institutional services. Bandits specialize in providing violent institutional services.

But it would be a mistake to view the dispensation of violence as some sort of work, for the bandits' code of honor forbids work: they must live off tribute. They see it as their moral obligation to exploit the morally inferior businessmen, who cheat and swindle each other, and whose word cannot be trusted. For the bandit, his word is his bond, and he is willing to back it up with his life if need be. As we will see, bandits can and do perform useful, sometimes essential functions, but to consider these as their "work" would pierce a certain veil and make their work impossible. This is similar to the fiction of disinterested exchange that must be maintained in gift economies: the moment gifts come to be treated as mere debts, the gift economy evaporates. Bandits act strictly to defend their honor, not to earn money, because the money is theirs "by definition." Still, most bandits were far from idle; according to Volkov, they, among other things, "intimidated, protected, gathered information, settled disputes, gave guarantees, enforced contracts [and] imposed taxes."[17]

What evolved in Russia during the 1990s was the cult of the ideal bandit—ready to deal, to kill and to die. Although a bandit must be ready to use violence, his main tool is language. Theirs is an oral culture, with minimal reliance on documents. Their most important utterances are performatives: expressions that are intended not to communicate a thought but to directly alter and transform the state of the world. Speech acts are used to give guarantees, enter into and enforce contracts and so forth. In their world, speech must be *konkrétny* (specific)— whether a threat or a promise, it must be backed up by an absolute willingness to carry it out. Talking nonsense or making empty threats or boasts is out of the question: a bandit must *otvechát' za slová*—be answerable for his words. Shooting off one's mouth is punished severely— by cutting off fingers.

The bandits' code of honor also requires sanctions against *bespredél* (lack of limits), which is the unjustified or gratuitous use of violence. Someone who resorts to violence without having a just cause may be labeled as *ótmorozok* (frostbitten)—a derogatory term, and a horrible curse, because anyone so labeled must be destroyed. Interestingly, in March 1999 Igor Sergeev, Russia's minister of defense, speaking of NATO bombing of Serbia, characterized it as *bespredél*. Vladimir Putin has used the term as well, though both have stopped short of labeling NATO as *ótmorozki*. Thus bandit jargon has now entered the official political lexicon.

The bandits initially operated as criminal protection agencies, but in 1992 protection rackets were more or less legalized, allowing them to drop the word "criminal." In any case, all of these agencies jealously guard their good reputations, which rest on their reliability in conducting business and in their resolve in the use of violence. Importantly, their reputations are not based on what their clients think, which they consider more or less irrelevant. Their reputations have to be maintained vis-à-vis other such agencies; credible protection results from posing a credible threat and from one's ability to resolve conflicts. The bandit lexicon uses a rather bland phrase—*reshát' voprósy* (to settle questions)—for the complicated set of services they tacitly provide. A criminal reputation built up through the use of violence is then used as an asset in conducting business as peacefully as possible. In order to "settle questions" with other criminal groups, they often have to give each other guarantees. While it is considered entirely legitimate for them to cheat businessmen, they don't tend to cheat each other, because this tends to result in very bloody retaliation.

Criminal groups have names, which are usually toponymic or ethnic designations (*pérmskie, kazánskie, chechénskie, kavkázskie*). Criminal authorities (*avtoritéty*) name themselves in the style of medieval nobles, taking as their surname their locality of origin. These names function as flags to which their troops pledge allegiance and under which they serve, and the phrase used when joining a criminal group—*vstat' pod flag* (to take position under the flag)—makes this association explicit. These designations play a critical role in laying claim to a territory and in negotiations between criminal groups. They are a mark of sovereignty. Once a name and the associated reputation are sufficiently well established, it can become a trademark that can be used separately from its founder (who can be dead, in jail or living in London courtesy of the Queen) and expanded through franchising.

The basic technique for founding a racket is to recruit a client. This is a three-step process. In step one, the racketeer creates a problem for the client. In step two, the racketeer offers the client a solution to this problem in exchange for payment. In step three, the racketeer assures the client that the problem will not recur as long as payments continue to be made. Extortion is a natural and spontaneous result of opportunity, which then just as naturally and spontaneously evolves into a protection racket: "The institution of the protection racket springs from the absence of a monopoly of force."[18] The initial act of extortion was often messy: "Unlike refined fictional extortionists, the real ones kidnapped [their] victims, put them in coffins, and placed the coffins on trucks for the 'last journey' to the cemetery."[19] But the difference between extortion and protection is a matter of degree. Singular episodes of extortion morph into a stable business relationship of protection, as a bandit "strives to establish permanent tributary relations with inhabitants of his domain and provides certain services that justify his demand for tribute."[20]

The recruitment process could be rough, or not, but it served an essential function; in the prevailing business climate, protection—called *krýsha* (roof)—was essential. If the creditor does not have protection and the amount of the debt is larger than the price of a contract killing, it is cheaper to kill the creditor than to discharge the debt. If you do not have *krýsha* but your competitor does, what is to stop your competitor's enforcement partners from shutting down your business? If a supplier takes your money but does not deliver, and you do not have *krýsha*, how do you get your money back? And so on and so forth. The proliferation of protection rackets was largely a response to an objective need: businessmen wanted to do business with people they did not trust, and in the absence of an effective legal means to enforce contracts, another system had to be improvised. And so it came to be that each new business had to pay protection money to one group or another. The fees started at a few hundred dollars a month and went as high as 20–30 percent of revenue. In spite of this, business owners viewed rackets as a minor problem, and preferred to deal with racketeers rather than the police, the tax collectors or the courts, seeing the racketeers as a viable and affordable alternative to all of the above. Moreover, "in Russia in the mid-1990s the very existence of the 'state' as a unified entity and of the public domain itself was called into question."[21] *Krýsha* is another term that has entered Russian business lexicon: "In current Russian business parlance...the term *krýsha* is used to refer to agencies that provide institutional services to economic agents irrespective of the legal status of providers and clients."[22]

Such institutional services should not be confused with formal justice. Recourse to formal justice was—and to a large extent still is— avoided because it cedes power to impersonal forces and destroys personal relationships, which are generally more valuable than anything else that is at stake within a given disagreement. Russia's businessmen tend to rely on their personal connections. Given the overall business climate, it is often hard to tell whether someone's activities have crossed the line into illegality, and if that is the case, then that person's trust could easily be compromised if it becomes known that, in case of trouble, one likes to get the officials involved. Most Russian businessmen saw litigation as a greater threat than organized crime, seeing the legal process itself as a form of punishment.

The tenuous legality of most Russian businesses needs to be viewed in context. Until 1999 Russia did not have a tax code, and taxes were levied by decree. The decrees were often mutually contradictory, their effects retroactive, the fines for noncompliance confiscatory. If they had been paid in full, most economic activity would have been stifled. Many tax penalties were illegitimate and were assessed to raise money, which the tax authorities then used to pay themselves bonuses. Businesses avoided contact with the state in order to avoid having to pay taxes, fees and fines, as well as the need to file paperwork. It is no surprise, then, that the shadow economy in mid-1990s Russia made up as much as 45 percent of GDP. The most distrusted Russian institutions were, and to some extent still are, city hall and the police. This is especially the case in small provincial towns, where corrupt local officials tend to be particularly entrenched. Those who have been harmed preferred not to go to the police but to "hire friends." People in Russia tend to use the courts exclusively to litigate against the state—because in such cases there is simply no other recourse.

Racketeering made legal

Private protection rackets started to proliferate in 1987. By 1992, when a wave of privatizations took place, rackets were legalized, and it became possible to operate a legal private protection company. The proliferation of rackets was a direct result of economic liberalization and rapid privatization of state property, a process inspired by Western economists, who, out of either stupidity or malice, favored a limited role for the government and an unlimited role for the mythical "invisible hand" of the marketplace. In essence, they were of the opinion that a market economy can work in the absence of "the institutions that make a market economy work: a system of clearly defined property rights, a swift and effective court system, and a credible police force that deters crimes."[23] Add to this the fact that the breakneck speed with which the Russian economy was being privatized created more temptations than any set of institutions could have handled, in effect rendering legal economic activity noncompetitive. Criminal groups stepped in to govern property transactions. The result was a wave of violence that swept the country, blurring the line between business and crime.

In 1995 the wave of violence crested. It was the culmination of a set of elimination contests between criminal groups, which ended in them consolidating into a smaller set of larger groups. In 1994 the rate of assassinations of criminal *avtoritéty* peaked at twenty and declined thereafter. By 1997 the process of consolidation was complete, and a curious transformation took place. Criminal groups spontaneously evolved from extortion and protection and moved on to stock ownership, control of enterprises, asset stripping and expatriation of capital. Many *avtoritéty* chose to settle in the West. A few invested in the Russian economy, set up holding companies and switched from coercion to legal capital accumulation. The cream of the criminal class became middle class. As this happened, the criminal groups formerly under their command underwent vertical disintegration. As the leadership integrated itself into the public order, mid-level and rank-and-file criminals became obsolete, although a few elite enforcers were kept around for special, secret missions. Outcomes varied; for the criminal elite this was the path to rapid social advancement, while for the common thug it was a one-way ticket back to the world of disorganized crime, which not unexpectedly spiked in early 2000, with a much higher incidence of burglaries and street crime. Some of the thugs went to jail, others were integrated into the world of "traditional" crime: drug smuggling, prostitution, gun running, financial fraud and so on. Mid-level criminals went into business or started working for the government, while for those on the up-and-up, Vladimir Zhirinovsky's LDPR (the Liberal Democratic Party of Russia) opened its doors to shady characters with checkered pasts, giving them an opportunity to enter politics. (But it cannot be said that Russian politics is packed full of criminals, unlike, say, Georgia, where a *vor v zakóne* by the name of Djaba Ioseliani made it as far as minister in the Western-supported regime of Eduard Shevardnadze.) Some Russian criminals also ingratiated themselves into polite society by becoming generous donors to the Russian Orthodox Church, and through overt displays of religiosity; they have financed many church restorations. (In turn, the diocese has on occasion turned to criminal groups to extract payments from parishes.)

In the meantime, the Russian state came roaring back, thanks to a radical innovation that converted the former Soviet enforcement ministries into a private protection industry staffed by former Soviet officials. Following the collapse of the USSR, the new Russian government distrusted the so-called *siloviki* or "power ministries"—Ministry of Defense, Ministry of Internal Affairs, Ministry of Foreign Affairs and KGB—because they had participated in the putsch against Gorbachev in August of 1991. During the early nineties, these ministries were defunded and constantly reorganized, causing many employees to flee to the private sector. Many subsequently resorted to criminal methods in providing *krýsha*, including *strélki* (face-to-face meetings with *avtoritéty* to "settle questions"), *probívki* (fact-finding missions conducted by any means necessary) and *razbórki* (shoot-outs, settling of scores), and using intimidation and violence to collect debts and settle disputes. Once they completed their learning process and acculturated themselves to the new environment, they became able to outcompete the criminals hands down. Instead of charging 10–20 percent of revenue, they collected a more modest insurance premium, offered a set of à la carte protection services and had many fewer issues finding common ground with their counterparts, who were often their former colleagues who were now also offering such services. Many larger companies chose to bring the protection function in-house: For instance, Gazprom, Russia's leading natural gas producer and one of the largest companies in the world, maintains a 20,000-strong private army headed by former KGB people. The world of private protection suddenly became, if not civilized, then at least professionalized.

The year 2000 marks the turning point where the rule of law became the government's top priority. Yeltsin initiated this transformation, but it was Vladimir Putin who spoke the words "dictatorship of the law" and actually meant it. By 2007 crime was down by double digits across most categories, with the notable exception of money laundering, which was way up. If you ask them, the Russian police will tell you that this is because they do such a good job: emphasize crime prevention, work with the youth, provide job quotas for released prison inmates and so forth. But they will readily concede that record-low unemployment and a healthy national economy have something to do with it too. To which I would like to add that Russia's huge police force (close to one percent of the population, which is much higher than in the USSR) and huge prison population (second only to the USA) have something to do with it as well. Be that as it may, the government is your *krýsha* now, and there will be no more *bespredél* because Putin, who is Russia's main *avtoritét*, said so on national television.

CHAPTER 3

Political Collapse

STAGE 3: Political collapse. Faith that "the government will take care of you" is lost. As official attempts to mitigate widespread loss of access to commercial sources of survival necessities fail to make a difference, the political establishment loses legitimacy and relevance.

Financial and commercial collapses are already potentially lethal. People lose their bearings and their sense of purpose, or decide to take advantage of those in distress, or fail simply through an inability to adapt to radically altered circumstances, and when that happens people get hurt. Financial and commercial collapses tend to be hard on those who failed to prepare, by putting aside objects that hold their value when the national currency hyperinflates and banks close and by stockpiling the necessary supplies to tide them over during the uncertain transition period, when the old ways of doing things no longer work but the new ones have not yet evolved. Both of these causes of potentially lethal circumstances can be avoided: first, by choosing the right kind of community; second, by laying in supplies or securing independent access to food, water and energy; and third, by generally finding a way to bide your time and ignore the world at large until times get better.

Political collapse is a different animal altogether, because it makes the world at large difficult to ignore. The potential for chaos is still there, but so is the potential for organized action of a very damaging sort, because the ruling class and the classes that serve them (the police, the military, the bureaucrats) generally refuse to go softly into the night and allow the people to self-organize, experiment and come together as autonomous new groups adapted to the new environment in their composition and patterns of self-governance. Instead, they are likely to spontaneously hatch a harebrained new plan: an initiative to restore national unity, in the sense of restoring the status quo ante, at least with regard to preserving their own power and privilege, at others' expense. In a situation where every person and every neighborhood should be experimenting on their own to find out what works and what doesn't, the politicians and the officials are apt to introduce new draconian crime-fighting measures, curfews and detentions, allowing only certain activities—ones that benefit them—while mercilessly putting down any sign of insubordination. To deflect the blame for their failure, the ruling elite usually also does its best to find an internal or external enemy. Those who are the weakest and the least politically connected—the poor, the minorities and the immigrants—are accused of dragging everyone down and singled out for the harshest treatment. This is conducive to creating a climate of fear and suppressing free speech. But nothing causes people to band together like an external threat, and, for the sake of preserving national unity, a failing nation-state often looks for an external enemy to attack, preferably a weak, defenseless one, so that it poses no risk of reprisal. Putting the nation on a war footing makes it possible for the government to commandeer resources and reallocate them to the benefit of the ruling class, further restrict movements and activities, round up troublesome youths and ship them off to battle and lock up undesirables.

Financial and commercial collapse creates an opening for those inclined toward the most miserable despotism. Once a despotic regime is established, the weak, demoralized, disoriented population almost inevitably finds itself incapable of rising in opposition to it, and the new despotism may become entrenched and quite durable, lasting for an extended period of time, during which the country is hollowed out and traumatized before collapsing through internecine strife or a battle of succession, or through increasing weakness that causes it to succumb to foreign occupation. The spectrum of possible responses to financial and commercial collapse stretches from despotism to chaos. There is a sweet spot of autonomous, anarchic social cooperation, with many small skirmishes and stand-offs but well short of all-out armed conflict.

Anarchy's charms

In the face of political collapse it is quite reasonable to expect that the good people of almost any nation will cower in their homes and allow themselves to be herded like domesticated animals, because their worst fear is not despotism—it is anarchy. Anarchy! Are you afraid of anarchy? Or are you more afraid of hierarchy? Color me strange, but I am much more afraid of being subjected to a chain of command than of anarchy (which is a lack of hierarchy). Mind you, this is not an irrational fear, but comes from a lifetime of studying nature, human as well as the regular kind, and of working within hierarchically structured organizations as well as some anarchically organized ones. The anarchically organized ones work better. I may be persuaded to accede to the specific and temporary authority of a superior (superior at a given task) but I find it problematic to blindly accept the authority of my superior's superior's superior. A bit of hierarchy may be temporarily justified while facing down a specific, temporary threat or while executing an ambitious task that requires a big, coordinated team effort. But once that's over, it's back to anarchy. Few of us enjoy taking orders from the sorts of characters who enjoy ordering people about, be they numb-nuts who rose through the ranks or pampered children of privilege, but to realize that there is an alternative we need to overcome our fear of anarchy. It works for the birds, the bees, the dolphins and the wildebeest—and it can work for you. There are many things that deserve to be feared in this world, but a pleasantly, congenially, efficiently organized lack of hierarchy is definitely not one of them.

The term "anarchy" is commonly used as a slur against things that seem disorganized, because most people (incorrectly) believe it implies a lack of organization. Anarchists are also confused with communist revolutionaries, and the typical anarchist is imagined to be an antisocial and bloodthirsty terrorist who craves the violent overthrow of the established order. Anarchy is also incorrectly conceived to represent the embodiment of a coherent ideology of Anarchism, making the argument against anarchy a straw man argument based on a false choice between an implied yet manifestly nonexistent system and a very real oppressively huge hierarchically organized scheme. The only grain of truth visible in all of this is that Anarchism as a political ideology or movement is, and has been for centuries now, rather beside the point.

Glimmers of anarchism could be discerned going as far back as the Reformation, in movements seeking autonomy, decentralization and independence from central governments. But eventually virtually all of them were drowned out by socialist and communist revolutionary movements, which strove to renegotiate the social contract to distribute the fruits of industrial production more equitably among the working class. In all the developed countries, the working class was eventually able to secure gains such as the right to unionize, strike and bargain collectively; public education, a regulated work week, government-guaranteed pensions and disability compensation schemes, government-provided health care and so on—all in exchange for submitting to the hierarchical control system of a centralized industrial state. Anarchist thought could gain no purchase within such a political climate, where the rewards of submitting to an official hierarchy were so compelling. But now the industrial experiment is nearing its end: trade union participation is falling; companies routinely practice labor arbitrage, exporting work to lowest-wage countries; retirement schemes are failing everywhere; pubic education fails to educate and even a college degree is no longer any sort of guarantee of gainful employment; and health care costs are out of control (in the US especially).

We can only hope that with the waning of the industrial age, anarchism is poised for a rebirth, gaining relevance and acceptance among those wishing to opt out of the industrial scheme instead of being pulled down to the bottom along with it. From the point of view of a young person seeking to join the labor force but facing a decrepit and dysfunctional system of industrial employment that holds scant promise of a prosperous future, opting out of the industrialized scheme and embracing the anarchic approach becomes the rational choice. Why toil at some specific, circumscribed set of repetitive tasks within a job if that job, and the entire career path, could disappear out from under you at any moment? Why not enter into informal associations with friends and neighbors and divide your time between growing food, making and mending things and helping others within the immediate community, and spend the balance of your free time on art, music, reading and other cultural and intellectual pursuits? Why bend to the will of self-interested strangers who have so little to offer when you can do better by freely cooperating with your equals? Why submit to an arbitrary external authority when a sufficiently cohesive and egalitarian community can be self-governing? All of these questions demand accurate and reasoned answers. If we find ourselves unable to provide these answers, but nevertheless expect our young people to go along with the industrial program, then we are attempting to coerce them to blindly submit to the forces of social inertia—nothing more.

The best way to approach the subject of anarchism is from the vantage point of a student of nature. Observe that, in nature, anarchy is the prevalent form of cooperation among animals, whereas hierarchical organization is relatively rare and limited in scope and duration. Prince Peter Kropotkin, a nineteenth-century Russian scholar and theoretician of anarchy, wrote convincingly on this subject. Kropotkin was a scientist, and having a scientist's eye for hard data allowed him to make a series of key observations.

First, he observed that the vast majority of animal species, and virtually all of the more successful animals, are social. There are animals that spend most of their lives as solitary individuals, but they are the exception rather than the rule, which is to live in cooperating groups. It is the degree and the success of cooperation that is the most important determinant of the success of any given species; gregarious, cooperative animals thrive while loners are left behind. The striking success of the human species has everything to do with our superior abilities to communicate, cooperate, organize spontaneously and act creatively in concert. In turn, the equally glaring, horrific, monstrous failures of our species have everything to do with our unwelcome ability to submit to authority, tolerate class distinctions and blindly follow orders and rigid systems of rules. Among the worst excuses offered by those who behave abominably are "I was only doing my job" and "I was only following orders."

Which leads us to Kropotkin's second observation, which is that animal societies can be quite highly and intricately organized, but their organization is anarchic, lacking any deep hierarchy; there are no privates, corporals, sergeants, lieutenants, captains, majors or generals among any of the species that evolved on planet Earth, with the exception of the gun-toting jackbooted baboon (whenever you see an animal wearing jackboots and carrying a rifle—run!). When animals organize, they organize for a purpose: birds form up to fly north or south, and spontaneously come together in colonies to rear their chicks; grazing animals gather together to ford rivers; prairie dogs post sentries that whistle their alarms for the entire town whenever any of them spots a predator; even birds of different species cooperate to repel and harass predators, with the biggest birds taking the lead while the smaller ones assist. Some groups of animals do explicitly sort themselves out into an order, such as a pecking order among chickens or an eating order in a pride of lions, but these are sorting orders that do not create entire privileged classes or ranks.

Consequently, animal societies are egalitarian. Even the queen bee or the termite queen does not hold a position of command; she is simply the reproductive organ of the colony and neither gives orders nor follows anyone else's. Because animal societies are egalitarian, they do not require any explicit code of justice or process of adjudication to maintain peace, since among equals the simple golden rule—do unto others as you want others to do unto you—corresponding to the innate, instinctual sense of fairness, provides sufficient guidance in most situations. A second instinct, of putting the interests of the group before one's own, assures group cohesion and provides a source of immense power. We humans have this instinct in abundance, perhaps to a fault; other animals follow it as a matter of course and do not decorate those who follow it with medals or put them on pedestals.

This clear understanding of cooperation, peace and justice, which springs forth through instinct in the egalitarian, anarchic societies that are found throughout nature, casts an unflattering light on written law. Kropotkin observes that systems of written law always start out as gratuitous, self-important exercises in writing down the unwritten rules that everyone follows anyway, but then sneak in a new element or two for the benefit of the emerging ruling class that is doing the writing. He singles out the Tenth Commandment of Moses, which states: "Thou shalt not covet thy neighbor's house, wife, manservant, maidservant, ox, ass, nor any thing that is thy neighbor's." Now, pre-literate societies, with their systems of unwritten, oral law, may vary, but all of them recognize that a wife is not at all like an ox, and all of them would recognize someone who tries to treat them as being the same before the law as a subversive or an imbecile. Recognizing that a wife and an ox are different, some societies may choose to let oxen wander about the community grazing where they may, so that they can be pressed into service as needed by anyone who wishes to do so, while stealing someone's wife may be a life-ending event for both the thief and the wife, causing the rest of the society to look away in shame. Other societies may regard borrowing an ox without permission as grand larceny, and borrowing someone's wife as legitimate love sport as long as the wife consents, but the jealous husband who then kills the two is charged with two counts of second-degree murder. The Tenth Commandment erases such distinctions and treats both the wife and the ox as individual property. Furthermore, it makes it a sin to regard the property of another with anything other than indifference, enshrining the right to own abstract individual property without limitation as a key moral principle. This is antithetical to maintaining an egalitarian society of a sort that can remain anarchic and self-governing, making it necessary to introduce police, the courts and jails to keep the peace in a society characterized by inequality and class conflict. Moses smashed the tablets once when he saw the Israelites worshiping the golden calf; he should have smashed them a second time when he saw them worshiping the idol of private property.

Kropotkin's third, and perhaps most significant, observation addresses a common misunderstanding of Darwinian evolution. You see, when most people say "Darwinian" it turns out that they actually mean to say "Hobbesian." Kropotkin pointed out that the term "survival of the fittest" has been misinterpreted to mean that animals compete against other animals of their own species, whereas that happens to be the shortest path to extinction. This misinterpretation of facts directly observable from nature has led to the faulty Hobbesian justification of the economic appetite as something natural and evolved, and therefore inevitable, giving rise to the conjectured laws of the market, which in turn favor nonempathic, exclusionary, brutal, possessive individualists. The result has been to enshrine a sort of mental illness—primitive, pathological, degenerate narcissism—as the ultimate evolutionary adaptation and the basis of the laws of economics. Thus an entire edifice of economic theory has been erected atop a foundation of delusion borne of a misunderstanding of the patterns present in nature.

Kropotkin provides numerous examples of what allows animal societies to survive and thrive, and it is almost always cooperation with their own species, and sometimes with other species as well, and almost never overt competition. He mentions that wild Siberian horses, which usually graze in small herds, overcome their natural aloofness to gather in large numbers and crowd together into gulleys to share bodily warmth when facing a blizzard; those who do not do so often freeze to death. Animals do fight for survival, but their fight is against forces of nature: inclement weather and climactic fluctuations that cause floods, droughts, cold spells and heat waves, and diseases and predators that reduce their numbers. They do not compete against members of their own species except in one respect: those who win the genetic lottery by generating or inheriting a lucky genetic mutation are more likely to survive and reproduce. Thus, it is possible to say that genomes compete, but this use of the term "competition" is purely metaphorical, while the dominant pattern, and the greatest determinant of success of a species as a whole, is one of cooperation taken quite literally.

Kropotkin's life was in many ways tragic. He was born into an aristocratic military family. His mother died when he was three, and his father remarried to a woman who took no interest in him or his brother. And so Kropotkin was brought up by the peasants attached to his father's estate (he was born twenty years before Russia abolished serfdom). The peasants were the only ones who took an interest in him or showed him affection, and he bonded with them as his family, and grew to be far more interested in the welfare of simple Russians than in that of his own class. Although he graduated from an elite royal academy that prepared him for a career at the imperial court, his interests in natural science immediately took him far afield into Russia's Far East.

Kropotkin eventually became a renowned scientist who advanced our understanding of the history of glaciers, a historian of revolutionary movements, the world's foremost theoretician of anarchism and, because of his lifelong, burning desire to do something to help the plight of the common man, something of a revolutionary himself. His memory has not fared well over the ninety years that have passed since his death. On the one hand, he suffered from being associated with the Bolsheviks, although he never spoke out in favor of state communism or dictatorship of the proletariat. On the other hand, a major effort has been made by Western capitalist regimes to denigrate anarchism and equate it with terrorism.

I would like to rehabilitate both Kropotkin and anarchy. People who bother to read Kropotkin's lucid and unpretentious writings quickly realize that he is first of all a natural scientist, who approached the study of both nature and human nature using the same scientific method. He was also a great humanist, and chose the path of anarchy because, as a scientist, he saw it as the best way to improve society based on the successful patterns of cooperation he observed in nature. He had no use at all for the vague metaphysics of Hegel, Kant or Marx and no use at all for the imperial state, be it communist or capitalist.

Kropotkin was an advocate of communism at the level of the commune, and based his advocacy on its demonstrated superior effectiveness in organizing both production and consumption. His examples of communist production were the numerous communist communities that were all the rage in the United States at the time, where the numbers showed that they produced far better results with less effort and in less time than individual homesteaders or family farms. His examples of communist consumption included various clubs, all-inclusive resorts and hotels and various other formal and informal associations where a single admission or membership fee gave you full access to whatever was on offer to everyone. Again, the numbers showed that such communist patterns of consumption produced far better results at a much lower overall expense than various capitalist pay-as-you-go schemes.

Kropotkin, in his usual data-driven way, was definitely in favor of grass roots communism, but I have not been able to find any statements he made in favor of communist governance. He spoke of the revolutionary change—change that required a break with the past—as necessary in order to improve society, but he wished that it would be a spontaneous process that unleashed the creative energies of the people at the local level, not a process that could be controlled from the top. He wrote: "The rebuilding [*perestroïka*] of society requires the collective wisdom of multitudes of people working on specific things: a cultivated field, an inhabited house, a running factory, a railroad, a ship and so on." Another of his more memorable quotes is: "The future cannot be legislated. All that can be done is to anticipate its most important movements and to clear the path for them. That is exactly what we try to do." (Here and elsewhere the translations from Kropotkin's quaint pre-revolutionary Russian are my own.)

Kropotkin's approach to the approaching revolution was also as a scientist, similar to that of a seismologist predicting an earthquake based on tremors: "Hundreds of revolts preceded each revolution… There are limits to all patience." Participating in the many revolutionary movements in Western Europe during his long exile, he monitored the increasing incidence of such tremors. (He spent a long time living in Switzerland, before the Swiss government asked him to leave, during which time he radicalized a large number of Swiss watchmakers, turning them into anarchists who, we must assume, practiced their anarchy with great precision.) Based on his observations, he came to see revolution as rather likely. Again, he wished for it to be an anarchic phenomenon: "We…understand revolution as a popular movement which will become widespread, and during which in each town and in each village within a rebellious region multitudes of people will themselves take up the task of rebuilding [*perestroïka* again] society." But he put no faith at all in revolutionary governance: "As far as the government, whether it seized power by force or through elections…we pin absolutely no hopes on it. We say that it will be unable to do anything, not because these are our sympathies, but because our entire history tells us that never have the people whom a revolutionary wave pushed into government turned out to be up to the task."

Based on this statement, I feel it safe to conclude that Kropotkin was not exactly a revolutionary but more of a scientific observer and predictor of revolutions who saw them as increasingly likely (and in this he was not wrong) and kept hoping for the best as long as he could. It also bears noting that he declined every leadership role that was ever offered to him, and that his participation in the Bolshevik revolution in Russia was nil; he returned to Russia from exile as soon as he could after the revolution of February 1917, but quickly removed himself to his home town of Dmitrov, north of Moscow, where he died in 1921. He wasn't exactly popular with the Bolshevik leadership, but they could not touch him because he was so popular with the common people.

Leaving aside the notion that Kropotkin was a Communist with a capital "C," it remains for us to show that he was not an Anarchist with a capital "A" either. My own personal working definition of anarchy, which has served me well, is "absence of hierarchy." The etymology of the word is ἀν (not, without) + ἀρχός (ruler). Kropotkin's own definition is as follows: "Anarchy represents an attempt to apply results achieved using the scientific method within the natural sciences to the evaluation of human institutions." You see, there are no Commie subversives here, no bomb-throwing Anarchists with capital "A"—just some scientists doing some science and then attempting to apply their very interesting results to the scientific study of human social institutions.

Kropotkin worked within the framework of nineteenth-century natural science, but his results are just as relevant today as they were then. Moreover, the accuracy of his insights is vindicated by the latest research into complexity theory. Geoffrey West, who was a practicing particle physicist for forty years and is now a distinguished professor at the Santa Fe Institute, has achieved some stunning breakthroughs in complexity theory and the mathematical characterization of scaling of biological systems. Looking at animals big and small, from the tiny shrew to the gigantic blue whale and many in between, he and his collaborators were able to determine that all these animals obey a certain power law; their metabolic cost scales with their mass, and the scaling factor is less than one, meaning that the larger the animal, the more effective its resource use and, in essence, the more effective the animal— up to a certain optimum size for each animal. Consequently, the growth curve for every animal is characterized by a bounded, sigmoidal curve; growth accelerates at first, then slows down, reaching a steady state as the animal matures.

What Professor West was able to discover is a small set of general laws—formulated as algebraic equations just as simple and general as the laws of Newtonian mechanics—that have been validated using data on trees, animals, colonies of bacteria, all manner of living things—and that provide amazingly precise predictions. As the size (mass) of the organism increases, its metabolic cost, heart rate and so on decrease as $m^{-\frac{1}{4}}$ while its lifetime increases as $m^{\frac{1}{4}}$. The 4 in the ¼-exponent comes from summing the three dimensions with a fourth fractal dimension. This is because all living systems are fractal-like, and all networks, from the nervous system to the circulatory system to the system of tunnels in a termite colony, exhibit fractal-like properties, where a similarly organized subsystem can be found by zooming in to a smaller scale. That is, within any fractal network there are four degrees of freedom: up/down, left/right, forward/back and, crucially, zoom in/zoom out.

Professor West then turned his attention to cities, and discovered that they can be characterized by similar power laws by which they too accrue greater benefits from increased size, through increased economies of scale, up to a point, but with two very important differences. First, whereas with living systems an increase in size causes the internal clock to slow down—the larger the size the slower the metabolism, the slower the heart rate and the longer the lifespan—with cities the effect of greater size is the opposite: the larger the city, the larger is the metabolic cost and the energy expenditure per unit size, and the more hectic is the pace of life. To keep pace with the metabolic requirements of a growing socioeconomic system, socioeconomic time must continuously accelerate.

Second, whereas all living systems exhibit bounded growth up to an optimum size, socioeconomic systems such as cities exhibited unbounded, superexponential growth. These two differences added together imply that cities must reach a point where they must move infinitely fast in order to maintain their homeostatic equilibrium: a singularity. But they reach natural limits well before they reach the singularity, and collapse. In short, socioeconomic systems are not sustainable. There is a crisp difference between natural, biological, anarchic systems that exhibit bounded growth up to a steady state and artificial, hierarchical, socioeconomic systems that show superexponential growth almost up to a singularity. Professor West was able to formalize this difference using a single parameter, β. In biology, $\beta < 1$, resulting in bounded growth; in socioeconomics, $\beta > 1$, resulting in explosive growth almost up to a singularity, followed by collapse.

Biological systems are collections of living cells that cooperate with each other. They are organized collections of cells—organized according to function—but there are no master and slave cells, they do not have rank and, with the exception of cancer cells, they do not compete with each other. There is a continuous progression from single cells to colonies of cells to multicellular organisms to colonies of multicellular organisms, all organized anarchically according to function, all accruing great benefits from their increased scope of cooperation, up to a limit determined by their environment. Even consciousness has no specific command structure; the complex behaviors that make us think that there are such things as consciousness and free will are emergent behaviors of cooperating brain cells; nobody is actually in charge. As I sit here concentrating on this, my right hand picks up a cup of tea and raises it to my lips without the rest of me having to pay any attention; another part of me thinks that I should take a break and visit the shops before it starts raining. If I do, then the decision will have been reached cooperatively because there is nobody to give the order and nobody to give the order to.

The difference between a living organism and a city is that while a living organism is organized anarchically, a city is organized hierarchically. A living organism is a sustainable, egalitarian community of cooperating cells that uses the economies of scale of a larger size to move more slowly and to live longer. A city is organized into various classes, some more privileged than others, and is controlled through formal systems of governance based on written law and explicit chains of command. The larger it becomes, the greater becomes the relative burden of police, the courts, regulation and bureaucracy, and other systems of overt control. Faced with these ever-increasing internal maintenance requirements, it can only achieve economies of scale by moving faster and faster, and eventually it has to collapse.

There are many conclusions that can be drawn from all this, but perhaps the most important is that collapse is not an accident; it is an engineered product. It is being engineered by those who think that a higher level of authority, coordination, harmonization and unity is always a net benefit at any scale. The engineers of collapse include political scientists, who seek universal peace through ever-greater military expenditure and dominance, in place of limited war. They include economists, who pursue stability and growth at all costs instead of allowing for natural fluctuations, including a natural leveling-off of growth at an optimum level. They include financiers, who seek uniformity and transparency of global finance and universal mobility of capital, and who, instead of allowing pyramid schemes to collapse as they always do, insist on government guarantees and bailouts, preventing productive capital from settling where it should—in communities and in human relationships based on personal trust. Last but not least, collapse is being engineered by theologians, who have fixed absolute notions of morality based on written texts, and who seek to distort or ignore human nature. All of these people are hopeless utopians attempting to base society on idealistic principles. Such utopian societies inevitably fail, while those that are cognizant of human weakness and are able to compensate for it can go on for ages. The greatest weaknesses we have in our nature are our propensities for forming hierarchies, following formal systems of rules and laws and listening to utopians.

Not only have anarchic (that is to say, non-hierarchical and self-organizing) systems been the norm in evolution and in nature but they have also been the norm in human societies through much of their existence. They have a great deal to offer us as we attempt to interpret a landscape dominated by the failures of various centrally controlled, rigidly organized, explicitly codified hierarchical systems based on complex chains of command that have come to dominate human societies in recent centuries. But what are we to do with all this excellent information? We live in a hierarchically structured society whose sometimes oppressive but always present top-down authority we cannot hope to escape. We may be able to accept that anarchy is the way of nature, but we must also accept that it is no longer (at least for the time being) the way of human nature—or, if you like, not the way of "the man"—the one who pays us a little something if we are helpful to him and orders us to be beat up or locked up if we are not. The political advocate of anarchy is at best an amusing disembodied voice on the Internet (who must be doing something or other more practical to please the hierarchy in order to be able to afford the free time and the Internet connection). At worst, the compulsion to advocate anarchism as a program of political reform is a sign of mental illness.

This is not to say that the theory that underpins anarchism is without any practical applications. It is just that such applications have nothing at all to do with politics. Just as anarchist thinking has at its source the scientific observation of nature, so must its applications to contemporary society start by observing the constructive role that anarchy normally plays within contemporary society, and then look for ways to extend it. Are there any examples of that? Yes, indeed there are! Whenever an existing hierarchically organized system becomes sufficiently ossified and dysfunctional to give an obvious edge to an improvised, anarchic, perhaps initially inferior alternative, there is a possibility that such an alternative will materialize out of nowhere, spread virally, become dominant and then, in turn, become hierarchical and ossified. Let's list some obvious examples.

The Protestant revolution is an obvious one. Once the Catholic church—a hierarchical organization par excellence, though built atop the wreckage of anarchic early Christianity—became sufficiently corrupt and obnoxious, putting up toll booths before the gates of heaven and so forth, a self-selected leader (Luther) led a revolt, providing a viable, though rather primitive, alternative, which then took over in many parts of the world and eventually sprouted its own hierarchical structures. The Russian revolution is another one: once the general senility and obsolescence of the Czarist *ancien régime* became compounded by its failed bid to take part in World War I to a point where it could no longer quell bread riots, a new self-selected leader (Lenin) stepped into the breach and provided an alternative which, though rather awful, provided a way forward for a time, until, seventy years later, the stiff and morbid hierarchy into which it had evolved was likewise tipped into the dustbin. More recently, when the first efforts at trade liberalization provided advantages of economies of scale, as well as labor and jurisdictional arbitrage, with which national enterprises could not compete, the trend became unstoppable, until there is now a single transnational business environment which is beyond any one nation's control. If history is any guide (as it sometimes is) the inevitable result will be that a dangerously centralized global financial bureaucracy, conceived in an effort to control the forces of chaos globalization has unleashed, will briefly attempt to dominate the scene before crumbling into dust under its own weight.

Equally significant (and somewhat less fraught) examples of anarchy in action can be found in the area of computer technology. There was a time when computers made by different manufacturers came with their own different and incompatible operating systems. The manufacturers liked this state of affairs, in spite of the fact that it greatly inconvenienced the users, because it created lock-in: switching from one manufacturer's hardware to another's involved an expensive and time-consuming rewrite of their software. Then it just happened that two minds at Bell Labs dreamt up a very simple and primitive operating system called Unix (the name was initially a joke) that was written in a language they invented called "C" that ran on a lot of different computers—and it virally took over the world. Then Unix became a commercial product, instantly going from anarchical to hierarchical. But anarchy triumphed again when it was rewritten, through various efforts, in a way that pried it away from grubby corporate hands.

Self-selected leaders played a big role in all this. Richard Stallman's GNU project (the acronym stands for "GNU is Not Unix") created GCC, a free "C" compiler, and rewrote a great many Unix utilities to be free as well. Linus Torvalds, a graduate student in Finland, didn't like the Microsoft Windows system that his university-provided PC was running (he thought it was crap) and so he wrote the Linux operating system, a Unix variant that initially ran on PCs but now runs inside a great many devices, from Android smartphones to WiFi hotspots and routers to the Google search engine to virtually all of the world's supercomputers. Eventually even Apple saw the light, and its OS X operating system is based on a Unix variant. Unix is now ubiquitous; the last non-Unix holdout is Microsoft, which is now clearly a dinosaur and sinking fast, while Linux-based Google and Unix-based Apple are eating its lunch. It started out as a nerdy joke and then went viral and took over; score one for anarchy.

There are many other such examples from many fields, but the pattern should already be clear: when a hierarchical organization—be it a church, a government or a corporation—creates a structural impediment, and when a solution, even if it is just a quick and dirty one, is found to circumvent that structural impediment, a leader self-selects to create that alternative. If the effort is successful and the alternative takes root and becomes rampant, in due course it gives rise to a hierarchical organization of its own. In an effort to expand and consolidate its control over the newly created domain, that organization then sets its sights on crafting a new set of structural impediments. But in time the deathly touch of hierarchy takes its toll, collapse occurs, and the cycle repeats. There doesn't seem to be a lot that can be done to break the cycle, although there is a way to stretch it out by placing the new invention in the public domain (in software, this is done via the General Public License and a few others) or by declaring it an open, public standard. This has the effect of negating, or at least reducing, the undue influence of any one corporate entity, which is almost always helpful because, first, corporations tend to be short-lived entities whose influence shortens the lifetime of the invention, and second, corporations pursue profit by any means, such as by working against the interests of others. But any significant invention is bound, over time, to come under the control of industry consortia, standards bodies, government regulators and other hierarchical entities, which eventually kill it. They may kill it with diligence or with neglect, but kill it they do, because in order for something to live forever and evolve freely it has to be organized anarchically, and that is a form of organization of which hierarchical organizations happen to be incapable.

I hope that this makes it clear what the practice of anarchism looks like. First of all, someone must blaze the trail; not seek a leadership position, not attempt to take charge or seize control, but simply go right ahead and do what needs to be done without asking anyone's permission. The goal is to create a viable alternative of which others can avail themselves freely. But for this to succeed, the leader must choose his target well: it must be a significant structural impediment that can be circumvented with finite effort. Crafting a quick and dirty solution that nevertheless embodies the right set of concepts to scale up and take over is quite a feat, and few people are capable of it, but it nevertheless happens quite a lot. It tends to occur with an individual working either entirely alone (in secret if need be) or with a few informal collaborators. The best targets are ones that can be circumvented through individual or small group effort, with minimal start-up costs and where the alternative can spread virally.

The nation-state fades out

It is our bad luck that so many of us happen to live within a political arrangement that is a lingering byproduct of the industrial age: the nineteenth-century industrial nation-state. What follows is a very brief summary of how it came together. Around the twelfth century the church and the aristocracy remembered the Roman imperial state and saw to it that it was reborn as a series of mini-Romes, come to replace the anarchically organized polities of the free cities that dominated the Middle Ages. Later, as rapidly industrializing Western empires jockeyed for dominion over the planet, they discovered that big is better than small (due to better economies of scale), homogeneous is better than diverse (making it possible to dictate one-size-fits-all solutions from the imperial center) and that, if you want to maintain tight political control, highly centralized is better than autonomous.

Each empire first processed the populations within its borders, dispossessing and destroying communities and forcing them to serve the representatives of the centralized state. They strove to eradicate all languages and dialects except the normative one, and to denigrate all sources of identity other than the patriotic, national one. To provide labor for the industrial experiment, farming families were driven off the land, eventually giving rise to the welfare state and a large urban underclass of underutilized wage laborers. Normally such an approach leads to collapse (it has done so in the case of all previous empires) but this time it was different because they were able to obtain what at first appeared as free energy, first from coal, then from oil, natural gas and nuclear, at a much lower cost than the benefit derived from using this energy, so low that this cost could be disregarded. These empires could, for a time, appear to be efficient and competitive, but only in a lopsided world in which a liter of gasoline, which holds the energy equivalent of a person-month of hard manual labor, still costs less than a liter of milk.

But in the early twenty-first century fossil fuel resource depletion has made the industrial nation-state inefficient and uncompetitive. It is now gasping for air and fighting for its life. Unfortunately, its death agony may turn out to be quite agonizing for many innocent bystanders. The current political arrangement, outdated though it is, is unlikely to voluntarily devolve into an artisanal, anarchic set of intensely local polities, along the lines of the prosperous medieval city-states like Hamburg, Florence and Novgorod, which it displaced some centuries ago. At best, it will need a gentle nudge in the right direction. In a truly beautiful outcome, national leaders, gently dissuaded from attempting to lead, will be kept at a secure location, made to appear periodically to give the royal wave to the crowd, and eventually stuffed, mounted and put on display in a museum of collapse history. At worst, the dying nation-state will opt for maximum destructive power in a futile effort to buy time.

The imperious nation-state is sometimes deadly for those who do not wish to bend to its ways, but it is almost always inadvertently comical. Its nationalist rhetoric is couched in the language of almost geological permanence, while its reality is inevitably that of an ephemeral, dream-like entity that winks in and out of existence over the course of just a few generations, its course often predetermined by the initial success, eventual decadence and inevitable senility of its ruling class. Its physical embodiments usually consist of a few threadbare symbols: a flag, an anthem, a few slogans and a few historical monuments. The Soviet national anthem, not untypically, started with words that, in hindsight, make it sound farcical: "The unbreakable union of free republics was bound together for the ages by Great Russia." The effectiveness of these symbols rests on a certain human vulnerability; there is a particular developmental stage at which young people instinctively seek a tribal identity, which is normally constructed by going through initiation rituals and rites of passage, and it is at this stage that they most easily imprint on a fake—an arbitrary set of hollow symbols—deftly substituted by public schools and other state-controlled institutions. The United States Pledge of Allegiance, which schoolchildren are made to recite with a hand on their heart (now that the original Bellamy salute, a.k.a. *Hitlergruß*, has fallen into disfavor) is not just a formality—it is a transformative act that creates a group of young people willing to follow a leader waving a certain flag just as surely as a group of ducklings followed Konrad Lorenz's rubber boots, having imprinted on the boots as their mother.

Some people also seem to like to follow those who wear boots. If there is a single symbol that communicates the essence of the industrial nation-state particularly well, it is the jackboot, sported by matching formations of jackbooted baboons, their rifles held at the ready. Look at any symbolic display of state power, such as a presidential motorcade, and the sine qua non decorative element turns out to be the cortège of jackbooted motorcyclists. Although some of the jackbooted baboons may have actually volunteered for bootlick service, beguiled by the patriotic psychodrama of nationalism, many others are mere mercenaries. Money is the key, because the ultimate purpose of the nation-state is to maintain a political system that can effect a perfect melding of industry, militarism and commerce; industry supports militarism by supplying it with large quantities of weapons, militarism supports commerce by conquering vast new resources and markets and commerce supports militarism by funding the next round of military spending. Since people are only willing to unify in the face of an external threat, but since national unity is a requirement to realize the economies of scale required by industry, nationalist politicians worked hard to develop myths of religious, cultural or racial superiority. The exclusive sense of identity thus created, which projected all that was primitive and degenerate in one's own nation onto a supposedly primitive and degenerate Other, compelled people to act as a single group. In our more politically correct age the rhetoric of imperial racism has been replaced by something less vicious and more vacuous; from "Exterminate all the brutes!" to "Freedom and democracy!" But the goal has remained the same.

Not all young people are so easily impressed by the nationalist farce. An effective antidote to the siren song of nationalism is an advanced, refined sort of tribalism: diaspora groups with a strong ethnic identity, such as the (non-Israeli) Jews, the Chinese, the Armenians and the Gypsies, are relatively immune to it. Knowing how to recognize the real thing makes it easy to spot a fake, even for the young, and as a result these groups are not easily swayed by the patriotic psychodrama and rarely agree to send their sons into the military (practically never in the case of the Gypsies). Other groups—such as the Cossacks in Russia and the Scots-Irish in Britain and North America—have not only fallen into the nationalist trap but have become stuck in it as in a tar pit, providing a reliable, renewable supply of imperial cannon fodder. The tribal antidote is also effective against many of the symptoms that surface as the nation-state begins to fall apart, such as the appearance of illicit economies, mafia politics, warlordism and the rise of violent non-state actors. It has been observed in many failed states, in Africa and elsewhere, that young men who have been excluded from their home communities are far more easily recruited by violent organizations and are far more likely to use violence on behalf of their patrons, even against the very communities that excluded them—assured that there would be no consequences. In such circumstances, it becomes a matter of necessity for communities to find constructive, responsible roles for their young men, and to make sure that they feel included and valued—but also judged. By no means all communities everywhere are capable of this; the amount of pre-collapse social capital determines the level of post-collapse consolidation and cooperation that can be achieved.

National language

The symbols and claims of nationalism are quite hollow—often little more than the banners, standards and myths of some conquering group—but they can be greatly amplified by adding a linguistic identity. As the Yiddish scholar Max Weinreich is said to have put it, "A language is a dialect with an army and a navy." A typical ploy of the imperious nation-state is to design and impose an imperial language— the artificial language of government-run schools and official institu- tions, which serve the explicit purpose of drowning out local languages and dialects. The rise of the nation-state has been bad for linguistic diversity: half of the world's remaining six thousand languages, many of which have been in existence for thousands of years, are not expected to survive this century.

By far the most ambitious project to build a national, and even a transnational language is the Chinese writing system, which largely de- couples sound from written form, giving it considerable universality. It also gives it longevity; the sounds of any language shift over time, but the Chinese characters remain largely immutable. A speaker of a lan- guage that is written using Chinese characters can continue speaking that language, but is forced to think in Chinese characters. At one time the area that relied on Chinese writing, at least for keeping records, included Vietnam (whose old, Chinese character-based literature has been lost because no one can read it), Korea (which started its escape from the Chinese writing system in the fifteenth century by designing the Hangul national writing system, but completed the process only in the twentieth) and, to a limited and idiosyncratic extent, Japan, with its two thousand Chinese-derived *kanji*. For a brief moment in AD 1241 the Chinese writing system was in use on more than one quarter of the Earth's dry surface. That was the year when the Mongol Empire's wave of conquest rolled as far west as the gates of Vienna. (The Mongols were a non-literate culture and, to administer their vast empire, relied on the services of hundreds of Chinese scribes and accountants enslaved in the sacking of Yanjing in 1215, who, of course, wrote in Chinese.)

The other major national, and then transnational, linguistic success is English, which has solidified its position as the main language for international communication and is making more and more inroads around the world. Here too generality and longevity of the writing sys- tem has been achieved by largely decoupling sound from written form. The English spelling system makes very few, if any, claims to adequately represent how English is spoken, proudly remaining the haphazard, nonsensical, idiosyncratic waste of everyone's time it has always been. More importantly, it forms a very large barrier to acquiring basic lit- eracy. Having to separately memorize both the spelling and the sound for many thousands of common word is the price we all have to pay for using a living fossil as a medium of communication. The result is that functional illiteracy rates in English-speaking countries are many times those of other developed countries—as high as 50 percent. Their very large prison populations are an almost direct consequence of illiteracy, with a large percentage of the inmates unable to integrate into society due to their inability to read and write.

But it is quite possible to write English phonetically, so the problem of putting the entirety of the English spelling system to a well-deserved death is strictly a political issue whose solution would be especially applauded by the many millions of people who have to learn English as a second or third or fourth language. While English spelling continues to reign, forcing millions of people to endure years of rote memorization, it produces the additional side-effect of inadvertent acculturation to specifically English ways of thinking: because of the time it takes to learn, students of English learn not only the language but also its cultural clichés, many of which have barely shifted since the days when English was the imperial tongue. Perhaps it is time to invent a new English writing system, based on Chinese calligraphy, which would have exactly one symbol to represent each lexically differentiating phoneme (there are, it turns out, only thirty-two of them, across all the major dialects). English is, after all, a simple little language that just happens to have a big dictionary. The two reasons it caught on so well as the lingua franca across the world are its extreme grammatical, phonological and morphological simplicity compared to all of its international competitors, and its international vocabulary. With 80 percent of its vocabulary specifically French, and quite a bit of the rest international, it is really just "French made simple." It's a sort of baby talk, great for scat singing ("Zip-A-Dee-Doo-Dah!"), that comes with a fat dictionary full of big foreign words nobody seems to know how to spell or pronounce, never mind use correctly. Yes, it has the strange retroflex approximant "r" (the IPA symbol for which is [ɻ], its queer shape a testament to its strangeness), which is why it is mostly silent, but that too can be taken for a charming little infantile speech impediment. Yes, it has some of the world's most fearsome consonant clusters—the word "strengths" is all one syllable—but that too is just the sound of a baby spitting up.

Beyond that, most of the trouble with English comes from its post-imperial attitude and its refusal to let go of its abominable spelling system in favor of something a linguist might design on a day off and that can be learned fully while attending a single adult education course at a neighborhood community center. It is highly recommended that this alternative English orthography start out by not flouting the alphabetic principle, according to which exactly one symbol (letter) unambiguously represents exactly one sound (phoneme) of the language. The current English orthography follows over seventy different "spelling rules," but there are about as many exceptions as cases that follow the rules, so in most cases rote memorization works better. The system simply isn't teachable as a system. Case in point: for about a century now a debate has been raging in the US as to whether students should be taught that letters represent sounds—or not! If that isn't sad, what is? In other parts of the English-speaking world, "phonics" has been accepted as the superior approach, but even there adult functional illiteracy rates are the shame of the developed world.

While at it, let's give up on the Latin alphabet; it's the twenty-first century, and Latin is still dead. The medieval monks who preserved it for posterity and tried to apply it to English clearly didn't know what they were doing. The Latin alphabet is missing ten letters that English needs (two vowels and eight consonants). Other Western languages have since upgraded their alphabets, but English is still proudly muddling along with Latin 1.0 Beta. Plus, those monks laid a trap for dyslexics; to see what I mean, hold the book upside-down and try to read this: "bdbpdpqbqdpdpqbdbdq." Even the mildest case of dyslexia can be exacerbated by English spelling, where one letter stands for multiple phonemes and multiple letters stand for one phoneme, the same word can be written in different ways ("ewe," "yew" and "you"), different words can be written identically ("moped" vs "moped" and "tear" vs. "tear," depending on whether there are wheels or liquids involved) and same letter combinations can represent many different sounds ("enough," "plough," "though," "through").

Now that all text is electronic and the question of how to render it on the screen or the printed page is strictly a matter of software, somebody really ought to do something about it: "break the spell," as it were, and leave the crazy old spelling system in the dust. For those who need to decipher a passage from an obscure old book, a smartphone app could eventually be provided; snap a page full of Old Gibberish and a legible version flashes up on the screen. The lack of a sensible, phonologically accurate English orthography is, in software terms, just a missing feature.

Taking care of your own

Unconditional surrender of your identity and your thought process to the imperial tongue is not always, and not everywhere, strictly required, and there are many ethnic groups that are generally bilingual or trilingual, jealously guarding their native home language. Just one example of widespread trilingualism was medieval Chechnya, which was once a major center of Sufi learning. There, everyone spoke their home language (one of the many North Caucasian dialects, which eventually coalesced into Chechen) as well as Turkish at the market and when conducting commerce and, to top it off, many people could speak and read Arabic, which was the language of learning and religion and was used in the mosques. Turkish influence slowly faded away to be replaced by Russian, but to this day Chechens living throughout the Middle East speak only Chechen with one another, and discipline their children if they attempt to speak anything else while at home. It is much the same everywhere; minority and diaspora groups jealously guard their language, knowing that the loss of language often spells the loss of identity. This in spite of the fact that doing so often incurs considerable risk (speaking a different language within a monolingual nation-state is always a political act), because the benefits of having a genuine source of identity that supersedes the synthetic, transient national identity almost always outweigh the costs. The advantages are many; among them is the ability to move within a circle of trust that automatically includes all the native speakers of the home language (since they can read each other and sense each others' intentions far more easily than those of the surrounding society) and the ability to code-talk in the presence of strangers, keeping communications private without having to make any special arrangements. Most importantly, groups that have their own language can use it to craft their own versions of consensual reality, separate from and in opposition to the mainstream one.

Not all groups have the strength of resolve and the group cohesion to maintain their separate linguistic identity in good working order. It takes serious effort to provide separate schooling for children and to maintain high community standards for the use of the home language, and groups that are struggling economically may not have the spare energy to devote to these tasks. It also takes a certain amount of determination to resist the pressure to integrate into and become assimilated by the mainstream culture. The result is that, in many cases, the home language degenerates over time, becoming polluted with a large number of loan words and expressions. Once a local dialect finds itself on this slippery slope, it is difficult to stop the process of degeneration. Since it is always easier to use a loan word than to come up with a native expression, virtually all creativity within the language itself ceases, and over time the home language becomes little more than accented English with a grab-bag of foreign function words and a bit of left-over grammatical glue used to cobble together sentences out of loan words. .

There are certain populations that are described as half-lingual: they do not adequately speak the mainstream language, nor are they able to communicate in the home language without relying on numerous loan words from the national language. If they return to their home country, what comes out of their mouths may very well be perceived as pure gibberish. One of the best examples of this trend is the Spanglish spoken by many Latinos living in the United States, which has become so prevalent that the Spanish Royal Academy has recently recognized it as a separate language. Luckily, Spain itself has a wealth of intact, living languages, including Castilian, Catalan and Euskara, but in some other cases the situation in the home country with respect to language may not be a whole lot better. Globalization has been forcing many changes on the world, including cultural and linguistic homogenization driven by the use of English and the Internet. Once a language becomes sufficiently polluted by loan words and loses its creativity, it also ceases to function as an alternative tool of thought and an independent representation of the world. The language becomes effectively colonized, along with the minds of its speakers. Soon thereafter it ceases to serve as a strong basis for group identity. Within a generation or two its use dwindles to a few stock phrases, and, shortly thereafter, the language dies.

State religion

A national language is a powerful tool for imposing a single, unified groupthink on a disparate and initially diverse population, and to make it behave like a single, hierarchically controlled entity, especially if that population is deprived of their own local languages and dialects, but it pales in comparison with the force of a state religion. Rulers have always recognized this, which is why Christianity, which started out as an anarchist movement, was quickly co-opted and became a tool in the hands of the Roman emperors, both Western (Roman Catholic) and Eastern (Byzantine Orthodox). It is also why the Protestantism of the initial Anabaptists, which started out as a popular peasant movement, was quickly co-opted when Luther and other Protestant leaders allied themselves with the nobles, leaving the Amish, the Mennonites and a handful of other exiled sects as the only politically independent communities of believers. Islam, on the other hand, started out as a political movement; the Prophet Mohammed was a businessman, a politician and a warrior and, of course, a religious leader who excelled at the art of bending people to his will, with religion as the most powerful weapon in his political arsenal. This is why Moslems fly into a rage whenever anyone jokingly intimates that their Prophet might have been a bit of a sharp dealer and that they are easy marks to be following his word (I have no opinion on this matter myself, of course). But his political/religious genius was such that even today, fourteen centuries later, two of the most toxic regimes on earth are Islamic theocracies: the Kingdom of Saudi Arabia and the Islamic Republic of Iran. These two states, representing the extremes of Sunni and Shia Islam, sow mischief over much of the world. The mischief they sow in turn finds an easy mark in the United States: terrorist attacks, which are mere pinpricks unable to truly hurt a mighty military empire, offend against the Americans' sense of infantile omnipotence and send them into an equally infantile rage. This is quite different from, say, the Russian reaction to terrorist attacks, which is, typically, "They can't kill us all." The American reaction is to kill Moslems indiscriminately, and this only makes matters worse.

If nationalist indoctrination is a dirty trick to play on children—substituting a fake, synthetic identity for a real one—then state-religious indoctrination of children is more like an actual crime, along the lines of child abuse through brainwashing and mind control. At the very least, children should be taken to the circus first, so that they can firmly grasp the concept of make-believe. Then they should be taken to a magic show, so that they get a chance to learn the meaning of "hocus-pocus." A trip to the theater is next, where they get to practice suspension of disbelief. A graduation ceremony is next, so that they get to see a rite of passage. Then it should be explained to them that a religious service is like a sort of make-believe hocus-pocus rite of passage that requires suspension of disbelief.

As their minds mature, children become capable of understanding syllogisms. All religions claim to be the one true faith. If there were one true faith, there would only be that one faith, and its truth could be proven and the truth of all the others could be disproven (since that's the process that defines truth). But there are many faiths. There-fore, the truth of any one faith is indeterminate. It's more of a mix-and-match than a kit of parts. Then tell them some actual truths. Back when the early Christians were feeding the lions at the Coliseum and on their days off were known as "the people without a book," it just so happened that the Jews had just lost their historical homeland of Palestine (again). Consequently, all of their holy books were on sale, so the Christians bought up the lot. Eventually they added some of their own. The Gospels are fabrications after the fact, written by pro-fessional ghostwriters (the ghostwriter who wrote for St. Matthew was excellent; others—mediocre). Emperor Constantine made every-one buy paintings on velvet of a stag by moonlight with a shining cross between his antlers (yes, I made that one up). Muhammad was a... never mind.

Also be sure to explain the concept of blasphemy. If a god is a pow-erful god and you insult him, he will smite you right back, correct? So if you insult a god and nothing happens to you, there are several logical possibilities: A. the god you insulted doesn't exist, B. the god is a weak god and can't smite you, C. the god in question is magnanimous and doesn't care if an insignificant being such as yourself insults him, or D. the god is a petty and vindictive god who holds a grudge for years and takes it out on the dead. Note that those who believe in god "D" are likely to be petty and vindictive themselves, and one should do one's best to avoid both them and their nasty little god.

Parents should do their best to shield their children from state reli-gion, be it Sunni, Shia, Russian Orthodox Christian or any other faith that is allied with and serves the interests of the state. (Children should also not be allowed anywhere near Catholic priests due to an unaccept-ably high incidence of pedophilia.) Religious institutions are just as flawed and fallible as any human institution, but they suffer from the additional moral hazard of starting out from a position of supposed, largely fictional moral superiority. Toss in a handful of politics and you have the perfect set-up for corrupting the minds, and bodies, of the young. The state prosecutor would rather kiss the monsignor's ring than prosecute him for child molestation, especially if he was himself molested as a child and would rather not be forced to confront the fact that his whole life has been based on a lie.

I hope that what I say will not be taken out of context: I have nothing against religion per se; I have everything against state religion, religion in politics and theocracy. In the next chapter, which examines social collapse, I have much more to say about the positive aspects of religion as a small-scale social organizing principle. But those positive aspects will come to light only after we have kissed the nation-state goodbye.

Life after the nation-state

The modern nation-state is a relatively recent phenomenon that emerged in nineteenth-century Europe. During the twentieth century it became dominant throughout the world. But recently it has started to fade: many nations have seen their sovereignty eroded by the forces of globalization, while many others have become weak states, and are verging on becoming defunct states. The World Bank publishes a list of nations lacking effective sovereignty. In 1996 there were eleven entries; in 2006 there were twenty-six. Not a year goes by that another nation-state does not get shunted to the weak/defunct track: last year it was Libya; this year, Syria. How far behind is Greece? Is Spain going to be able to hold on to Catalonia, Galicia and the Basque Country, even as it goes bankrupt? Is Scotland going to remain part of the United Kingdom after the independence referendum of 2014? It is too early to tell whether the increase in nonviable nation-states is linear or exponential, but a simple projection shows that if this trend continues to accelerate at the same rate there will be zero viable nation-states left by 2030 or so. My hope is that the majority of nation states skip the weak state phase and shoot straight for defunct, because, as it turns out, a weak state is far worse than a defunct state in many ways. This is because a weak state does not achieve much for its people, but it does stand in the way of local self-governance, whereas a defunct state can remain as a pleasantly innocuous ceremonial vestige in charge of museums, parades and historical reenactments (as with the British Commonwealth) or can be gradually consigned to oblivion due to lack of interest (as with the Commonwealth of Independent States, the empty husk that remained after the collapse of the Soviet Union).

Before the advent of the nation-state, there were city-states, confederations and, most transitory of all, empires. The city-states are by far the most successful political construct in human history. Before they were all but extinguished by Rome, a handful of relatively tiny towns in Greece gave rise to much of what makes up Western intellectual heritage. Similarly tiny specks of civilization—the free cities of Medieval Europe—were responsible for producing much of Western cultural heritage and for setting the stage for the industrial revolution. People in English-speaking countries have a skewed view of the Middle Ages because they associate them with miserable backward England rather than with glittering gems like medieval Florence, Hamburg, Pskov or Samarkand.

It would be just as expected, then, that as industrialism fades in a cloud of soot and smoke left over from a century-long fossil fuel-burning extravaganza, with it will vanish the nineteenth-century nation-state, taking with it all that is outlandishly huge, fraught with overweening ambition and immensely dangerous to human survival and life on Earth. In its stead will come a myriad of tiny polities, some squabbling with their neighbors, some living side by side peaceably, but all incapable of launching a single aircraft carrier, never mind starting a world war. But they might be able to build some beautiful cathedrals and opera houses, lavish resources on the arts and on schools of philosophy and use artisanal methods to produce everyday items that will put to shame the mass-produced plastic rubbish of today. This is because the rulers of small, regional states lack the resources to compete with their neighbors militarily, and instead compete by developing a superior culture.

The problem of excessive scale

In his excellent book *The Breakdown of Nations*[24] the maverick economist Leopold Kohr makes several stunning yet, upon reflection, commonsense observations. He points out that small states have tended to be far more culturally productive than large states, that all states go to war but that big states have disproportionately bigger wars that kill many times more people, and that by far the most stable and advantageous form of political organization is a loose confederation of states, each so small that none can dominate the rest. Kohr arrives at his conclusions by a process of reasoning by homology (viz. analogy) by analyzing many of the problems of modernity as different manifestations of the same underlying problem: the problem of excessive scale.

Most people can relate to the concept of optimal scale on an intuitive, visceral level; we know when something is abnormally big or abnormally small, and we tend to dislike abnormality. The exceptions, be they midgets or giants, are considered freaks. In living things, growth tapers off and stops when the organism has reached its optimum size. Pursuit of largest possible size is a quixotic one, like that of the farmer who tries to grow the largest-possible turnip. Terms like "jumbo shrimp" make children giggle. There was once a very successful and influential religious cult devoted to finding the optimum in all things: the Greek cult of Apollo, with its motto of μηδὲν ἄγαν—"Nothing in excess." Excess is never without cost, excessive size is no exception, and beyond a certain point the cost of excessive size becomes exorbitant. This point is lost on very few people, virtually all of whom happen to be politicians. For them, there is simply no limit to how big their nation-state should be allowed to become. When they think "bigger" they automatically think "better" and "more powerful," in spite of much evidence to the contrary. Incapable of understanding the concept of first diminishing, then negative economies of scale, they cannot understand why increased defense spending results in more military defeats, or why increased spending on education causes ignorance to spread and test scores to plummet, or why increased spending on health care results in an increase in morbidity and mortality. In their headlong pursuit of "growth" they work themselves into the cul de sac of excessive size, a predicament from which there is no escape except through collapse.

Kohr defines the effect of excessive size using the Law of Diminishing Productivity: if one adds variable units of any factor of production to a fixed quantity of another, at some point the effect of adding one more variable unit will decrease productivity rather than increase it. The best example of this law in action we currently have is with population as the variable unit and Earth as the fixed unit. Indications are that we passed this point some time ago, but the population continues to grow because, although productivity is being steadily diminished, it is still above zero. Kohr's ideas lived on in the work of E. F. Schumacher and others, but they have failed to gain enough traction to reverse the march to gigantism, followed inexorably by collapse.

Ironically, Kohr's effort failed precisely because of the vast scale of the contemporary intellectual endeavor. Kohr pointed out that most of the great advances in learning and the arts occurred in small communities—in ancient Greece, medieval Europe and other places where everyone knew everyone, where the entire sweep of human affairs could be taken in at a glance and where one could be well regarded as what was once called a Renaissance Man—a generalist. But the vast scale at which contemporary society operates makes it impossible for anyone to observe the whole of it with any degree of precision or insight, forcing everyone to specialize in one thing or another; the vaster the scale, the more circumscribed the realm in which one can gain sufficient expertise to understand what is happening and be in a position to predict what might happen next. The proliferation of experts who know almost everything about almost nothing is a sure sign that the pursuit of knowledge has been carried to an excessive scale, but the existence of these same experts makes it impossible to claw knowledge back from the brink of utter irrelevance, because that can only be done by a generalist. In turn, generalists are not allowed among specialists: to a specialist, as Kohr pointed out, a generalist is either irrelevant (unable to advance knowledge in the specialist's narrow field of expertise) or an impostor (someone not even interested in advancing knowledge in the specialist's narrow field of expertise).

To illustrate how this works (or, as the case may be, does not work) let us take the specific example of breast cancer. There are specialists in the genetics of breast cancer (which seems specialized enough for our purposes) who have recently taken to the airwaves in the hopes of drumming up support for extending their already rather expensive program of research. They have found some genetic markers for breast cancer which could potentially lead to more effective treatments given a great deal of further research. Some poor sane woman calls up and asks, "What about prevention?" (There didn't used to be so much breast cancer, you know.) One specialist starts babbling about the difficulty of doing studies of breast cancer prophylaxis therapies...before remembering that she is an oncological geneticist, dammit, not a historical epidemiologist! Now, let's suppose the impossible: someone managed to get a historical epidemiologist specializing in breast cancer on that same show. (It is difficult to have different areas of expertise represented on one show and still have it be interesting because the different specialists tend to politely ignore each other.) The historical epidemiologist would probably say that the evidence for lower historical incidence of breast cancer during centuries past is ambiguous because the diagnostic techniques we use today were not available then, but it's certainly the case that the rates for many types of cancer have doubled and even tripled since the early twentieth century, by which time doctors were certainly able to recognize tumors. So why is that? Well, the epidemiologist volunteers, the spike in cancer rates coincides with the introduction of a large number of synthetic organic compounds into the environment—ones that do not occur in nature. Another poor sane woman calls up and asks, "What about the carcinogenic pesticides found in breast milk?" What specialist do we summon next, a neonatal nutritionist, perhaps, who will tell us about the increased risk of cancer in breast-fed infants? (Sorry, that's off-topic!) Or an agricultural chemist, who will tell us that the pesticides are required to bring in the bountiful harvests we need to feed a growing, albeit cancer-riddled, population? Perhaps we should ask a politician? A politician would no doubt say that he will support all of these lines of research, so please remember to vote for him on election day.

Better yet, let's all take a short mental holiday (because by now most of us could probably use one) and ask a prince. Suppose the court scientist comes to the prince and says, "My prince, our women are developing tumors in their breasts at an alarming rate, and I have discovered why." (He is the only court scientist, but a very good one. He specializes in Knowing Much More Than Anyone Else.) "In this vial I have an extract of breast milk," he goes on, "which contains the same poisons your chemists are giving to your peasants to kill insects. I have fed these poisons to rats, and they too developed tumors. The poisons must be banned." The prince, his pampered hand resting lightly on a leather-bound volume by Niccolò Machiavelli, thinks to himself: "These chemists say that they are my friends, but are they really? Here is my chance to find out. If I ban these dreadful poisons, then they may comply willingly, but if they resist even for a moment, then I will condemn them as poisoners of women and children and clap them in irons and/or banish them from my realm in accordance with my *caprice du jour*! In either case, I will no longer have to wonder whether or not they are my friends." Aloud he says, "These poisons are an abomination," and to the palace guard, "Summon the chemists!" When the chemists arrive some minutes later, red in the face and out of breath, the prince, growing impatient, motions to the court scientist to get on with it. The court scientist repeats his words. "As you wish, my prince," the chief chemist says, "but don't your peasants need these poisons to kill the insects to feed the growing population?" The prince, now looking positively bored, turns to his scientist: "What would be better for us, a smaller but healthier population or a larger but sicker one...never mind, I just answered my own question. The poisons are hereby banned. Lunch, anyone?"

If a relatively specific problem, such as the task of banning cancer-causing pesticides, shatters into tiny, mutually unintelligible domains upon the submerged rocks of overspecialization, then what of the far more general problem of controlling scale at every level? It is simply not specific enough to register with any of the numerous specialists and specialisms on whose domains it impinges. There is a vast and desolate no-man's-land stretching between political science, economics, sociology, psychology, psychiatry, history and philosophy (to name a few) and this is the wilderness that our poor hero, Leopold Kohr, chose to wander. And although his book is a joy to read in spite of its sombre message, his fate was a sad one. He was trying to stop the cancer of unconstrained, uncontrolled growth after it had already metastasized and engulfed the entire planet. But thanks to Kohr's efforts we are able to realize that although the sick patient is the entire planet, the cancer is not necessarily in all of us. Instead of pointing at each of us, Kohr points at the global political juggernaut driven by a blind ambition of achieving global unity. Our task, it would appear, is to jump off this death-wagon without breaking our legs.

What drives the global juggernaut forward is the lust for power. Its power-hungry drivers have a particular blind spot: they cannot realize that beyond a certain scale further expansion undermines their power rather than enhance it. Writing in 1958, Hannah Arendt defined power as the human ability not just to act, but to act in concert. Power is amplified by enlarging the scale at which it is practiced, and politicians everywhere, in striving to increase their power, do so by striving for greater and greater political unity (but just short of a global union, because there must exist an enemy: it is politically necessary to be able to define an Other of whom we remain ignorant but onto whom we can project our own undesirable qualities). While problems of excessive scale are recognized and, at least in principle, prevented with regard to commercial monopolies, political monopoly of unified government is everywhere regarded as perfectly benign; but is it? Just as a commercial monopoly restricts material production, a political monopoly restricts intellectual production, and just as commercial monopolies tend to provide undifferentiated, standardized, shoddy goods, so political monopolies provide undifferentiated, standardized, shoddy policies and laws.

What is worse, large-scale political unions are inherently danger-ous. Small countries can only afford small armies and fight small wars. Only huge empires have the capacity to launch world wars, and only global superpowers have the ability to blow up the entire planet. Most wars are fought to establish or maintain political unity, and the larger the political union, the larger the conflict. What enabled the two world wars was the excessive scale of the European armies of the time. Any look at human history will show that wars are inevitable and recur with great regularity; if so, small wars are preferable to large wars, and the best guarantee that a war will remain small is if it involves small, rela-tively weak opponents. Also, any look at human history will show that all political entities collapse with great regularity; if so, many small-scale collapses are preferable to one giant collapse. Kohr refers to the program of uncontrolled political unification "the solution of spontane-ous collapse."

Kohr does admit the utility of unity, provided it is temporary and for a specific purpose, such as to face a natural disaster or an external threat. Political unity to the point of widespread willingness to die for the common cause arises spontaneously only in the face of an existen-tial threat. But it can also be coerced, and if state authority tends to be oppressive, then organizations of cooperating states tend to be much more so. Large, powerful states are inherently warlike, taking every op-portunity to project power both internally and externally in an effort to enhance it. These efforts result in the creation of impersonal systems of crowd living, be they militarism, communism or corporatism, that op-press the small group and the individual alike. The ability to wield mas-sive power with precision is deeply dehumanizing: "The most devilish designs of barbarism have not been conceived by illiterates, but by the most educated brains," Kohr writes. Beyond its overt monstrousness, the large state is simply not very good: small states are far more capable of exorcizing such social vices as rudeness, mendacity, inequality and hypocrisy, because they tend to increase in proportion to the size of the social unit.

According to Kohr, the small state has much to recommend it, especially if it exists in a loose but relatively peaceful confederation with other small states, none of them large enough to dominate the others (bringing to mind the outsized influence of Germany in the European Union). He points out that the smaller the sovereign group, the greater is each individual's share of personal sovereignty. An Icelander's share of state sovereignty is over four thousand times that of a Chinese: a sovereign giant compared to a sovereign dwarf. A sovereign dwarf is a mere statistic, a depersonalized average man and an embodiment of the god of collectivism, and such impersonal collectivism is, to Kohr, ignoble. To him, nobility (by which he means nobility of spirit) is never just "doing your job" in some abstract and perfunctory way, but engaging with each person, and democracy does not exist wherever a direct conversation between the ruler and any one of his subjects is no longer possible. To test whether you are living in a democracy, go and demand to see the president. If you find yourself questioned by the secret police and put under surveillance, or arrested and jailed, or put in a psychiatric hospital, then there is a teensy-weensy chance that you are not living in a democracy.

Although Kohr's work can be read as a warning of the dire consequences of excessive scale at every level, it can also be viewed as a message of hope for the future. The waning of the industrial age is making the maintenance requirements of gigantic political entities impossible to meet, and as they decay, collapse and devolve into much smaller and more local entities, the world may yet see a rebirth of states small enough to grant their members a reasonable share of personal sovereignty. Some of them may even become able to aspire to true, direct democracy and find ways to renew themselves, whereas the larger states can now only blunder along, biding their time. Kohr tried to get at this hopeful vision with this charming quote from André Gide: "Je crois à la vertu du petit nombre; le monde sera sauvé par quelques-uns." ["I believe in the virtue of the small number; the world will be saved by the few."]

The proliferation of defunct states

The triumph of the nation-state was made possible by the triumph of industry over artisanal production, especially in the area of weaponry. Industrialization gave the larger nations the means to produce vast

quantities of war matériel, in turn giving them the impetus to homog-
enize and standardize the population by imposing a single language
and educational system in order to be able to field a unified fighting
force. The transformation was profound: at the time of the French Revolution only 10–12 percent of the French population could be said to
speak French; in Italy the number of people who could be said to speak
Italian was even lower. It allowed a handful of European nation-states
to conquer the entire planet, before suffering the successive paroxysms
of the two world wars. As they retreated, they did their best to carve up
the planet into patches that, they hoped, would emerge as nation-states
in their own right. Many of these experiments at constructing nations
out of heterogenous ethnic raw material are famous failures: the Tutsi–
Hutu Rwanda, the Sunni–Shia–Kurd Iraq, the Moslem North and
Christian South Sudan, the permanent disaster area that is the Congo,
along with numerous less famous ones. But no matter how weak the
case for unity happens to be, it is a requirement that each patch of land
belong to some nation-state or other.

Take the example of the Republic of Abkhazia, a tiny speck of a
country on the Black Sea that, after the collapse of the USSR, fought
and won a war of independence against the newly hatched and rabidly
nationalistic nation-state of (former Soviet) Georgia. Abkhazia then
spent more than a decade in political limbo because the world at large
frowned upon its separatist ambitions. Meanwhile its remaining residents held a referendum and voted for independence, while at the same
time acquiring Russian passports. They wanted nothing whatsoever to
do with Georgia while realizing that full independence was but a dream.
In August of 2008 the Georgians lost their cool and attacked South
Ossetia (another limbo territory full of Russian citizens). For this they
were severely punished by Russia, which then de facto annexed both
territories. Since then the international furor over Abkhazia's refusal
to be part of Georgia has been buried. Clearly, the problem with the
world's refusal to recognize Abkhazia's independence had nothing to
do with Georgia; it had everything to do with independence. Now that
Abkhazia has been claimed by a nation-state, all is well and the matter
can be regarded as settled. And when we say "the world," let's be clear
that we mean the United Nations, the OECD and various other international organizations whose members are...nation-states. Member-

ship has its privileges, and one of them is the privilege of stomping on the heads of non-members.

Such is the pressure that every single patch of dirt on the planet should belong to some nation-state or other, even if it is weak or defunct or purely a notional artifact of the political map. Any patch of dirt that fails to coalesce with one of the neighboring tiles in the nation-state mosaic can, in principle, become its own separate nation-state, but then it must organize a national government for the purposes of seeking international recognition and entering into state-legal relations with other tiles. It is by now abundantly clear that not every former imperial possession does a viable nation-state make: the planet is littered with defunct or semi-defunct states that succumbed to internal conflict. The idea of carving up peoples according to arbitrary patterns set by previous imperial conquests and treaties is not a fruitful one.

It is often tempting to see the problems of these stillborn nation-states as problems of governance: if only the political arrangements could be worked out to everyone's satisfaction, democratically, of course. This approach rather glosses over the point that the world is full of tribes which have lived in close proximity for eons but generally do their best to avoid each other, perhaps only interacting in specific ways, for example by trading on market days, like animals that call a temporary truce when approaching a watering hole. Such tribes remain happy provided they can maintain their cultural, linguistic and social separateness while being able to insult their neighbors (not to their faces, of course). Failing that, they are happy to go to war with their neighbors until their separateness is restored. Forcing neighboring tribes to submit to a single government is tantamount to forcing them to fight. The problem is not with the lack of governance; it is with the mindset that centralized governance and political unity are necessary.

Here is a prescription for disaster. Take a collection of tribes that proudly hate their neighbors and treasure their ability to maintain their separate identity and way of life. Split them up into separate territories based on previous patterns of imperial conquest, being especially careful to make sure that the new borders cut across as many seasonal migration and trade routes as possible, to unnecessarily increase the amount of hardship. Hire a low-budget design agency to come up with a flag, an anthem and some other national symbols. Download a template for a national constitution off the Internet and spend an afternoon customizing it. But then you face a choice: organize a national government that pretends to be democratic and obeys the constitution, or just put the constitution in a glass display case and pick a dictator? These are both bad choices, but in different ways.

Dictatorship is a good form of governance in a bad situation. During the times of the Roman republic the senators would elect a dictator when faced with very serious crises, although a better practice was to elect a couple of consuls, so that their dictatorial powers would be divided between two competitors. The situation of being a recently formed, weak nation-state that confronts a political map crowded with established nation-states, many of them powerful, can be considered a crisis of such monumental proportions that the choice of a dictatorship may seem to be a wise one. However, the country rarely gets a chance to un-pick the dictator once the crisis is over. Perhaps the biggest problem with having a dictator is that dictators tend to either end up being Western stooges or getting overthrown by the West.

Here are some examples of dictatorial successes in holding non-viable nation-states together. The authoritarian Josip Broz Tito held Yugoslavia together and made it a pleasant place. Once it was left without his unifying presence, Yugoslavia descended into ethnic cleansing, genocide and civil war. Saddam Hussein succeeded in creating a prosperous Iraq out of disparate bits and pieces of the Ottoman Empire, with a large, thriving, well-educated middle class. Once he was overthrown, the country (if it can still be called that) descended into civil war, and is now an impoverished ghost of itself characterized by misery and permanent unrest. Muammar Qaddafi achieved similarly stellar results for Libya, and was for a time regarded as an honest broker and a peacemaker throughout Africa. He launched communications satellites in an attempt to break France Telecom's stranglehold on that continent. But he was overthrown, and now Libya is a war zone and a dangerous place for Washington's ambassadors. Hafez al-Assad (father of Bashar, the current dictator) held Syria together for thirty-odd years, but now it has descended into civil war.

Yes, dictatorship is at best problematic. But any nascent nation-state that decides to give democracy a try is sure to confront many problems as well. To start with, democracy is a tradition that cannot be conjured up on the spot or imported and installed like a piece of industrial machinery; it has to evolve in place. The best, oldest, most stable democracies have tribal roots and rely on direct democracy at the local level. A representative democracy is a degenerate case open to many kinds of corruption and abuse that may become bad enough to invalidate the entire project. In a representative democracy the electoral process involves forming national political parties which tend to become financially dependent on the dominant class in a process that disenfranchises those whose only ambition is to pursue local interests. On the other hand, violent confrontations over votes are likely when the elected representatives represent specific districts. An attempt to institute granular political representation in an already weak state dominated by non-state actors is a prescription for political violence. Add to this the fact that, in a heterogenous population, proportional representation gives the more powerful and numerous tribes the upper hand over the smaller, minority tribes, which do not readily accede to such an arrangement and look for opportunities to make mischief.

Secondly, democracies, young democracies especially, are easily corrupted by money, especially money from abroad. Much of the foreign aid that comes from the US, the EU, Japan and, more recently, China, has been spent on propping up weak governments, to the detriment of the governed. There is a long list of countries that have an impoverished, disenfranchised population lorded over by a government that is headed by corrupt officials who drive around in limousines and wear flowing robes and plenty of bling and command foreign-trained, foreign-armed militaries. It has been a long-standing pattern for such officials to accept Western loans, promptly deposit most of the money in their own personal offshore bank accounts, and leave the country saddled with the impossible task of repaying them. The same pattern of exploitation that corporate raiders practice in doing leveraged buyouts of public companies, where the raiders walk away with a great deal of money while the company is left behind as a hollow shell suffocated by debt, can be practiced with respect to countries, especially if they are democratic ones. It is only a slight exaggeration to say that democracy enables the process by which private property can be transformed into political power. If an authoritarian regime finds that individuals or corporations are using their private property to undermine its political power, the property in question is confiscated (nationalized). There is a very nice fellow by the name of Michael Khodorkovsky, who used to run a major Russian oil company but is now cooling his heels in a Russian penal colony. The reason he is there is that he did not appreciate this particular aspect of authoritarianism: he naïvely thought that his corporate wealth automatically gave him political leverage.

Although a nonviable nation-state run by an authoritarian government or a dictatorship is better at pushing back against neocolonial predation by other nation-states than a pretend-democracy, neither one is ultimately satisfactory. The solution that tends to emerge spontaneously is one of local self-governance that takes each small region out of the arena of state–legal relations altogether. If a region possesses a system of informal self-governance, refuses to allow selection of representatives, refuses to enter into treaties and rejects all claims of outside control or ownership with a credible show of force, then it effectively becomes, in the parlance of international law theorists, an ungoverned space. Such spaces are not necessarily lawless or even dangerous, but they are dangerous to outside forces wishing to advance their own interests to the detriment of the locals.

As more and more erstwhile nation-states pass through the weak phase and tip into the defunct column, they can collapse into durable disorder or endless civil war, but they can also collapse into local autonomy and self-governance and let national borders grow porous. Their human populations are then able to come out of the vegetative condition to which settled, civilized existence has consigned them and revert to their original, nomadic state. There is a none-too-subtle difference between terrestrial plants and animals; the plants do not move, while the animals do (and when they do, there is just one species that requires passports or visas to cross international boundaries). We did not colonize most of the planet by staying put; nor will we be able to stay put if we wish to adapt to life in a depleted, disrupted, rapidly changing natural, physical and social environment.

Government services disappear

Between the time we are born, diapered and weaned and the time we are retired, die and are cremated and/or buried, various things are done to us. We are delivered in hospitals and inoculated in clinics; we are educated; we are (made to feel that we are) protected from enemies foreign and domestic; we are made to work jobs, consume and recreate. These are things that define life in a nation-state, and the nation-state, in turn, defines life on the entire planet. If we go traveling, we need government-issued passports and visas to pass from the territory of one nation-state into the territory of another. If we are truly adventurous, we may travel to one of the nation-states for which the US State Department has issued travel warnings. As I write this, nine new countries were added to the list last month, and five the month before. Sudan, Libya, Afghanistan, Syria, Congo, Mali.... They are still nation-states, mind you, just not ones where the government controls the territory, or the night. But they are still nation-states, and a few million dollars in foreign aid to arm and equip whoever it is we want to be in charge will make it tick right along, don't you worry! There are just 33 out of 193 U.N. member nations that are on the list of countries to avoid in 2012, which is only 17 percent of the total, so let's not worry too much.

If you are adventurous and go to one of these places, you will find that you can still get from the airport to the government office to the hotel and back in relative safety and comfort. It's venturing outside the cities on your own and walking around the less prosperous neighborhoods without a bodyguard, especially at night, that gets dicey. As government power shrinks, there remains a core of central control that gradually diminishes toward the periphery, and you may want to find out where these boundaries lie and then avoid straying too far afield. Another good question to ask is, Who controls the night? It is quite usual to observe that after the sun sets and the government security people go home to sleep with their wives and/or sweethearts an entirely different contingent emerges from the shadows and takes over. The government security people know this, and go into hiding along with the sun because battling these shadowy forces is well above their pay grade; plus, more often than not, they have a private arrangement with them. They are rational, and are willing to sacrifice the fiction of national unity, piece by piece, on the altar of social harmony.

Leopold Kohr found a poetic way to express the split between unity and harmony, defining national unity as a single banner, a single anthem, a single constitution and "a single scream of anguish for all that is suppressed, excluded and ignored." Where this conflict does not lead to war (and most wars are fought to establish or to preserve national unity) there may be harmony, for a time, with the fiction of national unity preserved in the center during the day, when those supposedly in power try to maintain a cracked but still impressive political façade, while all that has been suppressed, excluded and ignored is allowed to rule the periphery and the night. The cost of projecting power over distance always causes empires to crumble starting with the periphery. It is only when the government forces not only retreat to the capital city but also start hiding during the day and sneaking around in armed convoys that the situation becomes recognized as a revolution.

Prosperous, stable nation-states cover contiguous areas of security and wealth. As they decay, they develop islands of economic and political exclusion that expand over time. In the US these are places such as Flint, Michigan, or Camden, New Jersey, or Fall River, Massachusetts, or many other defunct or nearly defunct cities and towns with high unemployment and hardly any government services. In the developing world, as the national government consolidates and expands its power over its territory, it creates islands of security and wealth that expand over time. The pattern is the same for the un-developing world. In its formerly developed portions, the islands of exclusion expand and merge, until what is left is a few islands of security and wealth. In the formerly developing portions, these islands shrink down to the last government compound where the remnants of the former ruling class cower behind blast walls and wait to be evacuated by helicopter.

Although people in the developed countries like to think that the problem lies elsewhere, this is no longer the case. The problem is no longer on their doorstep; it is in their living room, sitting on the couch enjoying a beer. As the formerly developed nations deteriorate thanks to economic stagnation, aging populations and a host of other problems, the locals are often slow to recognize just how far they have fallen. While they wait for better times to return, immigrants and migrant workers flood in from the formerly developing countries, which are plagued with a host of problems of their own, such as overpopulation, soil erosion and economic disruption caused by rapid climate change, and take whatever jobs are available, be it swabbing out toilets in offices or washing dishes. An uncomfortable standoff results. The host nations find that they can no longer function without imported labor, and, consequently, cannot withhold social benefits from the foreigners either, especially not from their locally-born children. They then start making a half-hearted effort to integrate the newcomers into the nation-state. Meanwhile, the refugees and immigrants often choose to make a virtue of transience, understanding full well that jobs can move at any time and that they will have to move with them, and so they develop an internal rhetoric of self-exclusion—a system of values that undermines both local society and the state. It is, by all appearances, a no-win situation: half-hearted, even resentful efforts to make room by one side, greeted with indifference toward something that is perceived as makeshift and temporary by the other.

The jig isn't quite up yet, but the trend is already unmistakable. Western liberal imperialism first imposed the concepts of territorial statehood and sovereignty on the entire planet, carving up the whole globe into colored tiles on the political map—each with its own banner, anthem, constitution, fetish of national unity and scream of anguish for all that is excluded—and then went right ahead and undermined the whole thing. Of all the prerogatives initially granted to sovereign states, saluting the banner and singing the anthem seem to be the only ones left. The prerogatives of national government are usually thought to include the following: printing and coining money and providing economic governance; maintaining law and order and waging war; providing for the welfare of its citizens; and choosing a development path. Once a nation-state loses the ability to exercise these prerogatives, it begins to lurch in the direction of a failed state, which can generally be defined by the following three "no's": no monopoly on the use of force; no ability to uphold the law; and no ability to deliver public services. Many nations-states are not quite there yet, but to see how far along they are, let us look each of their treasured prerogatives, and see how well they are faring in today's world.

Denationalization of currency

The government's prerogative of seigniorage—of reaping a windfall from the coining or printing of money—has been severely eroded by the financial markets, to the point where the government's responsibility to maintain a stable currency is no longer vested in governments at all. The European Central Bank and the US Federal Reserve now print money as needed, in order to bail out transnational banks on which they, in turn, depend. The US dollar, which is still at the core of the world's financial system, is fatally wounded, and the hemorrhage, in the form of runaway US sovereign debt, will in due course kill it. Just the US federal budget deficit (which is just one such funding gap out of many) is currently running at around $1 trillion a year—a number that puts it well beyond any hopes of containment. The gap cannot be bridged either by raising income taxes to 100 percent or by cutting all government spending except for Social Security and Medicare. The mechanism that allows it to be bridged at the moment is the purchase of US sovereign debt by the US Federal Reserve and by central banks around the world at yields that run well below the actual rate of inflation. The US government then spends the money, while the unhappy holders of US debt around the world have little choice but to let the value of this not-so-prized asset erode by letting it sit on their books while inflation eats away at it, because doing anything else with it would fuel inflation. How long this game can go on depends on how long the US can continue to browbeat the world into buying up and holding onto its debt, and this is anyone's guess, but the important point is that none of the participants—not the US government, not the foreign governments—can bring themselves to stop playing it, for that would risk bringing down the entire international financial system.

Beyond the formerly rather simple task of trying to not go bankrupt, it was once thought that governments were responsible for correcting the cyclical crises that affect all large economies—both capitalist market economies and socialist planned economies, because the USSR experienced cyclical economic disruptions just like the business cycles of capitalist economies. These cyclical crises seem to be the result of excessive scale, unaffected by ideology. On either side of the ideological divide, they were a symptom of the same degenerative disease of economic gigantomania. While it was previously thought that such imbalances could be corrected by making incremental adjustments to monetary and fiscal policy (though it was never entirely clear whether such efforts had ever been truly effective) it is now becoming clear that such efforts have the opposite effect: each new attempt at goosing up the economy by printing money expands debt faster than it expands the economy. The government of the United States, along with all the other governments that are tethered to it financially and politically, now have but one choice to make. They have no choice over whether to sink into a morass of unrepayable sovereign debt, but they can still decide whether to do so quickly or slowly.

But beyond just twiddling knobs on the fiscal and monetary machine to make it go faster, national governments have previously been thought capable of doing more to steer economic development; what of those efforts? In former times, governments exercised their prerogative to promote a particular development path, by supporting national champions, promoting import substitution or instituting corporate tax policies to incubate domestic industries. But more recently all such efforts have been neutralized by the increasing trend toward trade liberalization. A major unintended consequence of the effort by Western governments to form the entire world into a single market has been to give enhanced power to markets at the expense of governments, so that now trade is driven by global finance and global supply and demand, with government intervention only contributing at the margin.

By now, Western governments seem to have abdicated all thought leadership to those whom Susan George has called the "Davos Class," who have been led recently by those who sometimes ironically refer to themselves as "liberal communists." These are the golden boys of capitalism—who include Bill Gates, George Soros and the CEOs of Google, Intel and eBay, along with their court philosopher Thomas Friedman—and they have attempted to improve on their original ethos, which Adam Smith derided as "all for ourselves and nothing for others," by also endorsing anti-capitalist causes of social responsibility and ecological concern and targeting them with their private largesse. Gates and Soros have been champions of the "something for others" cause for many years now. Beyond sprinkling his largesse on the teeming masses, Gates espouses the theory of "frictionless capitalism"—a transnational, post-industrial, information-driven way of being—and believes that we are witnessing the "end of labor." Does this frictionless transnational capitalism spell the end of governments as meaningful economic actors as well? By virtue of serving global markets, transnational corporations become political entities, bypassing national governments. Faced with the golden boys of the Davos Class, who, with their armies of lawyers and accountants, can do no wrong, governments have little choice except to allow it to happen, as it were, frictionlessly, but what about the rest of us?

The problem here is that, except with regard to the privileged few, governance by non-state actors—whether of territorial spaces, cyberspace or financial systems—is implicitly equated with risks to state security. Around the world, security is becoming an ever-greater area of concern for governments, generally focusing on the security of states rather than of the human beings that inhabit them. Thus, even as governments do less and less, they continue to jealously guard their prerogatives by imprisoning those who ignore or circumvent their authority, and so we see a rise in prison populations, which predominantly consist of internal undesirables, minorities and foreigners, and which in due course become power centers in their own right. This is the flip side of "frictionless capitalism": prisons become command and control centers for criminal empires and cartels (it is safer on the inside), recruitment centers for terrorist groups, centers of political radicalization and incubators for intertribal and inter-gang affiliations. In many cases governments no longer control the prisons. A recent report estimates that 60 percent of México's 430 prisons are controlled by criminal gangs and drug cartels. It is unlikely that the situation is much different across the border in the US, where there are now more than 760 incarcerated inmates for every 100,000 citizens, the majority of them either African-American or Hispanic—surpassing the 560 per 100,000 that Stalin sent to the Gulags at the height of Soviet terror.

In turn, government officials who discover that they govern in name only are quick to realize a comparative advantage vis-à-vis their more scrupulous colleagues by tapping illicit, prison-centric economies as tools of patronage, blurring the line between public and private realms, and throwing open the doors to a full-scale criminalization of the state. As this process runs its course in more and more countries around the world, we witness the emergence of "feral cities"—marked by an almost complete lack of government services, by disease and environmental degradation, and with illicit but tacitly sanctioned economic activities as their centerpiece. It should come as no surprise, then, that the U.N. Habitat Report singled out urban slums as the "emerging human settlements of the 21st century." Presiding over these new settlements is a new class of political and economic entrepreneurs, who, in the absence of any constraining state authority, find plenty of incentives to form armed groups and engage in violent predation at the expense of the community. The process then turns full circle as these new violent entrepreneurs establish transnational links and, with the help of modern Internet and communications technologies, form dark networks which, through concealment, deception, corruption and circumvention, defeat international efforts at controlling them. Soon enough some of them might even start turning up at the annual Davos conference and laying out their own agendas, while the champions of the nation-state, should any still remain, look on in dumbstruck incomprehension.

What governments are good at

Lost in all of this is any concept of what national governments are actually good at. They *are* good at making sure that whatever crosses their national borders—be it people, money or goods—does so for the general benefit of their population. Although there are some exceptions, this generally does not include enabling free and instant movement of hot money, or enabling labor and jurisdictional arbitrage (governments have abdicated the ability to control these when they jumped on the globalization bandwagon, and falling off that bandwagon now would be simply too painful). National governments are also good at building and maintaining national infrastructure: roads and bridges, railways, the electric grid, a fast and reliable postal service and universal access to high-speed Internet. Some have done better than others: the United States has done miserably; Germany and South Korea—not so bad at all. They are good at primary education, basic health care, basic research, art, culture and historical preservation—all those things that free markets fail at so completely that the vast majority of free marketeers can no longer even grasp their significance. These are the things that governments can, in principle, do well, and that make a greater contribution to national success than all other government activities combined. And these are all the things that are now being sacrificed, across the world, in the name of fiscal austerity.

Warfare becomes self-defeating

Once upon a time the ability to wage war—to successfully resist aggression while simultaneously conquering new lands and expanding the realm—was considered to be an important activity for a nation-state. Now, however, states compete not for territory but for market share and, to a lesser extent, for market control, sometimes through military intervention but more frequently through the mere threat of military force. Defense of the realm is not really an important function of government any more. To the extent that the realm has to be defended, most of the contemporary threats come not from other nation-states but from non-state organizations such as terrorist and criminal groups. Of these, the terrorists pose the least serious threat, but they often provoke a disproportionate reaction because their attacks destroy a fiction which nation-states try to maintain at all costs: that they can exercise power with impunity because they can maintain a complete monopoly on military-style violence. The tiniest bit of blowback, in which a small terrorist group succeeds in scoring a purely symbolic victory against a mighty military empire, can result in a massive propaganda victory for the terrorists, recasting the conflict as a David and Goliath contest and causing Goliath to convulse in a fit of national hysteria, sometimes leading to military actions, such as the recent fiascos in Iraq and Afghanistan. The widespread availability of guerilla weapons, along with continuous improvements in guerilla tactics and asymmetrical warfare, have given rise to many successful new ways of frustrating the efforts of first-class militaries to control conquered territory. These new, asymmetrical methods of endlessly frustrating the adversary rather than attempting to prevail in an outright military confrontation, sometimes called "open-source warfare," have proven quite cost-effective: a successful campaign of this sort can be sustained indefinitely on a very small budget, but it costs a fortune to oppose, a fortune that deeply indebted Western governments no longer possess.

Where freedom of military action is not yet constrained fiscally, it is now constrained technologically and commercially: the vast majority of nation-states, if not all, now depend on others for their security, and require their collaboration in the manufacture and sale of weapons and in the licensing of defense technologies. The same trends toward globalization and market liberalization which have given terrorist groups and non-state violent actors unfettered access to war matériel and know-how have also eroded government control over organization and weapons. In an effort to remain militarily competitive with these groups while cutting costs, governments around the world have invested heavily in drone technology. So far, sixty-six countries have been provided with unmanned aerial attack platforms of various kinds, mostly by the US and Israel. Two aspects of drone technology stand out. First, the main objective of war is to persuade (not to force, for that is too expensive) the other side to lay down arms; but assassinations carried out using drones persuade the other side to take up arms—in revenge. We do not know who the drones kill, but we often do know who is killed in revenge for these killings. This makes drones all but useless for ending conflicts, but very good at expanding (because of inevitable mistakes in selecting targets) and perpetuating them. Secondly, it is a matter of time before drone technology goes open-source and becomes available to the other side, at which point it becomes a wonderful new terrorist weapon for asymmetrical warfare, with which to harass national governments with almost complete anonymity and impunity.

Add to this the now almost complete irrelevance of such big-ticket items as nuclear weapons and aircraft carriers. Since nobody is willing to risk causing a nuclear explosion, or even a nuclear accident, a rust-filled radioactive hole in the ground makes almost as effective a nuclear deterrent as a functioning ICBM humming along quietly in its silo. Aircraft carriers are sitting ducks now that there are two different ways to take them out (Chinese anti-ship ballistic missiles and Russian supersonic torpedos). The effectiveness of mechanized infantry is being eroded by the ever-increasing costs of keeping it fueled. Add also the spread and increasing effectiveness of war in cyberspace, via the Internet, where, due to the very nature of the terrain, shadowy non-state actors continue to run circles around governments. None of these trends portend anything positive for the continued ability of nation-states to successfully wage war. A time may soon come when nation-states, or what remains of them, exist at the pleasure of non-state actors, who may yet find uses for them in education, health care, cultural and historical preservation and the like. But their ability to act with impunity around the world or maintain a monopoly on domestic military violence will become a thing of the past.

The end of law and order

One of the most coveted and treasured prerogatives of the nation-state is maintaining the maximum possible amount of distance between its subjects by preserving what some like to call "law and order," because an estranged subject makes a docile and obedient subject, while group solidarity challenges the authority of the state. Unlike the informal community-based methods of arbitration that preceded it, the nation-state system uses the explicit threat of violence to defend the right of certain people (those who have curried favor with the government) to abuse, neglect and exploit the rest, and to prevent those who find themselves so abused, neglected and exploited from rising up and defending their interests. A particularly egregious example of this is the process by which some six thousand aristocratic families have come to own the vast majority of the land within the United Kingdom. This is the legacy of the numerous Enclosure Acts, by which common lands were stolen from their inhabitants and handed over to the aristocracy.

A similar process that went on throughout Europe from the twelfth century on, in which the rights of the formerly free city-states (which were responsible for a remarkable burst of cultural, social and economic development paralleled only by the city-states of ancient Greece) were eroded and eventually destroyed by the emerging nation-state, which was, in essence, a raising from the dead of the Roman imperial state through the efforts of the aristocracy and the Roman church. In due course, the older, local societies, which were based on common law and tradition and held together by local solidarity, were destroyed and replaced with a centralized administrative system of "law and order" which strove to mediate all interactions between people. While it endeavored to repress and dispossess the common people, locking them up in workhouses and factories or expelling them to newly conquered colonies, it also picked favorites, establishing monopolies in trade and commerce which allowed the favored few to build obscenely oversized fortunes that exist to this day.

The one exception is Switzerland, which has succeeded in preserving its confederacy and direct democracy, because no Swiss canton was large enough to dominate the rest, and because no political wedge could be driven between the city and the countryside. Just about everywhere else the emergence of national sovereignty was a sort of counterrevolution. Powerful aristocrats ensconced in their castle keeps, surrounded by powerless serfs, together with bishops in their fortress-like monasteries, surrounded by equally powerless monks, plotted and eventually took their revenge against an increasingly civilized world that was finding less and less use for their kind. It is a supreme irony that what most people now regard as civilization is in fact a Roman imperial revival staged by hereditary rural thugs and their religious sycophants who hailed not from any great center of civic life but from the howling wilderness of medieval castle keeps supplied by downtrodden serfs— hardly the epitome of civilization.

Initially, and even today in some parts of the world where the formation of the nation-state is relatively recent, religious legitimization and the ability to resort to violence were the two main sources of validation for the exercise of power. More recently, having a common identity has come to play an increasingly important role, but it is only effective in the context of providing services: the sense of belonging which the common identity produces has to be reinforced through access to certain communal necessities, such as food, shelter, medicine, security, education, an old age pension and so forth. In order to be effective, identity must be "identity with benefits." If it fails to provide any benefits, common identity only produces disrespect and contempt for those supposedly in charge. Also, insistence on a common identity has the effect of limiting participation, but does not automatically result in a common understanding of who should lead, and can hamper rather than enhance the exercise of power.

But once it is established, central authority becomes difficult to dislodge. Once local communities have been disrupted and destroyed, and the people no longer trust one another but are nevertheless forced to deal with strangers they distrust, they come to require protection from one another. Central authority, in the form of security, regulatory and judicial bureaucracies, then tends to become the most effective protection racket available. As long as it is remains powerful enough to suppress its competitors, it can keep random, opportunistic violence in check at the expense of perpetuating a system of organized, legally enshrined violence. In recognition of this, even those whose fortunes are continually eroded by central authority come to support it, because they come to see the alternative as being even worse. And there is indeed plenty of evidence that weak states, which cannot suppress organized crime, tend to produce the worst outcomes for their populations: worse than powerful states, which maintain a monopoly on violence, and worse even than no state at all.

As nation-states mature, they tend to move away from the brute force techniques of repression, dispossession and expulsion, and learn to achieve the same results—of preventing working people from accumulating wealth and taking back their local power—through the more subtle methods of regulation and taxation. These are subtle arrangements that are slowly arrived at in order to avoid drawing attention to them, and achieve their purpose during more prosperous times, but as the economy stops growing and starts to falter they drive ever-larger portions of the population into financial distress. The impoverished class then responds by acting to avoid regulation and taxation, and the result is an informal economy—unlicensed, unregulated, unofficial and uncounted. The state then inevitably responds by attempting to enforce prohibitions against it, making an informal economy into an illicit economy. An informal economy becomes an illicit economy when the state prohibits it without the means to enforce the prohibition (which is generally the case).

As this process runs its course, the expectation that the state is a working democracy that has the power to exclude violent non-state actors becomes largely baseless. Functional holes within an economy in which more and more people can find no legal way to survive create pressures and incentives for citizens to engage in criminal activities as survival strategies. Criminal gangs form, stockpile weapons, secure police cooperation and purchase political influence, then branch out into maintaining local order and providing social services. In one place after another—in Medellín, Colombia, in Rio de Janeiro, Brazil, in the parts of México most afflicted by the drug war, and in countless others—guerillas and drug traffickers collaborate with state officials and politicians, and the provision of governance by armed illicit actors in ungoverned urban spaces becomes the rule rather than the exception.

Although illicit economies threaten the state in the form in which it is legally constituted, the various criminal actors within illicit economies rarely want the state to collapse; instead, they desire accommodation. In turn, non-state local governance does not necessarily pose an existential threat to the state as long as the social groups that are key to perpetuating the state remain unaffected. Gated housing and private security services can be used as substitutes for state services for the ruling elite. And although, under such circumstances, the scope for the elite's constructive action becomes rather circumscribed, they can continue to enrich themselves by doing damage. For instance, they can institute draconian economic policies, then hire freelance enforcers while simultaneously selectively protecting those lawbreakers who make gratitude payments to their political allies. Such a strategy has the additional benefit of undermining existing illicit trades and, carried to an extreme, can steer certain illicit trades into becoming secret government monopolies.

But none of these developments is good for the economy as a whole, and as the economic situation continues to deteriorate, it is the communities with the most firmly established illicit networks that run the greatest risk of fragmentation and intercommunal violence once central authority finally collapses. Nor can these steps be retraced, because the development of the technology of illegality in a given locale—the establishment of smuggling networks, official corruption, crime syndicates, protection rackets, vested interests at high levels—makes illicit economies all but impossible to eradicate. Countless treasure has been wasted on foreign aid, which, of course, goes to governments, not to the people these governments are supposed to keep in line, in an effort to strengthen central authority and suppress illicit economies, with very little to show for it.

Once central authority does collapse, an area may lapse into chaos and warlordism for a time, disrupting both licit and illicit trade. Eventually new forms of governance begin to emerge. Governing forces such as the Islamic Courts Union in Somalia provided security and stability to illicit trade, making them popular with both the mafia and the general population. Such governing forces provide other benefits as well. Communities often lack ways of handling violent individuals and drugs and, given the choice between seeking to involve the ineffectual and corrupt police or turning to religious authorities or other non-state actors, such as a local militia, they choose the latter. In turn, militias are usually quick to establish internal policing systems and systems of military justice, in order to control their own members and preserve their internal hierarchy.

Just as it is misguided to expect that the state is a working democracy that has the power to exclude violent non-state actors, it is simply not the case that illicit economies lack governance. Illicit economies are just differently governed. The Sicilian Mafia is a particularly well-researched subject, and the research shows that it did in fact provide governance, primarily protection and enforcement of contracts. It is by no means the only example. Regardless of historical period or culture, the two key ingredients of lack of trust and lack of formal governance automatically produce reliance on mafia services. But beyond that, there are numerous situations in which formal governance may not even be applicable. Organizations that are capable of conflict resolution and dispute settlement and reconciliation are essential wherever rules and ownership are informal and improvised, and such organizations can only be effective if they have the means to resort to violence.

Beyond such traditional mafia services, it is to be expected that militias and other non-state groups that rule areas taken from the state—informal settlements and encampments, shantytowns, unofficial refugee camps and neighborhoods of cities that have gone feral—assume a broad range of roles, including infrastructure maintenance, policing, welfare and moral governance. In order to be effective and to stay safe, the thugs enforcing street order must be perceived as honest and fair by their constituent populations. Nor can they safely overstep the bounds of what their constituent populations can support without fear that a competitor will muscle in on their turf and take over. Without external disruptions, such as external attempts to reconstitute the nation-state and reimpose central authority, areas under non-state governance can persist in a steady-state condition that has been termed "durable disorder" and which, in the best case scenario, can be better than life in a weak, semi-defunct state. Such attempts may prove futile in any case, because the state cannot impose authority if the underlying pattern of self-governance is self-reinforcing and non-hierarchical. Such an ungoverned, or, when viewed from the inside, self-governed space can become an invincible fortress that can withstand repeated assaults by governments attempting to impose their sovereignty.

The end of the welfare state

Part of the legacy of the industrial revolution is the political polarization, which still prevails in developed, formerly developing and undeveloping nations, between capital and labor. The political forces arrayed on the side of capital have always wanted to treat labor as a commodity, driving down costs and demanding the freedom to move production to countries with the lowest wages. They have tried to prevent workers from forming unions and look for opportunities to break unions once they are formed. They have also tried to prevent governments from regulating working hours and conditions, imposing minimum wages or mandating family leave. On the other side, the workers have organized into unions, braving numerous bloody confrontations, in order to be able to bargain collectively for better wages and working conditions, and over the years have won a number of important concessions, such as laws that prohibit child labor and provide for a regulated work week, safer working conditions and so on.

The heyday of this era was in the 1950s, when an assembly-line autoworker in Detroit was able to earn enough to afford a house and a car, raise a family and then retire comfortably. That era is now over. The new era is one of permanently high unemployment, stagnant or declining wages, eroding workers' rights and economic insecurity. Jobs now move swiftly from one low-wage country to another. Just as consumers grew accustomed to poor-quality customer service from call centers in India, the call centers moved to the Philippines, and the quality of the service went down another notch or two. But the consumers have no choice: since the jobs have moved away from their own communities, first to India, then to the Philippines, they cannot afford to pay for better quality. The winners—for the time being—are the holders of capital, who can surf on a wave of destruction as it crests in one country after another; today the US and Europe, tomorrow China, India and Brazil. A very basic bit of insight—that the only real capital is social capital—has been all but lost.

The final battle of the labor movement, which is still being fought in the US, has to do with union jobs that cannot be outsourced to the other side of the planet: those of municipal and government workers, teachers and workers in public utilities and transportation. The ability to shift operations between countries neutralizes the political power of labor, except in the public sector and in extractive industries that compete for scarce resources under state control. Many of these categories of workers are in the process of losing their pensions—seemingly inevitably. Pension liabilities in the US are underfunded by well over a trillion dollars. But this is something of a sideshow, since most jobs in the US are now non-union jobs, and for these the trend is toward part-time, contract, temporary and freelance work with no security or benefits, while the few remaining salaried positions require a level of effort that includes remaining "online" during all waking hours and even during so-called "workations," resulting in quick employee burnout and a host of long-term medical problems.

Since the long-running standoff between labor and capital has resulted in labor being resoundingly trounced by the forces of capital, with globalization providing the bludgeon with which to beat labor back into submission, all that now stands in the way of a social explosion and open rebellion is the attempt by governments to maintain some semblance of a safety net. People who cannot earn enough to survive by working have to be paid not to work, and the only party who can do so is the government. Not surprisingly, then, social spending by governments has expanded the fastest. It has now reached its limits and, as in one country after another the holders of sovereign debt demand the imposition of austerity through cuts in social spending in return for continued financing, it is set to decline. All of the approaches to this situation that have been proposed so far appear to have been tainted by the subliminal policy assumption that the status quo is somehow good and valuable and deserves to be defended. It took a long time to secure the few paltry victories, so the thinking goes, and so we should stand firm and defend them even as the ground beneath our feet steadily sinks. But it will have to be admitted at some point that the state has lost control over labor relations: the Maastricht Treaty—the founding document of the European Union—once contained a social chapter that enshrined human welfare as an explicit objective, but it was obsolete even before the treaty was signed in 1992, and has not been ratified or implemented. If the European Union does not serve the interests of its inhabitants, even on paper, then whose interests does it serve? At some point an older truth will resurface: that money does not equate with power because power comes from the willingness to resort to violence, while few people are ever willing to offer their lives for mere money, especially when offered a better cause for which to fight.

In all of this, the state will definitely come out the greatest loser. Much of the financial news coverage throughout most of the world's largest economies that are classified as developed can be summed up as follows: states are going broke. There are several factors that drive this process. Falling wages due to leveling across countries, thanks to globalization, is one. Another is the fact that jobs are leaving: lack of collective bargaining power prevents workers from saving their jobs by blocking imports from low-wage countries that lack occupational safety or environmental regulations. Yet another is that the populations throughout the developed world are aging rapidly, with fewer and fewer wage-earners supporting more and more people who are no longer able to work. Add to this the fact that states have almost no ability to tax transnational corporations: companies such as Google and Apple, Amazon and Starbucks, have armies of accountants and lawyers to see to it that their wealth is parked offshore, in ways that make it immune from taxation. Nor do states have much of a way to regulate finance at all, having gambled it away in exchange for their continued ability to finance their surging budget deficits.

While governments continue to jealously guard their responsibility for taxation, their ability to raise taxes has been diminished over time. In effect, they have been forced into a tacit power-sharing arrangement with international criminal syndicates that administer transnational tax havens, because mobility of capital and the lack of a universal tax regime have made it almost impossible for states to tax transnational companies. While they still have the ability, at least on paper, to raise taxes domestically, political parties that raise taxes tend to be voted out of power, and so this is something that happens rarely. Also, localities and entire nations are forced to compete for private investment, and this limits their ability to raise sales, value-added or property taxes. With the tax structures remaining as they are (except for tax incentives that are commonly granted to attract transnational companies), the tax burden falls on citizens and local small businesses. These respond by entering the informal economy and keeping their transactions off the books as much as possible, further eroding the tax base.

Without savings or jobs, the welfare state becomes the only element left to bind the state and the people together. As it shrinks, clientelism and an abusive police presence remain as the only links between the excluded, disenfranchised population and the state. Consequently, substantial portions of the population come to live outside the legal system, where they depend on local strongmen for support and protection. In turn, these local non-state actors cannot provide social services without a local political monopoly and territorial control, if only over a few blocks, a courtyard or an alleyway. Such would-be local authorities have but two choices: intercede with the state on behalf of the community or replace the state entirely. In some cases, the state may be able to gain an extra bit of longevity through a judicious policy of benign neglect, serving the largely ceremonial function of legitimizing local autonomy.

Virtualized politics

As more and more nation-states around the world teeter and topple into the defunct bin, a lot of recent excitement has been artificially generated around Internet and mobile communications technologies as ways of enabling positive political change. A number of revolts have been branded as Twitter or Facebook revolutions (such as the one in Iran, during which most of the tweeting in question was done in English rather than in Farsi, and by foreigners, while the number of Iranians with Twitter accounts turned out to be vanishingly small). During the collapse of the Mubarak regime in Egypt a Google executive and cyber-activist, Wael Ghonim, was on the ground in Cairo and became something of a *cause célèbre*. We are being led to believe that new technology is what enables positive political change in places such as Egypt. But it seems that while a nation-state is intact (as in Egypt, which is still largely controlled by its military, which is still being propped up by the US), all of this Internet activism is largely for naught. On the other hand, once the nation-state has been tipped into the defunct column (as with Syria, where Western efforts to bring about regime change have finally tipped it into full-scale civil war), Internet activism is, again, largely for naught. If there is a sweet spot between the two scenarios, then it is yet to be discovered.

Suppose you wanted to achieve some significant political effect; say, prevent or stop an unjust war. You could organize gigantic demonstrations, with hundreds of thousands of people marching in the streets, shouting slogans and waving anti-war banners. You could write angry editorials in newspapers and on blogs denouncing the falseness of the *casus belli*. You could write and phone and email your elected and un-elected representatives, asking them to put a stop to it, and they would respond that they will of course try, and by the way could you please make a campaign contribution? You could also seethe and steam and lose sleep and appetite over the disgusting thing your country is about to do or is already doing. Would that stop the war? Alas, no. How many people protested the war in Iraq? And what did that achieve? Precisely nothing.

You see, the slogan "speak truth to power" has certain limitations. The trouble with it is that it ignores the fact that power will not listen, and the fact that the people already know the truth and even make jokes about it. Those in power may appear to be persuaded or dissuaded, but only if it is to their advantage to do so. They will also sometimes choose to co-opt, and then quietly subvert, popular movements, in order to legitimize themselves in the eyes of those who would otherwise oppose them. But, in general, they cannot be shifted from pursuing a course they see as advantageous by mere rhetoric from those outside their ranks. Some weaker regimes may be sensitive to embarrassment, provided the criticisms are voiced by high-profile individuals in internationally recognized positions of authority, but these same criticisms backfire when aimed at the stronger regimes, because they make those who voice them appear ridiculous, engaged in something futile.

Using rhetoric to shift those in power from their positions is like trying to win at chess by persuading your opponent to sacrifice his pieces because it is a reasonable, just and fair thing for him to do. As with chess, victory is achieved by moving in a way that restricts your opponent's choices. And, as with chess, the winning strategy is neutralized if your opponent is aware of your strategy ahead of time. Thus, attempting to enter into a dialogue with your opponent is a sure way to weaken your position by giving away your game plan.

In confronting the powerful, the need for secrecy is strengthened by the fact that, unlike chess, which is an overt game, the game of shifting those in power from their positions is best played covertly; it is advantageous to make game-changing events appear as accidents or coincidences, spontaneous rather than organized, and difficult to pin on anyone. Since a scapegoat is always found anyway, it is also advantageous if there isn't any identifiable organization with which it can be associated. Where an organization is required, it is best if it is transitory, fluid and anarchic in nature, and appears to be ineffectually engaged in some trivial, innocuous pursuit. In CIA parlance, it should at all times maintain plausible deniability.

Such a strategy just might be conceivable, provided the whole thing stays off the Internet. In previous, less networked eras, the work of the secret police was challenging and labor-intensive, but the Internet has changed all that. Anything you say on the Internet, whether in a private email, an unpublished document or posted to a blog, can now be used as evidence against you, or anyone else.

Back in the USSR, to spy on your conversations, the KGB had to come and install a bug in your apartment. That was quite a job in itself. One agent was assigned to track each of your family members, to find a time when there was nobody home. Another agent had to then stand watch, while a couple more would pick the lock, move a piece of furniture, neatly cut out a piece of wallpaper, drill a hole, install the bug, glue and retouch the wallpaper so that it looked undisturbed and put the furniture back in place. Then the conversations overheard by this bug had to be recorded, and someone had to stand by to swap the bulky reel-to-reel magnetic tapes. Finally, somebody had to go through all the tapes, listening for seditious-sounding snippets of conversation. Often the entire eavesdropping mission failed because of some trivial oversight, such as a deadbolt locked one turn too many or a cigarette butt of the wrong brand left in an ashtray, because it would cause the quarry to suddenly become careful, turning up the radio or the television when discussing anything important. Even if something vaguely seditious could be discerned, it sometimes happened that the person charged with listening turned sympathetic toward his quarry, in a sort of reverse Stockholm Syndrome, because the dissidents he was spying on turned out to be forthright, honorable, likeable people—unlike his own detestable superiors. And even if it was found, the seditious content had to be laboriously transcribed.

If it became necessary to map out the quarry's social connections, the process was, again, laborious. Transcripts of phone conversations and surveillance tapes had to be correlated against photographs of persons walking in and out of the apartment or seen talking to the quarry. Sometimes letters had to be steamed open and read to determine the nature of key relationships. If seditious documents, which were normally typewritten, were found, then an attempt was made to determine their origin based on the ownership of the typewriter, which could be matched by comparing minor imperfections in characters and small deviations in their alignment against a library of typed samples maintained on file, except that the documents were often typed through five layers of carbon paper, making the characters too blurry to make such identification possible.

Compare that to the situation in the US today, where CIA/FBI/NSA/Homeland Security is quite far along in forming one giant security apparatus that dwarfs the quaint old KGB in both intrusiveness and scope, though probably not in effectiveness, even though modern technology makes their job trivial to the point where much of it can be automated. There used to exist privacy protections written into US law, but they are in the process of disappearing as a result of new legislation. But whether or not a sweeping abolition of privacy rights makes it into law, your online privacy is already gone. Since the government can now detain you indefinitely without ever charging, trying or sentencing you, and has full access to your digital data, legal niceties make little difference. Nor does it matter any longer whether or not you are a US citizen: the firewall between CIA (which was supposed to only spy on foreigners) and FBI disappeared after 9/11, and although this practice violates several acts of Congress, you would be foolish to wait for anyone to do anything about it.

People now tend to communicate via cell phone voice calls, text messages, emails, posts to Facebook and tweets, all of which are digital data and all of which are saved. Relationships between people can be determined by looking at their Facebook profile, their email contacts and their cell phone contacts. If your phone is GPS-enabled, your position can be tracked very precisely; if it isn't, your position can still be determined fairly accurately and tracked once your phone connects to a few different cell phone towers. All of this information can be continually monitored and analyzed without human intervention, raising red flags whenever some ominous pattern begins to emerge. We are not quite there yet, but at some point somebody might accidentally get blasted to bits by a drone strike while texting when a wrong T9 predictive text autocompletion triggers a particularly deadly keyword match.

A lot of commerce now happens online, while most retail point of sale systems are now computerized and most people use credit or debit cards rather than cash and often use "rewards cards" even when paying with cash. Thus everything you buy can be traced to you, and your purchasing patterns can be analyzed to determine such things as whether or not you are pregnant. In a recent scandal, the Target chain committed the *faux pas* of offering discounts on baby products to women who did not yet know they were pregnant, based on their recent purchases of such things as unscented face cream, larger-size bras and various soft, plush items.

Thanks to vastly increased computational power, the emphasis is now shifting from enforcing the law by identifying transgressions to flagging as aberrant any sort of behavior that the system does not quite understand. That is, it is not looking for violations of specific laws, but for unusual patterns. One such pattern might be an attempt by you and others to go electronically dark for a time. Suppose you are walking to a park, and, before getting there, you switch off your cell phone. And suppose several other people walk to that same park at the same time, and also switch off their cell phones before getting there. And suppose none of you called or texted each other beforehand. Well, that's an obvious red flag for conspiracy! Video from surveillance cameras installed in that park will be downloaded, fed through facial recognition software, and the faces matched up with the cell phones that were switched off. Now you are all connected and flagged as attempting to evade surveillance. If this aberrant behavior is observed during some future time of national emergency (as opposed to the usual permanent "War on Terror"), drone aircraft might be dispatched to take you out. All of this might happen without any human intervention, under the control of a fully automated security threat neutralization system. It's a Catch 22: stay off the Internet and you are sure to be too socially isolated to organize anything; get on the Internet and you are immediately exposed; do a little of each, and you suddenly start looking very suspicious and invite additional scrutiny.

If you are a bit savvier, you might be able to come up with ways to use the Internet anonymously. You buy a laptop with cash and don't register it, so that the MAC address can't be traced to you. You use Internet cafés that have open Internet access or pirate open wifi connections from somewhere. You connect to web sites outside of the US jurisdiction via SSL (HTTPS protocol) or use encrypted services such as Skype. You further attempt to anonymize your access using Tor. You think you are safe. But wait! Are you running a commercial operating system, like Windows or Mac OS X? If so, it has a back door, added by the manufacturer based on a secret request from the US government. The back door allows someone (not necessarily the government, but anybody who knows about it) to install a keystroke logger that captures all your keystrokes and periodically uploads them to some server for analysis. Now a third party knows all of your communications and username/password combinations.

Suppose you know about back doors in commercial operating systems, and so you compile your own OS (some flavor of Linux or BSD Unix) from source code. You run it in ultra-secure mode, and nervously monitor all incoming and outgoing network connections for anything that shouldn't be there. You encrypt your hard drive. You do not store any contact information, passwords or, for that matter, anything else on your laptop. You run the browser in "private" mode so that it doesn't maintain a browsing history. You look quite fetching in your tin foil hat. You are not just a member of Anonymous, you *are* Anonymous! But do you realize how suspicious this makes you look? The haggard look from having to memorize all those URLs and passwords, the darting eye movements.... Somebody is going to haul you in for questioning just for the hell of it. At that point, you represent a challenge to the surveillance team: a hard target, somebody they can use to hone their skills. This is not a good position to be in.

Internet anonymity doesn't have much of a future. It is already all but nonexistent in China. You land in Beijing, and need a cell phone. To purchase a SIM card for your cell phone, you need to show your passport. Now you SIM card is tied to your passport number. You go to an Internet café. There, Internet access is free, but to connect you need a password that is sent to your cell phone via SMS. Now your passport number is tied to everything you do while on the Internet. Can you remain anonymous? Not too much, I would think.

But even if you could remain anonymous, are you still rebellious enough to challenge the status quo through risky but effective covert action? My guess is that you are by now quite docile, thanks, again, to the Internet. You don't want to do anything that might jeopardize your access to it. You have your favorite music and books in the cloud, your online games, your Facebook friends, and you can't imagine life without them. For many people, the Internet is also the way they get sex, either voyeuristically, through porn, or by finding people to have sex with. And I have observed that men, even if normally rebellious, become quite docile if they think that they might get to have sex. (Women tend to be more docile than men in any case.) Overall, there seems to be a taming effect associated with Internet access. People might still feel rage, but they express it by posting nasty comments on blogs or engaging in flame wars on newsgroups.

There is supposed to be such a thing as Internet activism, but a better term for it is "Slacktivism," a word used by Evgeny Morozov in his book *The Net Delusion*. He is a Belarussian activist whose work is funded by George Soros's Open Society Foundation, which I find creepy, plus he spends a lot of time trying to give policy advice to the US government on ways to promote democracy abroad—a funny-smelling subject as far as I am concerned, pots calling kettles black and so on. He does list a lot of amusing SNAFUs, such as the State Department spending money to train Iranian bloggers to use software that's been embargoed by the Treasury Department. But the point he makes about Internet activism is important: it is too easy, too low-risk (unless you happen to be in Iran or Syria or Belarus) and, in general, futile. Should it ever rise to the point of posing a threat to the status quo, it is easily neutralized by authoritarian governments, Western corporations or a combination of both. The world's biggest censors are not China and Russia, says Morozov, they are Apple and Facebook. In all, Internet activism is a powerful time-waster, a boon for repressive, authoritarian regimes, a tar pit for foreign Internet neophytes and a delusion for Western politicians and activists.

Does the idea of achieving some significant political effect still seem interesting? What if I told you that you could achieve that same effect with just a bit of patience, sitting Buddha-like with your arms folded, a beatific smile on your face? The idea is not too far-fetched. You see, the Internet is a very resilient system, designed to let packets flow around any obstruction. It is, to some extent, self-regulating and self-healing. But it depends on another system, which is not resilient at all: the electric grid. In the US, the grid is a creaking, aging system that now exhibits an exponentially increasing rate of failure. It is susceptible to the phenomenon of cascaded failure, where small faults are magnified throughout the system. Since the money needed to upgrade the system no longer exists, blackouts will continue to proliferate. As the grid goes down, Internet access will be lost. Cell phone access is more likely to remain, but without the grid most people will lose the ability to recharge their mobile devices. Information technology may look shiny and new, but the fact remains that the Internet is around 40 percent coal-fired and 20 percent nuclear-powered.

Beyond the purely technical issues with the electric grid, there is also a problem with finding enough energy to power it. A lot of America's electricity comes from coal that is of increasingly poor quality. The volumes of coal are staying more or less constant, but the energy density of the coal is decreasing over time. The anthracite that made the age of steam possible is all but gone. The lignite and brown coal that have replaced it are sometimes closer to dirt than to coal. At some point it will become a net waste of energy to mine them and transport them to a power plant. Already the inferior quality of coal is causing giant balls of clinker to accumulate in the power plant furnaces, causing extensive downtime and millions in damage. As for other sources of electricity, many of the aging nuclear power plants are already unsafe while the mirage of energy independence, to be achieved by "fracking" for shale gas and other equally ineffective dirty tricks, is not going to save us. Moving forward, the amount of time the electric grid is available in any given place will dwindle, and with it the amount of Internet access.

As the electric grid goes down, there will be a great deal of economic disruption. But in terms of the surveillance system, two effects are virtually guaranteed. First, people will once again become very expensive to track and monitor, as in the olden days of the KGB. Second, people will cease to be docile. What keeps people docile is access to the magic shiny world of television and the Internet. Their own lives might be dull, grey, hopeless and filled with drudgery, but as long as they can periodically catch a glimpse of heaven inhabited by smooth-skinned celebrities with toned muscles sporting the latest fashions, listen to their favorite noise, watch a football game and distract themselves with video games, blogs or cute animals on Reddit's /r/aww, they can at least dream. Once they wake up from that dream they will look around, then look around some more, and then they will become seriously angry. This is why the many countries and regions that at one time or another ran short of energy, be it former Soviet Georgia or Bulgaria or the Russian far east, always tried to provide at least a few hours of electricity every day, usually in the evenings during "prime time," so that the populace could get its daily dose of fiction, because this was cheaper than containing a seriously angry populace by imposing curfews and maintaining around-the-clock military patrols and checkpoints.

And so, if you want to achieve a serious political effect, my suggestion is that you sit back Buddha-like, fold your arms, and do some deep breathing exercises. Then you should work on developing some interpersonal skills that don't need to be mediated by electronics. Chances are, you will get plenty of opportunities to practice them when the time comes, giving seriously angry people something useful to do. By then nobody will be keeping tabs on you, because those doing the watching will have grown tired of looking at their persistently blank monitor screens and gone home. Then they too will become seriously angry— but not at you.

Case Study: The Pashtuns

Among the world's many ungoverned spaces, there are few as long lasting and as able to withstand the relentless onslaught of empires as the Pashtun tribal areas, which straddle the porous and largely notional border between Afghanistan and Pakistan, including the Pakistani tribal area of Waziristan. To invaders, this is an invisible yet impregnable fortress that has withstood all attempts by centralized government authorities to impose their will. The term "ungoverned" is, as usual, misapplied here: the Pashtuns have an alternative system of governance whose rules preclude the establishment of any centralized authority. At over forty million strong, they are one of the largest ethnic groups on the planet. Their ability to resist the British, the Pakistanis, the Soviets and now the Americans/NATO makes them one of the greatest antiimperialist success stories on our planet. What makes up the shell of such an uncrackable nut? This is an interesting question, which is why I have decided to include an exposition on the Pashtuns, the toughest nut in the whole tribal nutsack.

An equally interesting question to ask is, What compelled a succession of empires to continue to make futile attempts to crack it, throwing life and treasure at the task of conquering a rugged, fiercely independent, inaccessible and mostly worthless piece of land? Wouldn't it be much easier to just leave the Pashtuns alone and continue using rifles against Pygmies armed with ripe fruit? The compulsion to conquer and to subjugate is by no means new, and tribes have continuously conquered and subjugated other tribes since prehistoric times, but with the emergence of global empires a new element seems to have been introduced: complete intolerance of complete independence. Every pocket of the planet, no matter how small, has to be assigned to an internationally recognized state that has been bound to other states through treaties and state-legal relations. The global political order can no longer tolerate a single white spot on the political map. Its imperative seems to be to force every single group of humans to at least sit down at the negotiating table, at which the most powerful (or so they think) always have the upper hand, and to sign legally-binding documents. The existence of any such white spot poses an existential threat to the entire system, which is why the efforts to eliminate it are often disproportionate to either its value or its threat. Like space aliens, great big empires swoop in and say, "Take me to your leader!" And if there is no leader, and the only bit of foreign policy this particular tribe ever happens to have developed is exhaustively described by the words "go away and leave us alone," then a misunderstanding inevitably results and things end badly for both sides. Appointing a local stooge to sign legally-binding documents on behalf of the ungoverned territory that is supposed to behave like a nation-state does not work.

It would appear that the state cannot impose its authority on an area if its underlying, local system of governance is non-hierarchical, self-enforcing and decentralized, and has a strong tradition of uniting solely for the purpose of ganging up on outside threats and an equally strong tradition of attempting to avenge all wrongful deaths (such as a family member who has been killed by an American Predator drone). This happens to be the case with the Pashtuns. Their ancient and eternal code of conduct is Pashtunwali, or "The Pashtun Way." The reason for following Pashtunwali is to be a good Pashtun. In turn, what a good Pashtun does is follow Pashtunwali. It is self-reinforcing because any Pashtun who does not follow Pashtunwali is unable to secure the cooperation of other Pashtuns, and has very low life expectancy, because ostracism is generally equivalent to a death sentence. Among the Pashtuns, there is no such thing as the right to life; there is only the reason for not killing someone right there and then. If this seems unnecessarily harsh to you, then what did you expect? A trip to Disneyland? Needless to say, the Pashtuns cannot be seduced with offers of social progress and economic development, because that is not the purpose of Pashtunwali. The purpose of Pashtunwali is to perpetuate Pashtunwali, and at this it is apparently very, very good.

Pashtun society is classified as segmentary, a subtype of acephalous (leaderless). The main figures of authority are the elders (*maliks*) who serve a local tribal chief (*khan*), but their leadership positions remain at all times contingent on putting the tribe's interests first. All decision-making is consensus-based, severely restricting the scope of united action. However, when faced with an external threat, the Pashtuns are able to appoint a dictator, and to serve that dictator with absolute obedience until the threat is extinguished.

Pashtunwali defines the following key concepts: honor (*nang*) demands action regardless of consequences whenever Pashtunwali is violated. It is permissible to lie and kill to protect one's *nang*. Revenge (*badal*) demands "an eye for an eye" in case of injury or damage, but crucially allows payment of restitution to avoid bloodshed. Incarceration is considered unacceptable and unjust under any circumstances. It is seen as interfering with justice, since it complicates the process of exacting revenge and precludes the payment of restitution. This is why Afghanistan has been the scene of spectacular prison escapes, where hundreds of inmates are freed in a single military-style attack; the attackers' goal is not just to free prisoners but also to later kill them or collect restitution from them. The law of hospitality (*nanawatai*) demands that any Pashtun must welcome and provide sanctuary to anyone who asks for it. As a matter of *nang*, the guest must be kept perfectly secure and safe from all harm while a guest. Once over the threshold and no longer a guest, he can be sniped at one's leisure should such an action be called for. Laws against harboring fugitives, serving as accessory after the fact, impeding official investigations and so forth are meaningless and attempts to enforce them automatically result in *badal*.

The local Pashtun governing body is the *jirga*, which is convened only on special occasions. It takes its roots from Athenian democracy, although some scholars argue that it predates it. The participants arrange themselves in a circle, and everyone has the right to speak. There is no one presiding, in accordance with the principle that no one is superior in the eyes of Pashtunwali. The decision is based on a majority consensus. Those who defy the decision of the *jirga* open themselves up to officially sanctioned arson and murder. It is significant that the *jirga* does not allow representation: it is a direct rather than a representative democracy. It is also crucial that the *jirga* reserves the right to abnegate any agreement previously entered into, making treaty-based state-legal relations with the Pashtuns impossible. Lastly, only those who follow Pashtunwali can participate in a *jirga*; all outsiders are automatically excluded.

This should give you some idea of why Pashtunwali presents an intractable problem for any empire that wants to dominate the Pashtuns. Now let us briefly glance at the long and tangled historical record of such attempts.

Empires break their teeth

The first modern empire to tangle with the Pashtuns was the British, who optimistically tried to impose the Indian Penal Code on them. When the Pashtuns refused to recognize this code as just, the result was a considerable amount of carnage. The British then abandoned attempts at imposing a system of justice and resorted to administrative means instead: their Closed Border Policy attempted to segregate the plains tribes from the hill tribes. This policy failed to stop the carnage and was abandoned after thirty years. Eventually the British were compelled to resort to accommodation by recognizing Pashtun tribal law. Then they bled profusely and departed in unseemly haste, leaving the Pashtuns to the Pakistanis, who mostly practiced accommodation as well. The Taliban movement, which is predominantly Pashtun-led, was recognized by Pakistan. Pakistan was content to allow Pashtun self-governance until September 11, 2001. Since then they have been compelled to at least make a show of imposing authority on the Pashtuns, in order to at least appear to cooperate with their American allies, although little remains of this cooperation today.

The Soviets blundered into Afghanistan in a misguided effort to defend socialism against regressive counterrevolutionary tendencies in accordance with the Brezhnev Doctrine. They made a futile attempt to eradicate ethnic and religious identities through a strategy of suppression, and succeeded, for a time, in consolidating control of urban areas while the predominantly Pashtun resistance established footholds in the hills surrounding the capital Kabul. They also relentlessly bombed the Afghanistan-Pakistan border to create a no-man's land. In doing so, they failed on a grand scale, creating a very large refugee crisis and thus ensuring that their enemies had plenty of international support. Once, thanks to the efforts of the CIA (working closely with Osama bin Laden) the Pashtuns acquired Stinger anti-aircraft missiles, the Soviets gradually lost the ability to continue the air campaign.

The Soviets' effort to win the Pashtun hearts and minds was likewise a spectacular failure. Pashtunwali demanded revenge for the Soviets' military actions from even the most ambivalent Pashtuns. The few elders the Soviets were able to co-opt through intimidation or bribery swiftly lost the support of their followers. The Soviets withdrew in 1988, having made zero headway, and having lost the political will to succeed. It was a costly conflict with no benefits.

The Americans (and a few NATO troops) are currently in the process of repeating the Soviet experiment, with very similar results. Here is a nice little fact to illustrate this point: on March 18, 2012, Hamid Karzai, the American-imposed President of Afghanistan and an ethnic Pashtun (but an obvious apostate from Pashtunwali) denounced the Americans as "demons" engaged in "Satanic acts." The Americans swiftly reacted…by saying nothing and doing even less. Then they trotted out some well-spoken media robopundits who said that Afghanistan is still, potentially, "a good war." Thus, the result of the American invasion of Afghanistan is predictable: the Americans will pretend it never happened. When forced to discuss it, they will remain delusional. But mostly it won't be in the news, and Americans will no longer know, or care, what happens there. The US initially blundered into Afghanistan under the delusion that they would find Osama bin Laden there (while, if you believe the news, Osama was in Pakistan, living quietly next to an army college). If jet airliners start crashing into skyscrapers again, odds are some other tribe will get "bombed back to the Stone Age."

An approach that works

It is difficult but not impossible to constructively engage the Pashtuns: during better times, the Pakistanis came closest to doing so. They freely offered the few important gifts the Pashtuns were willing to accept and appreciate. They offered the Pashtuns a sense of participation by giving them a big audience and a voice. They provided an unlimited time horizon for engaging the Pashtuns as permanent neighbors, building traditional ties and long-term relationships. These activities were informed by an understanding that attempts to impose order without legitimate authority are bound to fail, coupled with the realization that with the Pashtuns any such legitimate authority must of necessity come from within and remain autonomous and decentralized.

Part of what made such accommodation succeed is the fact that Pakistan is a weak state with limited resources. But as long as there are mighty military empires stalking the planet (not for much longer, we should hope) we should expect that one of them will periodically come along and, just like the ones that came before it, break its teeth on Pashtunwali. You might think that they'd learn from each others' mistakes, but then here is a simple rule for you to remember: the intelligence of a hierarchically organized group of people is inversely proportional to its size, and mighty military empires are so big, and consequently so dumb, that they never, ever learn anything.

CHAPTER 4

Social Collapse

STAGE 4: Social collapse. Faith that "your people will take care of you" is lost, as local social institutions, be they charities or other groups that rush in to fill the power vacuum, run out of resources or fail through internal conflict.

Along with finance, government and globalized commerce, social institutions are failing us. More and more people in the developed world are being excluded from the productive life of their societies, condemned to subsist on various hand-outs, odd jobs and, if they are lucky, earning a little something in the ever-expanding informal economy. In the countries that are not as highly developed, patterns of international investment are increasingly cutting off local populations from the resources they need to survive as land is bought up by international conglomerates and turned into industrial farms to produce exports. The resulting temporary gains in agricultural output come at the cost of disrupting the local populations' traditional relationship with the land, while destroying the fertility of the land itself through soil depletion and erosion. Almost everywhere in the world societies are fracturing along class lines. With each passing year, larger and larger shares of capital are being concentrated in fewer and fewer hands, while at the same time throughout the world, governments—the guarantors of the property rights that enable such concentrations of wealth—are growing weaker and weaker. Once political chaos makes property rights too expensive to defend, the value of that highly concentrated paper wealth will be greatly reduced.

To my mind, social collapse is not a political or economic or technological problem for the elites to solve, but a cultural one. There are billions of people in the world who survive on less than a dollar a day, and yet many of these people are happier and lead more pleasant, carefree and fulfilling lives than many of the people in the developed nations, including the ones who are working for the international aid agencies and NGOs struggling to help them. Having a different set of values and expectations enables poor people in poor countries to lead leisurely, social, rich lives in conditions much worse than those that cause rich people in rich countries to lead exhausting, sleep-deprived, lonely, poor lives. As everyone becomes progressively poorer, the people in rich countries have much more to learn from the rest of the world than the other way around.

All of the coping mechanisms that exist to deal with societal failure are designed to treat it as the exception rather than the norm; there is no safety net designed to catch entire societies as they fall. International aid, charity, disaster management, peacekeeping efforts and military interventions are designed to handle singular, localized, limited crises and cannot be expected to be useful within an international landscape of constant and accelerating collapse. Few places are likely to remain sufficiently insular to escape the onslaught of internationally displaced groups driven from their land by a variety of forces, from political unrest to economic dislocation caused by globalization to habitat destruction created by rapid climate change. Some who see the inevitability of this onslaught react by attempting to isolate themselves, by building a well-stocked "doomstead" in a remote area. This may work for a few people; for the rest, it might be better to abandon the idea of finding a safe *place* to be, and to concentrate instead on discovering a safe *way* to be—in company with others.

The limits of community planning

Let us imagine how an enlightened, well-meaning group of people might attempt to construct a safe place in which to ride out social collapse. After some preliminary organizing and planning activities, they set out to attempt great things: establish community gardens and farmers markets, lobby for improved public transportation, bike lanes and sidewalks, promote ride-sharing initiatives, weatherize existing homes and impose more stringent construction standards for new ones, construct windmill farms and install solar panels on public buildings, promote the use of composting toilets and high-efficiency lighting and so on. In the midst of all this organizational activity neighbors get a chance to meet, perhaps for the first time, and discover a commonality of interests that leads them to form acquaintances and perhaps even friendships. As neighbors get to know each other, they start looking out for each other, improving safety and reducing crime. As the community becomes tighter-knit, it changes in atmosphere and appearance, becoming more fashionable and desirable, attracting better-educated and more prosperous residents. News of these vast improvements spreads far and wide, and the community becomes a tourist mecca, complete with food festivals, swank boutiques and pricy bric-à-brac shops and restaurants.

The undesirable element is priced out of the neighborhood and is forced to decamp to a less desirable neighborhood nearby. This they may not even particularly mind; these are the many people who live with a legacy of abuse and neglect, of poverty, destitution, lack of educational opportunities, alcohol and drug abuse, violence and depression. Given their set of problems, there is an upper limit to how great life can be for them, and to attempt to fit in among the lovely and the talented and pretend that life is grand only causes them additional stress. Life at the bottom can be strangely soothing and comfortable, and offer opportunities to drown their sorrows and forget their troubles, one day at a time, that the more prosperous, busy, upscale neighborhood cannot.

In their new, downscale haunts, there is, of course, trouble; the poor have little choice but to suffer high levels of crime, but are typically afraid to ask the police for help, having learned from experience that the police are more likely to harass them than to help them, to arrest and imprison them for minor offenses and to round them up and deport them if they happen to be illegal immigrants. They also learn to be careful around members of local gangs and drug dealers. Since official jobs in the neighborhood are scarce, they seek informal, cash-based employment, contributing to an underground economy. Seeking safety in numbers, they self-organize along racial and ethnic lines, and promote their common interests by forming mafias that strive to dominate one or more forms of illegal or semi-legal activity. Growing up in a dangerous, violent environment, their children become tough at a young age, and develop excellent situational awareness that allows them to steer clear of dangerous situations and to know when to resort to violence.

As the collapse scenario unfolds around them, both of these communities are harmed, but to different extents and in different ways. Supposing that they are both in an English-speaking country, which is likely to be afflicted with the irrational belief that the free market can solve all problems on its own, even problems with the availability of critical supplies such as oil, we should expect that at some point fuel supply disruptions will make themselves felt. Once fuel is no longer delivered to either of these communities (although some fuel is likely to still be available on the black market, at prices that very few people can afford), things start to shut down. A lack of supplies and maintenance at every level causes electricity to shut off, water pumping stations to cease functioning, sewage to back up (making bathrooms unusable) and garbage trucks to no longer collect the garbage, which piles up, breeding rats, flies and cockroaches. As sanitary conditions deteriorate, diseases such as cholera, dysentery and typhoid reappear and spread. The medical system requires fuel for the ambulances and running water, electricity and oil-based pharmaceuticals and disposable supplies for the hospitals and clinics to operate. When these are no longer available, the surviving residents are left to care for each other as best they can and, when they fail, to bury their own dead. Along with the other municipal and government services, police departments cease to function. Particularly important installations are guarded by soldiers or by private security, while the population is left to fend for itself.

The effect of this shutdown on the two communities is markedly different. The first community is better equipped for emergencies. People there have laid in crisis supplies of food, water and fuel, installed backup electrical generators and solar panels at key facilities and put together a list of emergency procedures to follow. But being more prosperous at the outset makes a sudden transition to squalor, destitution and chaos much more of a shock. Their relative prosperity and excess of needed supplies also makes them a target for many requests for help from less fortunate communities nearby, and, failing that, a much more desirable target for looters. Used to living in safety and enjoying the protection of a benign and cooperative police department, the residents are not acculturated to the idea of countering violence with violence. Their response is more likely to take the form of a fruitless policy discussion rather than an attempt to strike a practical balance between safeguarding supplies and avoiding an escalation of violence. Unaccustomed to operating outside the law and having few connections with the criminal underworld, they are slow to penetrate the black market, which is now the only way to obtain many necessary items, such as food, cooking fuel and medicines, and may include items that had been previously looted from their own stockpiles. Worse yet, they once again become estranged from one another. Their acquaintances and friendships were formed within a peaceful, civilized, law-abiding mode of social behavior. When they are forced to turn to scavenging, outright theft and looting, prostitution, black market dealing and consorting with criminals, they can no longer recognize in each other the people they knew before, and the laboriously synthesized community again dissolves into individuals and nuclear families. Where neighbors continue to work together, their ties are likely to be weak, based on altruistic conceptions of decency, mutual benefit and personal sympathies—a far cry from the clear do-or-die imperatives of blood ties or clan or gang allegiance that prevail on the other side of the tracks.

The second community is already accustomed to hardship and, not having quite so far to fall, can take the transition to mayhem, destitution and squalor in stride. The prevalence of illegal activity prior to collapse smooths the transition to a black market economy. Already resistant to the idea of relying on police protection, the residents are relieved when the police disappear from the streets, and a great deal of unofficial and illegal activity that previously had to be conducted in secret bursts out into the open. With the police no longer stirring the pot with arrests and confiscations, local criminal groups now find themselves operating in a more stable environment and are able to carve up the neighborhood into universally recognized zones of influence, and this allows them to avoid unnecessary violence. The children, who are already in the habit of roaming the streets and harassing and mugging strangers, now come to serve as the community's early warning system in case of an organized incursion. (Not that too many strangers would want to venture into such an area unaccompanied by a trusted local, given its fearsome reputation.) Lastly, the prevalence of illegal drug dealing means that the community already has a trained cadre of black marketeers who, now that official commerce has collapsed, can diversify and branch out into every other kind of commerce. Their connections with the international narcomafia, whose representatives tend to be well organized and heavily armed, may turn out to provide certain benefits, such as an enhanced ability to move people and contraband through the now highly-porous national borders. If the narcomafia ties are sufficiently strong, a narcobaron may take the community under his cartel's explicit protection, founding a new aristocracy to replace the now disgraced and powerless former ruling class.

The new rules

Community organizing is quite wonderful, and can provide some of us with a perfectly pleasant way to while away our remaining carefree days. As a useful side effect, it can provide individuals with valuable training, but it does next to nothing to prepare the community for collapse. A safe and congenial environment for you and your children is obviously very nice, much better than trying to survive among social predators. But humanity is not immune to the laws of nature, and in nature one can usually observe that the fewer are the wolves, the lamer, fatter and more numerous are the sheep. The central problem with community organizing is that the sort of community that stands a chance post-collapse is simply unacceptable pre-collapse: it is illegal, it is uncomfortable and it is unsafe. No reasonable person would want any part of it.

The most important element of preparing for collapse is to devise a plan to force through a swift and thorough change of the rules by which society operates. Under emergency conditions, the previously enacted rules, laws and regulations will amount to an essentially lethal set of inflated standards, unachievable mandates and unreasonable restrictions, and attempting to comply with them or enforce them is bound to lead to inaction at best and armed conflict at worst. The current way of changing the rules involves lobbying, deliberation, legislation and litigation—time-consuming, expensive activities for which there will be neither the time nor the resources. There are few non-destructive ways to decomplexify complex systems, and while systems that have physical parts fall apart by themselves, a legal framework is a system that, even in an undead state, can perpetuate itself by enslaving minds with false expectations and hopes. By default, the procedure for those who wish to survive will be to universally disregard the old rules and to make up new rules as they go along, but this is bound to cause mayhem and much loss of life. The best-case scenario is that the old rules are consigned to oblivion quickly and decisively. The public at large will not be the major impediment to making the necessary changes. Rather, it will be the vested interests at every level—the political class, the financial elite, professional associations, property and business owners and, last but not least, the lawyers—who will try to block them at every turn. They will not release their grip on society voluntarily, so it is best to make plans to forestall and thwart their efforts. When taking part in community organizing activities, if your envisioned community is to survive the transition to a post-collapse existence, it is important to keep in mind one vital distinction: is this community going to operate under the old rules or the new rules? The old rules will not work, but the new ones might, depending on what they are. You might want to give the new rules some thought ahead of time, perhaps even test them out under the guise of emergency preparation training.

Keep in mind, though, that even if all of your best-laid plans come to naught, community regenerates spontaneously, given time, space and a commonality of interest, provided it is not too oppressed. As industrial economies continue to shrink and shed jobs, more and more people will be squeezed out to the margins of the consumerist universe and, finding they have more time on their hands than they know what to do with, will start to reengage with other people in similar situations. Since their needs will often be coincident or complementary, they will form various types of temporary and informal groups. There is certainly a great deal that all of us can do to help, but first we should stop working so hard on destroying community, as we have been doing by leading overwhelmingly specialized, regimented and commercialized existences.

Social reclamation

Societal failure takes many forms. There are the educational systems which, in keeping with contemporary fashion, mainly train students to take tests (not a practically useful or marketable skill), then attempt to teach them jobs which, more often than not, do not or will not exist. The best outcome that education can achieve—an educated person, versed in liberal arts and basic science—is now commonly regarded as a useless luxury. But even basic numeracy and literacy are increasingly out of reach, with rates of functional illiteracy in the English-speaking countries as high as 50 percent, and the prisons bursting with people who cannot rejoin society because they have not been taught to read and write their native language.

There are the travesties of continued insistence on economic growth at any cost, of inflated standards which make it impossible for people to meet their basic needs if they lack the money for the upscale, high-end products and services, of extreme but impersonal interdependence where everyone is forced to rely on and to trust strangers and foreigners, of a system of globalized finance which forces everyone to gamble with their savings—be it their retirement savings or other investments. This system of legalized gambling is rigged so as to pool localized, personal risk into centralized, systemic risk that will, sooner or later, bring down the entire economic system.

The outcome of all this is that in most of the densely settled, economically developed parts of the world, human relationships have been reduced to the commercial, client-server paradigm. The intergenerational contract, where parents and grandparents bring up children who then take care of them in their old age, and which is actually an evolved trait of the human species, has been largely broken. There is extreme alienation that reduces conversations to scripted interactions on topics that are considered safe, along with transience, both in where people live and in the people with whom they associate. There is a steady replacement of local culture with commercial culture, packaged as a set of popular but short-lived cultural products.

Faced with all this, the natural response for many people is to want to turn their backs on society. But we are social animals and to remain healthy we need to be part of a small, close-knit group. A few people still have that, while the rest must content themselves with the addictive ersatz offerings of commercial culture: shopping, sports, and entertainment and the Internet.

How do we opt out of societies that are falling down around our ears without being left alone? How does one start a tribe from scratch? One probably doesn't; in fact, starting anything from scratch is often a bad idea. A much better idea is to reclaim, reuse and repurpose fragments of existing social institutions. As societies fail, their cultures do not vanish, at least not immediately. Rather, they end up on the proverbial scrapheap of history. That scrapheap, for lack of anything else, will have to be our treasure trove of ideas for us to rediscover and revive.

Religion as organizing principle

What institutions do we have that could help us accomplish this, ones that predate this now failed society, as well as the countless other societies that have failed before? Religious ones. Religious institutions have turned their back on more societies than we can count, and survived. Moreover, they have repeatedly provided a survival mechanism where all else had failed.

A well-studied example is Rome after the collapse. Rome went from a majestic imperial center to a papal swamp. The barbarians destroyed the baths and the fountains, but left the aqueducts running. Over the following decades, the aqueducts filled Rome with water, turning it into a malarial swamp. The Roman forum was used to graze goats and to mine marble by stripping façades and smashing statues, which was then burned down to lime to make mortar for building churches and monasteries. What followed was an age dominated by religion, which eventually coalesced into the Holy Roman Empire. It has been endlessly remarked that it was neither holy nor Roman nor an empire, but the dominant role of religion set the rules by which everyone had to play, even its rulers: no warfare was permitted on Sundays or feast days or in churches or monasteries, which were treated as sanctuaries, or on church property, which was considered sacrosanct. The result was several centuries of very small-scale, silly little operetta wars, in which not too many people were hurt. The last surviving echo of this age was the Christmas ceasefire during the First World War.

What makes religion unique among human institutions is its ubiquity (all cultures have it in one form or another) and its lack of compartmentalization. The secular universe is always broken up into specialties. Look at your typical college or university: there is marketing, communications, economics, political science, sociology, psychology and so on, and each discipline has its circumscribed set of concerns. In comparison, religion is a total system that encompasses every aspect of human existence. Moreover, religion (when placed in a position of authority) is able to place limits on the secular realm, rejecting those parts of it that it finds harmful or useless. Religions also have the uncanny ability to demand and be granted social exemptions and become, to a considerable extent, a law onto themselves.

The role of religion tends to increase in times of adversity. Immigrants, exiles and diaspora communities are often held together by a church, a mosque, a synagogue, an ashram. This effect usually wanes as times get better, but the institutions never quite go away, and come roaring back as times get worse.

The subject of religion is something of a minefield; there is something in it to offend just about everyone. Atheists are offended when told that missing out on religious experience means ignoring a big part of what it means to be human, and that by ignoring religious experience they ignore and repress their own innate irrationality. This is a dangerous move, and an unnecessary one, since religion is there to steer our irrationality into a wide, safe channel.

On the other hand, religious people are offended when told that there is a physiological basis for their belief, and that it has to do with the development patterns of the human infantile brain: God's omnipotence is an infantile lack of limits and illusion of omnipotence, while the concept of hell has its source in infantile rage. Religious myths such as Eve being made from Adam's rib or Athena leaping from the head of Zeus, fully armed and ready for battle, are projections of the distorted, infantile body image. The idea that gods have families—causing Christians to pray in the name of the Father and the Son—probably stems from our innate primate tendency to favor the offspring of the alpha male. As infants acquire language, develop an ego and are socialized, their pre-symbolic impulses are repressed. But this repression is never complete, and if the ego is ever damaged, these impulses resurface as psychotic delusions. Religion provides a safer way of channeling them and expressing them in socially acceptable ways without attempting to rationalize them. It is an essential safety valve for the overwrought human psyche.

To me, atheism is a perfectly valid belief (or, if you like, belief system). Everyone must believe something, because our brains are wired to believe, and spontaneously hallucinate explanations for things, even where there aren't any, as is generally the case with financial markets, which are always heading either up or down for no reason at all. Everyone believes in a creation myth of one type or another. The atheist creation myth is the Big Bang, which says that the universe came into existence 12.75 billion years ago. Alternatively, you can believe that the world was created by a deity in six days of work, after which he then took a day off. Or, if you are one of the Oogla people described by Douglas Adams, who live in the Oogla tree and subsist on Oogla nuts, you believe that the universe was created when the Giant Pixie sneezed, in an event that became known as the Big Sneeze. We cannot *not* believe because our brains use belief to filter our perceptions of reality; all of our perceptions and value judgments are based on what we believe. And our beliefs are mostly based on what we were told when we were young, impressionable and unquestioning. Some of them are outlandish; for instance, people believe that suburban real estate in the United States will continue to be valuable, because they will continue to be able to drive there. It is very important to remain rational about most things. Faith is not a good substitute for reason, although it can be quite helpful when reason fails us.

From the points of view of their practitioners, theology and astrophysics and humor/science fiction literature are very different genres, but as for the rest of us, who make up about 99.9 percent of humanity, it is a matter of choosing what we want to believe. We walk up to the great salad bar of faith and decide what to put on our plate. The practitioners try to restrict our choices (they are, after all, in competition with each other, and are forever hoping to establish a monopoly on faith) but in the end it is all up to us to pick a god, or gods, or fashion some new ones in our image. Heresy is fun!—so much fun that they used to burn people at the stake to keep them from engaging in it. This makes it very important, politically, to keep the various divinities from cornering the market: Catholicism and Islam—you are on notice!

Getting back to what religious faith might be, to us non-specialists, the various creation myths, be they religious or scientific, are just different stories, accepted *on faith*, without proof or evidence. But there is one type of story that you get to play a role in, rather than just watch television. There are no historical reenactments of the Big Bang that I am aware of, no little Big Bang mangers with the Three Subatomic

Particles in attendance, set up to commemorate the birth of the universe on its birthday.

Religious belief offers us a connection. The word "religion" comes from the Latin *religere*, to reconnect. Religion gives us a part to play. Scientific belief makes us a research subject, a specimen or, if we are young and still daydream, a great scientist about to be awarded the Nobel Prize. Science has its uses, of course. Science has its utility. It can also inspire awe. The Large Hadron Collider which discovered the Higgs boson (nicknamed "the God particle") is an awe-inspiring scientific experiment; it is also a nine-billion-dollar, seven-mile-long tunnel to nowhere. There are much cheaper ways to inspire awe, while giving people a role to play at the same time; a role that expands in bad times.

The minimal functions of religion are limited to what one priest once described as, "Hatch 'em, match 'em and dispatch 'em": baptism and chrismation, marriage and last rites. The maximal functions might be carried out by a network of monasteries that oversee agriculture and construction, regulate commerce, control politics, limit warfare and offer education, medical treatment and all manner of advice. This describes, among many other things, medieval Europe, as well as Tibet prior to the Chinese invasion.

There is a long-standing tradition of exempting religious organizations from rules governing civil organizations. These run the gamut from taxation to labor laws and land use laws, to lax law enforcement (which is why the Roman Catholic church in North America has not been summarily shut down to prevent further incidents of child molestation). There are many special exemptions grandfathered in, from the Christian Scientists being exempt from "Romneycare" in Massachusetts to the Amish in rural Pennsylvania being able to behave in ways that would have alarmed Child Protective Services were they living in a city. An exception that proves the rule is the Branch Davidian sect in Waco, Texas, which was torched out of existence by the FBI; if you stockpile illegal firearms and impregnate underage women whom you hold captive, the government will eventually go after you in the most heavy-handed and incompetent way imaginable, but not before much soul-searching accompanied by a full-scale media frenzy.

Cults are a bad problem specifically because political authorities are afraid to go near them. Americans, in particular, practically have it in their DNA to avoid a confrontation with anything even vaguely religious. Political confrontations are transient while religions, with their various grudges and superstitions, are able to persist on an almost genetic basis. Also, religions often help governments do their job (or, as the case may often be, help them *not* do their job) of helping take care of the sick, the old and the indigent. Religious organizations face the fewest barriers to expanding their functions in bad times. Willy-nilly, they turn out to be the organizations most capable of creating alternative living arrangements during a time of permanent crisis.

Religious institutions are sustainable and resilient, as evidenced by the fact that they tend to outlive cultures, empires and civilizations. Although not all of them achieve it, life in balance with nature is imperative for a religion if it wishes to survive, and although there is always the threat of realpolitik in any human endeavor—and religions are no exception—religions offer wider latitude for moral challenge (unless they are largely dead) than secular organizations.

The social functions of religion are particularly significant within the American context. In other parts of the world, conscientious atheism can be perfectly moral, even scrupulous, because for an atheist morality and ethics can be ends in themselves, without being motivated by some metaphysical or supernatural external force. But the US was founded for religious reasons, and political tolerance of religious differences is enshrined more fully than any other freedom. Given the steady erosion of civil liberties, the creation of an untouchable financial/political elite beyond the reach of the law, and acceptance of fraud at every level, any attempt to mount a moral challenge via the legal system is futile. At the same time, religious freedom will prove to be very difficult for American politicians to whittle down. It is where they will fall down if they even try. Should they decide to, they should first try taking away the right to bear arms, as a practice run.

Religion does have a negative side, which we should not ignore. This mostly has to do with identity games. Give an idiot a flag to wave, teach him an anthem to sing and some patriotic drivel to repeat unquestioningly, and he will march off to battle to kill other such idiots who are marching under a different flag. Religions provide ample scope for such identification, and religious idiots tend to be even more ardent than political idiots. But at a higher, non-idiotic level, different religions tend to work and play well together. A priest, a rabbi and an imam walk into a bar…and what do you suppose they discuss? Who is the one true god? Not likely; they are far more likely to compare notes on whatever happens to threaten or oppress all of them, and to share stories of their troubles. Religious tolerance and religious freedom are different words to describe exactly the same thing. Freedom *from* religion is just as important; the atheists deserve to have their own church. It can be an open-air church, to save money, and it can stand empty.

Note that I have not delved into the specifics of any one religion. I have used the word faith, in an offhand way, but have refrained from using the s-word (spirituality). My point is that we have religious institutions, or traditions, that are able to survive just about anything. We also have a society that is disintegrating, a corrupt, unreformable political system that will ruin many lives and an economy that is failing to provide the necessities for more and more people. Why should we fight battles that have already been won? Religious institutions have already succeeded in fighting political institutions down to a reasonable truce, which the politicians are rightly terrified to break. Let us not start from scratch; let us work with what we already have.

Charitable giving and taking

Beyond various kinds of religious institutions, which, in the United States especially, are well-positioned to escape government scrutiny and oppression and create and sustain alternative living arrangements apart from the surrounding social decay, lie various kinds of charitable organizations, many of them also religious. As I have already pointed out, charitable donations, endowments and other forms of largesse are handouts designed to please the benefactor. Rather than give rise to gratitude or a desire to reciprocate, they breed resentment, dependency and unjustified feelings of entitlement. Charity, grift and extortion form a single continuum of perversely motivated exchange within power relationships based on privilege backed up by the threat of violence. A gift that can never be reciprocated is a form of abuse or an insult. Charity is really a sort of imposed hypocrisy—a system of domination in which those who have the upper hand pretend to offer help in the most humiliating way possible.

However, in an environment where the state attempts to tax all transactions but makes an exception for charitable giving, charitable organizations offer a legal, unencumbered and largely unregulated form of exchange that can be used to build allegiances and circles of trust.

For this to happen, the work of charity has to be made personal—not directly mediated by institutions, except superficially, on paper, to abide by legal requirements. This work must become an unwritten, largely unspoken contract between two persons or two families. Rather than a breezy, superficial way to do good by sharing your excess with those anonymously in need, it must be part of a relationship: one party pledges to support the other in any way it can; the other party pledges to support the first in any way *it* can. Such relationships take time to build, but they often start out as simple acts of volunteering to help, followed by taking more than a superficial interest in those you try to help. Perhaps the most difficult part of making such a transformation is in finding a good balance between playing a socially sanctioned role (of dispensing charity) and, at the same time, acting as yourself among your friends.

What society?

This is a short chapter, and it is short for a reason, because what happens after social collapse is up to you. Society exists, until it doesn't. Take a society that is held together by a set of institutions, a common code of behavior, a set of laws (enforced though violence) and a set of class privileges enshrined in separate living arrangements and paper wealth (again defended through violence). Now render all of these distinctions meaningless through as simple a device as an extended power outage lasting more than a month, followed swiftly by lack of access to transportation fuels and consumer goods. Where is that society now? Poof!—and it's gone, perhaps forever.

But it is precisely in such situations that people spontaneously come together and self-organize to help each other. In fact, many people are naturally at their best and most helpful when facing an emergency or a crisis, and most able to attract others to a common cause. But what could previously be viewed as a single, monolithic entity—Society writ large—dissolves, perhaps forever, and is reconstituted in a much more practical, humble, local form: "societies" in the plural. Whether, and to what extent, these societies ever decide to coalesce into something larger is a practical concern. Such lower-case societies, in the plural, can start with just a couple, or a family, or a couple of families, and grow from there. The logic by which the whole becomes greater than the sum of its parts is inescapable and compelling, and the process occurs spontaneously wherever officialdom fails to step in and impose its own fragmenting, isolating, impersonal order. This chapter has inadvertently taken on some religious overtones, so we might as well end it on a religious note, from Jesus, who was clearly quite an accomplished anarchist organizer: "For where two or three are gathered together in my name, there am I in the midst of them." (Matthew 18:20)

Case Study: The Roma

While attending third and fourth grade at a school in what was then the outskirts of Leningrad I happened to have an unlikely desk-mate. We sat in rows, at paired desks, wearing our school uniforms. The seats were assigned. In an effort to make the children behave, the better-behaved boys were paired up with girls, while the few particularly troublesome boys were seated together in the back, where nobody but the teacher could see them. They were regularly thrown out of the classroom for speaking out of turn, throwing things, starting fights and so forth, and would spend the rest of the class standing outside the classroom in the cold, drafty, dimly lit hallway.

There wasn't a spot for me in this scheme, since at the time I was mainly home-schooled by my grandmother. I would show up on first day of school, and a week or two later I'd come down with severe sniffles or a nasty-sounding cough, and get yanked out of school and sent to the country house to recuperate. My grandmother did not believe in home-work assignments; my homework was to read cover to cover and memorize all the textbooks the Ministry of Education saw fit to provide for that school year, and to do all the exercises at the end of each chapter. I proceeded at a steady rate, only slightly bored, putting in a solid three or four hours of schoolwork a day, then going skiing or sledding or playing fetch with the dog for the rest of the day. I then showed up back at school a month or so later, fully recovered and ready to stand up at the blackboard and answer any and all questions put to me, to the extreme annoyance of both the teacher and the class. Two or three weeks later the cough would come back, or I would start sneezing again, and the cycle would repeat.

There was no good place for me to sit during my brief sojourns in the classroom, so I ended up with the riffraff at the back of the room. Since I had already done the reading, I knew all the answers, and my hand pretty much stayed up the entire time, but, being rather small and seated at the back of the class, I was easy for the teacher to ignore. After a while, delirious from boredom, I would resort to shouting things out from my seat, and get disciplined. The riffraff I was seated next to, who understood nothing and cared less, would pick fights with me. I would get rowdy right back at them, and get disciplined for that as well. And so it went.

Finally, something clicked in our pathetic teacher's overtaxed brain, and I was relocated to the very, very back of the classroom and told to sit next to a tall, taciturn fellow, who was never called upon during class and never spoke to anyone during recess. He was at least three years older than me and had been kept back for several years for doing no schoolwork whatsoever. He would come in, sit down, not bother with any books or writing implements, and just sit there gazing at the teacher the way cats gaze at fishtanks. Something of his serenity rubbed off on me and my mood improved. With my back against the rear wall of the classroom I was virtually invisible and could read, doodle or day-dream at my leisure. The boy (or was he already a man?) seemed to take a liking to me. Although he never condescended to speak to me, he would helpfully poke me in the ribs on those rare occasions when my name was called, saving me the indignity of being disciplined yet again, this time for not paying attention in class.

And then one day he did speak to me.

"So," he said, "your grandfather is a professor of Russian literature?"

"Yes he is," I replied.

"Our people don't like books."

"Who *are* your people?" I asked, astonished.

"*Tsygane*," he said with an inscrutable smile. Gypsies.

"So how do you know things if you don't read?" I asked.

He pointed at his head. "We remember everything."

I said a few words about the wonderful things to be found in books. "Do you realize that none of that is real?"

I said a few more words about things that apparently weren't real.

"That's enough!" he said dismissively. And that was that.

There wasn't much of anything for us to talk about after that, but we tended to spend recesses together, standing around with nothing better to do. He was an island of tranquility in a ceaselessly churning sea of restless idiots briefly released from confinement. Plus, when I was with him, nobody would even dream of bullying me. Both the children and the teachers were afraid of him, and found it safest to completely ignore him—which was precisely what he wanted. He was simply biding his time, as his entire million-strong people have all had to do, on and off, for over a thousand years.

And then one day we met outside of school. We lived in the same apartment building—one of those Soviet-era concrete high-rise monoliths—on the same floor and in identical apartments, but accessed through adjacent stairwells. The entrances were hard to tell apart without counting them off, because the numerals painted on the wall near the doorways had long washed off. I usually navigated my way across the pockmarked wasteland between school and home by setting course by a certain old woman who always sat on the bench in front of our doorway, but on that particular day she had mysteriously relocated one door to the left. I went past her, took the elevator to what I thought was our floor and knocked on the door of what I thought was our apartment.

My Gypsy desk-mate opened the door.

"What are you doing here?"

To answer his question, I had to step into his apartment. You see, it is a Russian taboo to carry on a conversation across a threshold, and it seemed strange to ask somebody to leave their dwelling so that you can answer their question. To a Russian, a question asked across a threshold is equivalent to an invitation to enter. At that point I was mugged by his many, many siblings (I didn't have time to make a precise count of them). My pockets were empty and they were disappointed. Seconds later his mother marched out of the kitchen and ordered me out of the apartment. As I was to learn later, by avoiding one taboo, I had broken another: to a Gypsy, having a Gadjo (a non-Gypsy) set foot inside their dwelling invites *mahrime* (a state of defilement or pollution). To my Slavic ear, Gadjo has always sounded like "vermin." To avoid *mahrime* in case of an unavoidable visit from a Gadjo—be it a policeman or a school official—Gypsy households usually have a special Gadjo chair, on which nobody ever sits except a visiting Gadjo. If food is to be served to such a Gadjo visitor, Gypsies use special plates that they then smash and throw away, together with any utensils the Gadjo had used.

A short while later we received a return visit. My mother was at home by herself when she heard a knock on the door. Outside stood a Gypsy woman, who asked for a glass of water, so that she could tell my mother her fortune. My mother, curious to see what would happen, fetched a glass of water while the Gypsy stood outside, and handed it to her. The Gypsy took the glass, waved her hand over it, and an ugly black thing materialized in the water. Then the Gypsy started waving her free hand in the air and exclaiming loudly, at which point she and several other Gypsies, who had been waiting in the hallway, swarmed into the apartment and fanned out across the rooms, where to their certain disgust they found a whole lot of books and not much else. They made off with a packet of tea from the kitchen, and that was all. One of them grabbed my mother's purse, but when my mother gave chase and threatened to thrash them all to tiny pieces they gave the purse up instantly and fled.

This, it turned out, was a fairly typical Gypsy gambit. Another involved knocking on the door of an unsuspecting person, and, when the door opened, laying a swaddled infant across the threshold, then swarming in. The theft was always petty, there was never any violence, and the Gypsies were always quick to run if there was any threat of violence or of having to confront the authorities. Since the Russians are themselves normally reluctant to get the authorities involved (the police to this day are informally referred to as "werewolves") the threat was usually an empty one, but effective nevertheless. No one saw the Gypsies as particularly threatening. Aside from their petty thievery, flimflam and swindles, they were sometimes falsely accused of kidnapping children, which is, in fact, something that Gypsies would never, ever do: they do not adopt Gadjo children for fear of *mahrime*.

Who are they?

At this point, you may be curious to know, Who exactly are the Gypsies? Accurate information about them is not particularly difficult to find, but neither is it widely disseminated. Many academic libraries contain a shelf of books, of various vintages, offering ethnographic, linguistic and sociological analyses of the Gypsy "problem." Some libraries even contain an entire shelf of bound tomes of *Études Gitanes* that, to my mind, contain altogether too much information and discourse on the Gypsy *problématique*. A few slender monographs in the English language, listed in the bibliography, are quite sufficient for our purposes.

The English exonym Gypsy and the French *Gitane* are both derived from Egyptian/*Egyptien*, which is something that Gypsies are most certainly not. The Slavic/German exonyms *Tsygane/Zigeuner* are probably derived from the Greek for "untouchable," and are somewhat closer to the truth. The people in question came out of India at some unknown point in time, then passed through Persia, Greece and Armenia, as well as other countries, as is evident from Farsi, Greek and Armenian borrowings in Romani, their language. What they call themselves, to themselves, is Roma. In their dealings with Gadje (the plural form of Gadjo) the Roma will usually do their best to obscure their ethnic identity. They are not identifiable in a national census, but researchers estimate their numbers at around one million in the Russian Federation, well over a million in the US, and as many as twelve million worldwide. They are quite widespread in Europe, especially in Bulgaria, Romania, the Balkans, Italy, France and Spain.

Throughout their history, the Roma have been a nomadic people, ranging all over Europe and, more recently, the Americas. Although economically dependent on the surrounding population, they have always taken great pains to remain completely apart from it socially. Roma identity is an *internal identity* that is not disclosed to the outside world. It is a birthright reinforced by upbringing and socialization into a community that caters to its members from cradle to grave. Roma are not known to adopt Gadjo children. It is possible to marry into a Roma family and participate in the life of a Roma community, but it is not possible to become Roma. The children from such a mixed marriage may become Roma if so brought up.

Although the Romani language has been written down, this has had minimal effect on the Roma themselves, who continue to adhere to a strictly oral tradition, with a rich folklore that includes creation myths, a religious tradition loosely based on Christianity and a purely oral internal system of jurisprudence. Among the Roma, literacy correlates negatively with wealth and status, occurring least often among the wealthiest. The literate play subservient, low-status roles such as corresponding with Gadje and forging paperwork and documents. The effort of keeping everything in one's head seems to result among the Roma in excellent memory and a sharp and lucid mind, which are all very helpful in stealing, lying, cheating and swindling—major advantages which ignorant educationalists tend to miss. As the US Poet Laureate Robert Pinsky likes to say: "This is important, *don't* write it down!"

To paraphrase Lenin, "If you want to make a Gypsy omelet, you must be willing to steal a few eggs." If there is one thing that defines the Roma, it is their relentless pickpocketing, swindling, scamming, horse-rustling and poaching, all of which they have elevated to the status of high art. Children are taught to beg and steal from an early age. Even their dogs are prized for their ability to steal, especially meat from butchers, but also to run into an enclosure on a farm, kill something quickly without being noticed and drag it back to the caravan.

But the Roma also work, usually in gender-segregated teams called *kumpania*, but sometimes as families. Their traditional occupations include fortune-telling and horse-trading, but they also engage in various types of recycling activities, such as gathering and selling scrap metal and rags, and a few types of construction work, such as roofing and paving. There are also many capable craftsmen among them. Perhaps most significantly, the Roma are brilliant musicians. Music is their most important means of self-expression, and they have inspired entire new musical genres in many of the countries through which they have traveled. One of the better-known Roma musicians is the jazz guitarist Django Reinhardt. In Russia, the Roma contributed to the development of the popular genre of Gypsy romance. Director Tony Gatlif detailed the history of Roma music in the 1993 French documentary *Latcho Drom*. The most recent addition to Roma music is the 2012 album *Champagne for Gypsies* by Goran Bregović; he and his Gypsy *Wedding and Funeral Band* are wildly popular throughout Europe.

In keeping with their overall strategy of systematically selecting or rejecting specific elements from the surrounding society, the Roma refuse to be proletarianized and try to remain completely independent of wage labor. The lowliest Roma beggar is a self-employed entrepreneur. Nor do they employ others. Furthermore, they do not work alone but as part of a *kumpania*, where all winnings are remitted to the *rom baro*, the "big man" (or woman), who then divides it up equitably among the membership. The Roma sometimes accept Gadje into the *kumpania*, and, since they hold no regard for Gadjo law, they are happy to take in former convicts, especially ones who put their time in jail to good purpose, saw it as a valuable networking opportunity and picked up a few tricks of the trade.

The units of Roma society are *rasa* (i.e., the Roma), *natsia* (most recent country of origin), *vitsa* (clan) and *familia* (extended family). There are a few subcategories of *rasa*, but the distinctions are far from crisp and the main intent of this category seems to be to separate the Roma from the Gadje. *Natsia* seems relatively unimportant socially, although Roma coming from different countries initially speak different dialects of Romani, having absorbed some amount of vocabulary from the local languages. *Vitsa* is much more important, since all those belonging to a *vitsa* must at all times fulfill their obligations of mutual self-help. The Roma like to say that "Money will never be allowed to come between us Roma," by which I believe they mean the Roma belonging to a given *vitsa*. *Familia* is a social and economic unit, and includes three or four generations, including any adopted children, all female in-laws and some male in-laws. Orphaned children are normally adopted by grandparents, who also often lay claim to grandchildren in cases of divorce. When twins are born, one is always adopted, usually by an aunt or an uncle, since it is considered unhealthy to bring up twins together.

All earnings are pooled and given to the family elder (man or woman) who then distributes them according to need and merit. The Roma accumulate status and authority as they age, and a patriarch or a matriarch, whose word is law, rules each *familia*. The deference paid to the elders provides for the cohesion and the welfare of the entire *familia*—essential in the absence of any formal financial arrangements, pensions, retirement funds, police protection or government social services. The elders are also far less likely to spend money frivolously, not necessarily because of their great wisdom, but more or less automatically: as one ages, one's temptations inevitably grow fewer, weaker and farther between, and one's concerns shift to one's children and grandchildren. This strategy also avoids a great deal of conflict: since the elders are obeyed automatically, and since they are unlikely to fight each other physically, the worst that happens is a heated exchange between two elders, held in private, and the conflict resolved in secret.

Law and politics

However, serious conflicts can and do happen, both within and outside a given *vitsa*. For these situations the Roma have their own system of jurisprudence, based on an orally conveyed body of law. The first step in adjudicating a conflict is to summon a *diwano*—a judicial conference of elders. Often the decision of the *diwano* is carried out voluntarily without further proceedings. If this does not happen, the next step is to convene a *kris*—a judicial council, which takes the form of an open meeting at which anyone can speak, presided over by some number of judges, and with the decision reached by some number of jurors, all of whom are elected by those assembled. The decision reached by the *kris* is, again, generally carried out voluntarily; if this does not happen—and this is the only recourse the Roma ever make to Gadjo justice—the disobedient party is falsely accused of some crime and arrested. The case never goes to trial, because the accusers withdraw their accusations or simply fail to turn up, but the humiliation of arrest is generally enough to bring about compliance.

But the authorities rather than the Roma initiate virtually all other official confrontations. Most authorities tend to treat the Roma as a minor nuisance—a source of petty crime, loitering, littering and so forth. They tend to frown upon the nomadic lifestyle and the lack of proper documentation (identification papers, car registrations, tax receipts and insurance policies are often missing, and, when found, turn out to be fake). They are suspicious of people living entirely within the cash economy. The educationalists frown on Roma children not being sent to school, and, when they are forced to go to school, are scandalized by their refusal to learn to read or write. But they generally find that it is cheaper to deal with the Roma by not prosecuting them rather than by prosecuting them, with some spectacular exceptions. The Nazis tried to exterminate them, alongside the Jews; the Soviets resorted to mass imprisonment and a total ban on nomadism; the French, to mass expulsion. But given their resourcefulness, adaptability, strong internal cohesion and high birth rate (starting from an early age) the Roma always bounce back.

Roma strategies for dealing with official confrontations involve evasion, dispersal and disappearance, and their success in pursuing these strategies rests on their ability to relocate. Their first line of defense is in hiding their identity. Each Roma person has three names. The first name is chosen by his or her mother at birth, but kept secret until the child is old enough to understand that this name is not to be divulged to anyone, under any circumstances. Thus, to maintain a Roma identity is to participate in a conspiracy. The second name is the Romani name, which is used strictly within the *familia* and the *vitsa*. This is the name by which the Roma know each other. It is never divulged to Gadje. Lastly, there is the name that they use with the Gadje. Certain surnames are popular with the Roma; in the English-speaking countries, Adams, Roberts, Williams and Smith are common ones. (These are not family names since they do not correspond to *familia*, they are not necessarily shared between husband and wife and they may not be passed on to their children.) And so each Roma has a secret name (which none of us can ever know), a Romani name, such as Ruslan or Zemfira, and a Gadjo name, such as Bob Adams or Cathy Smith. The Gadjo names change constantly based on location: it is a common Roma practice to be known by a different surname in each place they visit. If Gadjo authorities try to put together a case against a Roma, they have to collect physical evidence from multiple locations and cross-reference it to a physical body, which, if not already in their custody, is likely to be long gone, never to return, or to return under a different name and guise, and then the wild goose chase starts again.

The second line of defense when confronting authorities is their self-denigrating, polite, self-effacing stance: "We are poor illiterate migrants, we just want a safe place for our children to grow up," and so on. The men act downtrodden, the women act unfairly put upon. When threatened with eviction from a particular location (the authorities' favorite strategy) they play for time. And then they vanish. Which brings us to their third line of defense: the disappearing act. The entire caravan can be made ready to move within an hour or two. The Roma cultivate the ability to make a quick group decision without any deliberation or melodrama, and to keep it secret. Their itinerary is also kept secret, if it exists at all, because the Roma explicitly condemn planning ahead. In direct opposition to the methods of bureaucratized, literate Gadjo society, which fetishizes planning and communication and cannot make a move without preparation, coordination, public discussion and official approval, the Roma can change direction, as a group, at a moment's notice, in response to events as they unfold.

If the authorities decide to engage the Roma politically as a group rather than confront them individually, and seek among them a leader or a representative, they are treated to a different form of misdirection:

they are presented to the "Gypsy king." Individuals self-select themselves for this role, mostly based on their low status and lack of anything better to do. This "king" may be a Gadjo married to a Roma woman, and/or a "house Rom": a man who lives with his in-laws. What motivates him to step forward to act as the "king" is the ego gratification of being treated as a figure of authority while wasting the Gadjo outsiders' time. The real authority is the *rom baro*—the "big man," also a self-selected individual, whose identity is never divulged to the Gadjo outsiders.

Children and marriage

Roma children are included in the life of the tribe to the fullest extent possible. They learn from adults and from each other by directly participating in the economic and political life of the *familia* and the *kumpania*. Infants are not regarded as important. All Roma are nominally Christian (interestingly, the Romani word for God is *Devel*, and addressed as "*Devla!*") and all of them are baptized, with the choice of Christian denomination considered unimportant. Once baptized, children are freed from taboos of cleanliness until puberty. Until they reach puberty, they are also exempt from all sexual prohibitions. Roma adults regard the sex lives of children as a taboo subject for discussion, turning a blind eye until their children reach puberty, and allowing them to be as obscenely foul-mouthed and perverse as they like, although girls are required to marry as virgins. This cultural trait may explain why the Roma are in so little need of psychoanalysis.

This special dispensation ends at wedding time. A Roma bride's wedding night is traditionally spent not with her new husband but with her mother-in-law, who uses the opportunity to conduct a thorough brain dump on all that a new wife needs to know about the proper way to have sex, including the myriad taboos she needs to obey to avoid becoming *mahrime* (contaminated), or, worse yet, doing the same to her husband. Although the Roma sometimes have a reputation as libertines—and sometimes even cultivate one as part of an exotic external image—with all of their taboos they are really quite chaste, and tend to marry as virgins. Roma girls sometimes impersonate prostitutes, cheerfully and artfully, as part of a scam, where the customer ends up sexually unsatisfied and somewhat poorer, after paying someone restitution for insulting that someone's daughter or sister, who was, of course, only playing, the poor child—but there is never any actual sex with Gadje.

Children are also useful politically. As I mentioned, they can be used directly from birth to symbolically jam doors open, to facilitate home invasions. As they get older, they learn to beg, spy and ask questions that would be insolent or insulting if posed by an adult but are disarming coming from a child. If an official shows up and tries to evict the family, it is quite effective to field a small army of young children, some barely bipedal and pulled along by the others, who gang up on that official on his way in, hanging onto his sleeves and pant legs, tearfully crying "Please, Sir, don't evict us!" while deftly relieving said official of his wallet and wristwatch. Of course, as soon as these items are discovered missing, the children helpfully run around and quickly "find" them: "Here, Sir, I think you dropped this!" Given such treatment, most officials quickly realize that they've been tasked with something well beyond their pay grade and restrict their actions to delivering bits of paper—violation notices, citations, summonses, cease and desist orders, writs, eviction notices and other products of Gadjo lawyers' fevered imaginations—which the Roma promptly burn. The Roma women—invariably calm, polite and diplomatic when confronted by authorities—play the role of long-suffering, harried mothers doing their level best to keep the situation under control. The most officials get the courage to do is arrest a few Roma men and lock them up for a while. Roma men endure imprisonment stoically and cooperatively, and are quickly paroled for good behavior. In the meantime, the women are left alone to bring up the children—as Roma.

Roma girls are considered marriageable as soon as they start menstruating. However, a considerable amount of time may elapse between betrothal, a fairly elaborate ritual, at which the groom's family pays a significant bride price—*daro*—much of which is spent on the wedding, which is an even more elaborate ritual that goes on for days. (The Roma have recently taken to posting their big fat weddings on Youtube; I find them fascinating.) Immediately after marriage, the "young wife," called *bori*, joins her husband's family, and until she gives birth she remains a trainee/intern tutored and bossed by her mother-in-law. Only when she gives birth to her first child does she become a *romni* (wife proper). However, a Roma wife, whether *bori* or *romni*, remains ultimately under the control of her father, who may recall her if the marriage does not work out, or if her services are required by her parents' *familia*, though once the marriage takes place under no circumstances is the *daro* ever refunded. Divorces and subsequent marriages are informal affairs, and never involve Gadjo courts. In the case of divorce the children may go to either parent or to the grandparents. The first marriage is a rite of passage; subsequent marriages are not.

Wealth

While many Roma appear, most of the time, to be quite poor, with no possessions beyond a camper, an old car or truck with which to tow it and the clothes on their back, many of them are in fact quite wealthy. They accumulate wealth in the form of jewelry and other items of value. When a betrothal is negotiated, the *daro* can range into hundreds of thousands of dollars, with the subsequent wedding a lavish banquet lasting several days.

Some Roma have given up nomadism, and the wealthier ones have built themselves opulent palaces packed with crystal, handwoven tapestries, expensive furniture and statuary and state-of-the-art electronics. In Bulgaria, Romania and the Balkans these wealthy Roma have established themselves to the point where they are no longer concerned about having to stay on the move; nor are they shy about flaunting their wealth. In most other places, however, they stay mobile and their wealth remains hidden.

Many Roma appear to be wearing what looks like excessive and perhaps tasteless costume jewelry, which, when they are arrested, goes into the inmate's property envelope in the prison safe. The few prison wardens who actually bothered to get the contents appraised were surprised to find that their value ran into hundreds of thousands of dollars: the costume jewelry was solid gold and platinum with real, large diamonds, rubies and emeralds. Since the Roma refuse to have anything to do with banks or other Gadje institutions, the approach of wearing much of their net worth directly on their person while remaining on the move is actually quite reasonable.

Separatism

The Roma, with their compulsive drive to maintain their separateness at all times, maintain a very strict division between an inner realm, which is kept pristine and free from contamination, and an outer realm, which is dominated by the Gadje and is considered permanently contaminated. An elaborate set of customs and taboos controls the purity of the inner realm, which generally stops at the threshold of the dwelling, be it a tent, a camper or a house. Some Roma households have drawn the ire of neighbors and the authorities for covering their back yards with trash. Similarly, they have been known to trash campgrounds. However, the inner realm can also expand, and does so whenever the Roma can claim a patch of ground as their own. If they know that they can stay at a given spot for as long as they like, as a group, then that spot is spontaneously cleaned up, because the boundary of the inner realm expands from the threshold of the dwelling to the bounds of the encampment. This inner/outer distinction can be seen in their tendency to camp in a circle. While many official campsites take pains to provide the campers with as much privacy as possible, the Roma explicitly destroy it, taking down and burning fences. When camping together, they try to position themselves so that everyone can see everyone else, and they never draw their curtains. But when they are living among the Gadje, the curtains are invariably drawn.

This elimination of privacy within the inner realm is both an internal and an external security measure. Internally, if everyone is being watched by everyone else, then no one can transgress with impunity. Externally, any threat is easier to spot given more eyeballs, and easier to communicate when everyone is within everyone else's view and shouting range at all times. They tend to pick locations that are externally visible, preferring an exposed spot directly on the edge of a major road to a secluded spot deep in the forest: being exposed to public disapproval does not make them vulnerable; being hidden does. Thus, the Roma do not hide; rather, they hide *who they are*. This forces them to maintain constantly shifting external roles and can produce a dangerous sense of unreality and self-degradation, which they battle by protecting their inner self through a set of rituals that reinforce group integrity. Their many pollution taboos are part of a coherent cosmology, and are symbolic rather than practical, designed to serve as a constant reminder of their eternal vulnerability to contamination. The most polluting rites of passage are birth and death. Menstruation is also considered highly contaminating.

The Roma abide by an elaborate set of ancient taboos concerning food. Food must be prepared fresh from scratch, and the table at which meals are eaten must be maintained in pristine condition with no extraneous objects. A flower vase or a statue is acceptable, but placing a keychain or a cell phone on the dinner table makes it *mahrime*. Each

person's plates and eating utensils are washed and kept separately, and .
dried using a separate cloth. A clean tea towel drying on a clothesline
by itself serves as a flag of ethnic purity. Food can only be prepared
while wearing an apron—not to protect the clothes from the food, but
to protect the food from symbolic contamination by the body. And, of
course, nothing is quite so contaminating as the Gadje: at the dinner
table a Gadjo guest is given a special seat on which no one else sits and
eats from a special plate which is later smashed.

The Roma maintain a crisp distinction between the upper and the
lower body: the upper body is considered clean (especially the head,
and kissing full on the lips is considered perfectly fine) while the lower
body is considered contaminating. Roma men often go around stripped
to the waist, but would never even consider putting on a pair of shorts,
even in the most sweltering heat, while Roma women may dance
around topless and breast-feed openly but always wear skirts that cover
the knees and keep their knees pressed together whenever there are
men present. Water and containers used to wash clothes cannot be
mixed up with those used to wash dishes, and dishes cannot be dried
using towels that had ever been used to dry the body.

The price the Roma pay for maintaining their precious separateness is a sort of Obsessive-Compulsive Disorder at the level of an entire
ethnic group. But then it seems that, while serious psychiatric disorders
are rare in individuals, they are very much the rule in ethnic groups,
political parties, economies (both market and planned) and entire nations—and in this the Roma are exceptional perhaps in degree, but not
in kind, to the rest of humanity.

"Gypsiness"

The Roma in any given area or country may either flourish or languish,
depending on what might be termed the "Gypsiness" of the social environment. They did very poorly indeed in Nazi Germany, where they
were victims of genocide along with the Jews. They have done consis-
tently well in the US, where they easily blend into a multi-ethnic, transient population, and where living on the road is an accepted lifestyle,
although the recent trend toward extreme bureaucratization and ubiquitous surveillance is probably starting to cause them problems. They
like to tell people that they are Lebanese—a good choice if your aim

is to confuse, since the Lebanese are barely a nation and definitely not identifiable as an ethnic group.

The Roma did poorly in the Soviet Eastern Bloc, where they were forbidden from traveling and were forced to work in factories. But a remarkable change of Roma fortune took place with the collapse of the Soviet Union, allowing many Roma to quickly amass great wealth, to such an extent that many of them have since built opulent palaces. In all, the Roma do poorly in a rigidly governed and regulated society, and do well in a disordered, disorganized society, in which there are many empty economic niches for them to temporarily fill and then move on. Thus, there is every reason to expect that the Roma will thrive both during and after collapse. And there is every reason to expect that, as the various collapse scenarios unfold, nomadic groups that adopt some of the practices of the Roma will do better than they would otherwise.

CHAPTER 5

Cultural Collapse

STAGE 5: Cultural collapse. Faith in the goodness of humanity is lost. People lose their capacity for "kindness, generosity, consideration, affection, honesty, hospitality, compassion, charity." Families disband and compete as individuals for scarce resources. The new motto becomes "May you die today so that I can die tomorrow."

The term "culture" implies different things to different people. Some only think of it in terms of "cultural events" such as a symphony orchestra performance or an art exhibition. Others include literary and visual arts, along with other formal, non-utilitarian disciplines. Yet others see culture through the lens of nationalist pride—Culture with a capital "C"—and speak of great "cultural achievements" and "cultural monuments."

All of these diverse approaches to culture are exciting and inter-esting, and the collapse of Culture with a capital "C" is a fascinating topic, but perhaps it is not one that should be given the highest prior-ity. Taking a minimalist approach, let us try to answer the following question: How little culture does it take to make a physiological human into someone we are ready to recognize as a "normal" human in any sense of that vague and troublesome word? What cultural elements are necessary and sufficient for humanity to exist? There is a widespread tendency to obsess about development—cultural, scientific, economic, social—and to ignore the unpleasant reality that all such development places a burden on the natural environment that has already gone far past unsustainable. But there is a certain lack of willingness to discuss just how far we can scale back on development in order to secure a bet-ter chance of biological survival for our progeny.

Development requires plentiful natural resources—ecosystem re-sources such as fresh water and food, natural resources such as fossil fuels and minerals—and these are all becoming increasingly scarce. Add to that the continuous large increases in weather-related disruptions that are being caused by climate change, and it becomes apparent that we are running short of the ingredients we need to maintain a complex society and, with it, a complex culture. But all of our eggs are in the basket called "development"—from new, more energy-efficient technol-ogies to investments in renewable energy to better vaccines and medi-cines to fight off new and virulent diseases, we are waging total war against nature, forgetting that, no matter what we do, no matter how mightily we struggle, nature always wins in the end. A more sensible ap-proach is to let nature take its course, and be ready to survive in a state that is as close to feral as can be made survivable, and ready to evolve, or devolve, based on what our environment demands of us, not on what we demand of it.

Such an approach allows for a much simpler definition of culture, but one that is both useful and vital: culture is how people relate to each other face to face, plus the learned ways in which they interact directly with the physical world around them. Do they display kindness, gen-erosity, consideration, affection, honesty, hospitality, compassion and charity? If so, is the scope of these ancient virtues limited to just the self, or the nuclear family, the extended family, the clan, the tribe, other tribes, the surrounding ecosystem? I took this list of virtues from Colin

Turnbull, who wrote a book about the Ik—an African tribe in which most of these virtues were almost entirely missing. The Ik are sufficiently interesting that an entire case study is devoted to them, which follows this chapter. Based on his study of the tribe, Turnbull made a larger point, which was that these personal virtues are also all but destroyed in Western society, but that for the time being their absence is being masked by the impersonal institutions of finance, commerce and government. In the wake of financial, commercial, political and social collapse, do we become the Ik? And if so, is that a fate better or worse than death? Colin Turnbull has fearlessly tackled this question for us; but can we look at his answer without flinching?

The civilized world is a cold world. Its citizens are theoretically expected to fend for themselves, but in reality they can only survive thanks to the impersonal services of finance, commerce and government. What will happen to us once these impersonal services are no longer available? Will we have our humanity to fall back on, or will we go the way of the Ik? Society only allows us to practice the warm virtues from Turnbull's list among family and friends, and perhaps among neighbors in a few particularly idyllic (or contrived) situations. But that is a start, and from there we can expand this circle of warmth to encompass more and more of the people who matter to us, and we to them.

Beyond this circle of warmth lies a wider circle of trust. We can enlarge this circle, by trusting people in small ways, where little is put at risk, then including them if they prove trustworthy and excluding them if they do not. Trust is as much about exclusion (of those we discover to be menacing, dishonorable, disagreeable or untrustworthy) as about inclusion. To trust is to surrender, and beyond the circle of trust lies the battleground of mistrust from which trust is wrested through risk and toil. But to begin to build a wider circle of trust, we must first establish an even wider circle of recognition. One subtle type of mental violence that abounds in the civilized world manifests itself in the act of refusing to acknowledge someone's existence. We may believe that it makes us safer to walk past people without saying hello or making eye contact. That is certainly true if our look is blank and indifferent, and it is then better to avert your gaze than to look, and in effect to say, "I do not recognize you." That definitely does not make you any safer. But if your look says "I see you, you are OK," or even "I recognize you," then the effect is quite the opposite. It can, among other things, instantly reduce the chance of violence. In his amazing book about the legacy of European colonialism, *Exterminate all the Brutes*, Sven Lindqvist makes the stunning observation that violence renders one unrecognizable. The aggressor, whether active or passive, becomes a stranger. But the opposite is also true: the aggressor, once recognized as such, quite often finds it far less necessary to remain aggressive.

Humans and other animals

Human infants are marked by what biologists call "extreme altriciality": our babies are not only born completely helpless but remain so for an extended period of time, requiring, compared to other mammals and even to other primates, an extraordinarily long period of parental care—three years at a minimum—before acquiring the full set of behaviors they need to function autonomously. Human babies need to be taught to walk, talk, eat and communicate—things that other animals know largely through instinct. They need to be taught how to navigate the physical world, how to make sense of their own emotions and how to relate to others. And all of these lessons comprise the minimal subset of culture without which the usual developmental sequence cannot be completed.

There have been cases of feral children raised by wolves, bears and other animals. Orphaned human babies are sometimes adopted into non-human families, and thrive, to a point. They fail to develop an upright gait and walk on all fours. They lack language, and are only able to signal, as do other animals. They lack a variety of basic cognitive abilities that are considered normal, because such abilities require the use of symbols, which is only learned in the context of acquiring a language during a critical developmental period. It is unclear whether any of these feral children are able to breed and rear feral children of their own. In all, these cases do not seem to make good role models for a viable feral humanity of the future. The missing ingredient is human contact; without it, human abilities, both physical and cognitive, fail to develop. But it does point out that we are, after all, just animals. If a human mother is not available, a dog or a pig may serve as a viable surrogate, on the physiological level. Add some amount of human contact to impart a bit of culture (with a lower-case "c") and what emerges is a fully-fledged human.

There have been other cases where children of a few years old were adopted by animals. John Ssabunnya, a Ugandan, ran off into the bush when his father killed his mother. Instead of dying, as one would expect, he was adopted by a group of monkeys, which took care of him for three years. In a similar case, in 1996, a year when packs of stray dogs roamed the streets of Moscow, four-year-old Ivan Mishukov ran away from a dysfunctional, alcoholic home and spent two years begging in the streets, where he befriended one such dog pack, eventually becoming their leader. The dogs kept him warm during the long cold winter nights and defended him.

These cases, extreme though they are, being the inverse of the normal pattern, point out something we already know: that it is normal for human families to include non-human members—dogs, cats, chickens, pigs, ducks, geese, parrots, goats, donkeys, horses, monkeys and so forth. It does not seem quite so normal to us for non-human families to include humans, but why should that be? How do we know which of these two patterns will prevail in the future? Are we simply being biased in favor of our own species? Are the herders that follow the migrations of their herds part of an animal society, or are the herds part of human society? In absence of other nearby humans the question becomes academic. Whether as hunters or as herders or farmers, we need other species to survive. Our current widespread practice is not one of integration or cooperation with other species, but one of domination, exploitation and parasitism, and it's proving to be so environmentally destructive that not only are we driving other species to extinction at a record pace, but our own survival is in doubt. What if we tried to achieve a symbiosis instead?

What makes us feel superior to other species is our ability to use language and symbolic reasoning: if you weren't human you wouldn't be reading this. Language gives us the ability to count and calculate, remember and communicate exact measurements and quantities; it allows us to indicate objects not present at the time and even to describe objects and situations that do not exist; to determine cause and effect relationships, formulate and test hypotheses and so forth. Language allows us to develop and pass on procedures for making tools, clothing, shelter and other artifacts that allow us to overcome some of our physiological limitations. Taken together, all of this gives us the collective ability to outsmart animals much stronger, faster and physically more dangerous. But it is a double-edge sword: language also allows us to irradiate ourselves by building nuclear power plants which then melt down, to put ourselves at risk of immediate extinction by stockpiling thousands of nuclear weapons, and to threaten the existence of all life on the planet by poisoning the oceans and the atmosphere with products of our fossil fuel and chemical industries. In the final analysis, perhaps we, and all life on Earth, would have been safer if humans had not evolved language. Perhaps the use of knowledge that language enables, taken to an extreme, only allows us to achieve a higher overall level of suicidal stupidity.

There are some physiologically and cognitively normal humans who lack language: this is the usual result of not being exposed to language during the critical period in early childhood. Children are born with the ability to acquire language, or languages, that they are exposed to, and this happens to a large extent automatically. In some cultures, infants are spoken to constantly. In others, they are regarded as unimportant and uninteresting and largely ignored; their physiological needs are attended to, but little effort is expended in attempting to communicate with them. But the vast majority of them learn to speak anyway. Deaf-mutes spontaneously develop systems of home signs to communicate; if there is a community of deaf people (even of just two individuals) a language spontaneously develops among them in a phenomenon known as idioglossia. Twins sometimes develop a private language of sorts; this is called cryptophasia. In short, among us humans, language just happens.

This is not surprising, since we appear to be wired for it from birth. There is quite a lot of literature on so-called language universals, but it seems like a conflicted and vexed subject, more philosophy than science. The language universals that are obvious and non-controversial are very few. One is syllabification (i.e., babbling, something babies spontaneously do)—all oral, spoken languages consist of syllables, which consist of phonemes, which, in turn, consist of a vowel or a diphthong preceded and/or followed by one or more consonants. The second is the existence of things called words: there is a specific area of the brain (Wernicke area) that is responsible for handling vocabulary. Lesions in this area cause Wernicke's aphasia: the tendency to confuse and forget words, and to lose the ability to perceive and convey meaning. The third is the existence of phrases: another area of the brain (Broca's area) is responsible for arranging words together into phrases and sentences. Lesions in this area cause Broca's aphasia which manifests itself as agrammatism: the tendency to scramble sentences and make grammatical errors. But most of the discussion about language universals seems to avoid these obvious universalities, and instead centers on the rather abstract matter of syntax. Noam Chomsky is the great Syntactician, the undisputed champion of Universal Grammar, but he has recently conceded that his creation is a mere potentiality that may not be realized in any given language.

The limits of language

What caused Chomsky to qualify his claim to linguistic universality was the recent research into Pirahã, a language spoken by a small group of hunter-gatherers in the Amazon. Pirahã is a highly unusual language: its form is so redundant that it can be either whistled, whispered or hummed without loss of meaning. It is grammatically quite complex, with many verb suffixes that can convey a wide range of meanings, but, most notably, it lacks recursion—the ability to say things like "This is the cat that killed the rat that ate the malt that lay in the house that Jack built." Since recursion is considered to be a key element of Universal Grammar, this was taken by some to mean that Pirahã is not a complete language, possessing a finite set of possible phrases rather than an infinite set of possible sentences. Another notable feature is that in Pirahã the source of information is obligatorily marked with reference to known individuals using a specific set of verb suffixes. Taken together with the impossibility of saying something like "St. Matthew said that Jesus said that...", this feature makes the Pirahã immune to proselytizing by missionaries: all of Scripture is automatically ruled inadmissible on a technicality. Lastly, the Pirahã lack the ability to count and, in spite of wanting very much to learn to use numbers, to avoid being cheated when trading with other tribes, have been unable to do so. They appear to have one word to signify quantity, which can mean both "few" and "many," the gradation between the two being a subtle tonal difference. They can probably compute as well, their computations being analog rather than digital in form. In spite of these linguistic limitations, the Pirahã are a carefree, thriving little tribe, get on splendidly with each other and seem happy with their lot in life.

These recent discoveries concerning the Pirahã have revived arguments in favor of linguistic relativism, called Whorfianism, after its

proponent, American linguist Benjamin Lee Whorf. Whorfianism espouses the idea that linguistic categories determine cognitive categories (in its strong, by now thoroughly disproven version) or influence
them (in its weak, still controversial version). There was already a lot of
empirical support for the weak version before the Pirahã came along.
Based on the presence of certain obligatory grammatical markers for
distinctions such as number (singular/plural), tense (past/present/
future), gender (male/female/neuter), direct/indirect speech, condi-
tional, subjunctive, perfective/imperfective and so on, languages limit
the ambiguity of utterances, and lend a certain automatic precision to
both thought and expression. This is more of a statistical effect; if a
language obligatorily marks hearsay, then people are more likely to distinguish hearsay from evidence in daily life. But even if it doesn't, then
people can still understand the distinction once it is explained to them,
and act on it.

The strong version of Whorfianism has been disregarded more or
less as a matter of general principle, because there is nowhere to draw a
boundary around a language. Universal Grammar presupposes that the
number of possible sentences in any language is infinite, and therefore
each language is capable of expressing an infinity of meanings. Pirahã
throws a monkey wrench into this logic. If one tribe of hunter-gatherers
can happily get by with such an "incomplete" language, summarily
dismissing all evidence that their language does not express, then language does in fact determine cognition in a directly observable, non-
theoretical way. Furthermore, if there is one such language, then there
can be any number of other such languages, dialects or idiolects out
there as well, whose speakers are able to function biologically and socially while remaining blissfully unaware of the many things that tor-
ment our overburdened, overeducated psyches.

Moreover, it then starts to seem likely that languages, not in some
abstract and timeless sense of their full logical potential, but in terms
of actual utterances spontaneously uttered by their native speakers in
response to each other and their environment, span a large range, from
a fixed stock of phrases, as with the Pirahã, to the turgid and pedantic
academic prose of linguistics journals. Introduce a linguist into the mix,
however, and the situation changes: in attempting to elicit from native
speakers responses that would be in line with the principles of Universal Grammar, the linguist changes the picture. Native speakers of most

languages can be trained to produce responses in support of Universal Grammar, just as tigers can be trained to jump through blazing hoops, even though such tricks bear little resemblance to their behavior in their natural environment.

The Pirahã possess some ability to communicate with outsiders using a very limited subset of Portuguese. They make no attempt to learn Portuguese grammar, and simply use Pirahã with Portuguese words substituted. This type of language, known as a pidgin, develops spontaneously between groups that do not share a common language. Pidgins tend to be limited to a particular domain, such as trading, and lack expressive power. They are expressly incomplete, and nobody speaks them as their native language.

Except that sometimes groups of children learn to speak pidgin as their first language, in which case they have no choice but to turn it into a complete language. This process, which has occurred countless times, is called creolization, and the result is a creole language. The better-known contemporary examples include Haitian Creole (based on French) and Cape Verdean Creole (based on Portuguese), but, in fact, most Romance languages such as French and Spanish started out as creoles, derived from Latin-based pidgins that the conquering Romans used to communicate with the local tribes. English was incompletely pidginized and creolized in the aftermath of the Viking invasions and the Norman conquest, shedding a great deal of its grammar and replacing some 80 percent of its vocabulary with French, but retaining some irregular verbs and a few other grammatical vestiges that creoles typically lack. The process of pidginization and creolization results in the shedding of a great deal of grammar and vocabulary. Linguists are usually able to tease out examples to bolster claims that any given creole is a complete language. However, based on my own observations and experience, I am willing to say something that I am sure many people will find politically incorrect: in their actual daily use patterns, creoles can be quite limited. Creoles are simple, limited and easy to learn. In an environment where thinking complex, nuanced thoughts is a waste of precious energy, such spontaneously formed languages may be the right tool for the job.

In recent decades, thanks to rapid economic globalization, cultural homogenization and widespread penetration of the Internet, a new wave of pidginization has swept the world. The de facto contact language of the world is now Broken English. Throughout the world children are growing up hearing and speaking Broken English, and are spontaneously transforming it into various pidgins and creoles that they use among themselves. Some of them later learn a more complete version of English, but as the process of global economic decline accelerates, one should expect that such educational opportunities will dwindle, and that an assortment of English-based pidgins and creoles will appear in many parts of the world. To what extent these creoles qualify as complete languages—and to what extent their limitations affect the cognitive abilities of their speakers—will have to be determined on a case-by-case basis.

Spoken memory

One of the most significant uses of language is for remembering narratives. All cultures have a tradition of storytelling, which can be as simple as the ritual of having one (usually older) person speak while a group of (usually younger) people listens, but it can also take the form of long epic poems set to music accompanied by dance or puppet theater or shadow play. (Shadow play is particularly efficacious; the puppets cost nothing to make, pack flat for travel, and the stage set-up consists of a curtain and a lantern, but the result, in skilled hands, is most impressive.) These are the forms in which cultural knowledge was transmitted from the old to the young. It may seem amazing to us today, but in pre-literate societies the experience of listening to such epic recitals was treated as extraordinarily significant, to such an extent that at least some of the audience would take the trouble of committing the entire text to memory, to recite it later.

With the appearance and spread of writing, the burden on memory was lessened. The stories were committed to paper instead of to memory. It is an unfortunate fact that paper is more perishable than memory; the oldest stories we have—the myths and the epic poems—had existed for thousands of years, passed down orally from one generation to the next, before they were written down. Silent reading, which is now considered the norm, was slow to develop, and for a long time the use of written texts was for reading them in public in spite of failing memory. Even when people were reading to themselves, they moved their lips. An ability which is not exercised tends to atrophy, and, not surprisingly, the ability to read and write has had a very significant deleterious effect on people's ability to remember. Calculators and computers produce a similar effect on the ability to do mental arithmetic. Extensive use of spell checkers has largely erased people's ability to write without the aid of a computer. The ease with which information can be retrieved by search engines has reduced the amount of information people retain. The pattern is always the same: start walking with a crutch—develop a limp.

A second deleterious effect of literacy is that it causes the amount of information to expand in wild profusion, without causing an increase in knowledge, because the people who have access to this information remember less and less of it. Bodies of law, scientific and other research and analysis, engineering specifications and the like force us to base our decisions on a corpus of knowledge that is now too big to fit into anyone's head or to communicate orally in a finite lifetime. Most people no longer possess knowledge but merely convey information. The paradoxical effect of too much information is that everyone is forced to wallow in confusion and ignorance, growing more and more helpless. As technology improves, manual information-processing functions are automated, jobs eliminated, and we are left behind, our minds clogged with a disjointed collection of useless trivia.

Tribes that choose not to emphasize literacy and favor diligently maintaining an oral tradition realize many advantages. A system of justice based on a verbally transmitted codex and case law automatically limits the size of the legal system. Ignorance of a law, once it becomes sufficiently widespread, does become a valid excuse, and laws are discarded once they become sufficiently obscure. None of their precious resources are wasted on teaching children to read and write using an ancient and cumbersome orthography, or on maintaining and duplicating a body of written knowledge. When they enter into agreements, contracts or treaties, these are not committed to paper, making it easier to quietly cancel them once they outlive their usefulness.

During the recent decades much of our information (what we, perhaps mistakenly, continue to call "knowledge") has been migrated to digital media: the progression has been from brain to paper to plastic. This plastic is rather long-lived: as minute particles of chemical waste, it persists in the environment for centuries. But its useful life is limited to just a few years. With plastic, the distinction between a useful product and a piece of trash depends on whether it is cracked, dented, scratched, or, in more and more cases, whether it has ever been used before. Information encoded in the form of microscopic magnetization spots or laser-etched pits on bits of plastic is not particularly durable, and untold reams of "knowledge" have disappeared without a trace because the media on which they were recorded can no longer be read. Even when the data are intact, there is an even bigger problem: information technology is a very power-hungry beast, its power generated largely from burning coal, natural gas and diesel, and from the decay of enriched uranium. It relies on scarce and quickly depleting ores, rare earths and other minerals, and depends on a steady supply of electricity, which is becoming a rarity in many parts of the world. It is also vulnerable to a very unpredictable but recurring sort of disruption: we are one large solar flare away from having our collective memory erased.

There is a danger that the long road from oral culture to written culture to digital culture will end with groups of humans helplessly clutching their dead smartphones, no longer knowing where they are, who anyone is or even where to have lunch. They have learned to cope with being bombarded with millions of bits of information every day, much of it meaningless or irrelevant, but remembering almost none of it, because, you see, there was no need: the information was always at their fingertips.

The best way to make a body of knowledge live on forever is to teach it to children. If it's a story, set it to a rhythm, make it rhyme, give it a melody and a young mind will absorb it like a sponge and spontaneously reproduce it in its entirety—no rote memorization necessary. If it's facts about the natural world that they need to learn, then venture out into it with them, have them smell and chew their way through it while learning what each plant is called, and they will associate the look, the smell, the taste and the sound into a durable synesthetic memory. Or you can let them spend countless hours playing with pencils and pieces of paper, staring at screens and pushing buttons, while learning very little beyond how to be helpless, physically useless and reliant on second-hand understandings and on technology that won't be around for very long. We have the necessary technology right in our heads! Why don't we teach our children how to use it?

The second best way to preserve a body of knowledge is to preserve it in a written form that children can be taught to read and write quickly and easily. The current English spelling does not qualify; it cannot be learned as a system, but can only be memorized as a set of idiosyncratic renderings of words that are only vaguely related to the way the words sound. This process of rote memorization takes some ten years of formal schooling—a ridiculous amount of time, considering that Italian or Vietnamese or Russian orthography can be learned in about two years. The rates of functional illiteracy in the English-speaking countries are already very high and heading higher. It is about time somebody addressed this problem by providing a workable alternative while the lights are still on and all the information is available in digital form. The solution is part linguistics, part software engineering and part running acid-free paper through a printing press.

The isolated human

It is a human cultural universal that people live not as individuals but as groups, and the most common type of group is the family. There is a wide range of cultural variation, from large clans numbering in the hundreds that operate as single economic units to people living as urban singles who may or may not briefly meet even their closest relatives for Christmas. There are also numerous situations where family ties wither away and are replaced with other types of association: collegial groups, clubs, gangs and so on.

Although it was hardly an option through much of human history, modern highly developed industrialized societies make it possible for people to subsist as almost complete loners, serving some specialized job function, paying for all goods and services and limiting their interactions with others to fun and recreation. Such people are, in fact, ideal from the point of view of the state: they are easy to track and pay taxes on everything they use or do. They are unlikely to ever pose a serious threat to the state by forming the sorts of associations that might threaten it. Loners rarely cause more than a single incident's worth of damage. In a society full of loners, their connections with others are too weak to organize because organizations, especially ones that act in opposition to the state, require trust. As technology advances, the technocrats running the state apparatus can dream of eventually replacing them with robots or computer programs. Of course, if the citizenry, through schooling, training and the right sorts of behavioral reinforcements, can be conditioned to act like robots or computer programs, then such expensive upgrades can be avoided. Human organo-robots cannot operate 24/7, require food, bio-breaks and days off, and there is the sticky issue of scrapping them upon retirement. But they have one major advantage: they do not need to be manufactured because they have the amazing ability to spontaneously reproduce.

But there is another problem: making their offspring wards of the state and bringing them up baby farm-style does not produce good results. What does produce good results is something that modern technologically advanced industrial society considers outmoded: an extended family. A nuclear family, with just a mother and a father, is not quite enough to raise even a single child without at least some help and support, which is normally provided by aunts and uncles and grandmothers and grandfathers. Although it is possible to organize a replacement for extended family using friends and neighbors, it must be understood that to do so is to go against nature, for the institution of the grandmother, it turns out, is an evolved human adaptation and an integral part of the human reproductive strategy. You see, there is only one primate species that experiences menopause, and that's ours. Normally nature is quite reluctant to sacrifice reproductive ability, and females of other species continue to ovulate over their entire lifespan. And so there must have been evolutionary pressure for the evolution of menopause: one's own reduced fertility must have been more than made up for by the increased viability of the offspring produced by one's daughters. Massive amounts of anecdotal evidence as well as statistical results from recent research into the question indicate that this is the case: children who are brought up with the help of their grandmothers have better outcomes.

This allows us to say with some confidence that the normal pattern in human culture is an extended family encompassing at least three generations. Of course, what is normal, never mind what is ideal, is often not what results from economic and social pressures. Societies that are explicitly structured to give priority to the individual, accommodate nuclear families only grudgingly and provide little to no additional support for sustaining extended families make the ideal, or even the normal, human living arrangement into something of a challenge. But it must be understood what sort of challenge it is: it is a challenge against nature. Societies that do not nurture and support the extended family as an essential human institution, one that is older, and more valuable, in biological terms, than the individual or the state, will inevitably have worse outcomes than societies that do, and, when stressed, will be the first to fail. The reasoning behind this is straightforward: humans evolved a superior reproductive strategy involving extended families; those who follow this superior reproductive strategy thrive; those who do not follow it may thrive too, for a time, but only under ideal laboratory conditions.

For the time being those who have plenty of money, as well as those who make barely enough by working all the time and leaving no time at all for their children, have the option of hiring professional caretakers for their children: nannies, governesses and daycare specialists. This results in something the psychologist Kathy McMahon described to me in conversation as "model prisoners of war": obedient, ambivalent, alienated humans. Those who choose this method of bringing up children might as well just pay for the welfare of some anonymous orphans. The result is the same: they are paying strangers to bring up other strangers. It seems like a particularly labor-intensive way to arrange to be lonely while growing old.

The primacy of family

If the idea of the primacy of the extended family seems alien to some of us now, it should be remembered that until quite recently it was regarded as perfectly commonsense and obvious. Most countries in the world are only a few generations removed from a time when they were governed by a family: the royal family. It was indeed an extended family, which jealously guarded the purity of the bloodline and did its best to arrange marriages to create valuable alliances between royal houses and to accumulate as many titles of nobility as possible. Monarchy seems like an outdated and outmoded form of governance to us now, but de facto petty monarchs do still reappear with great regularity. In some countries the monarch is called president—president for life, and then his eldest son is elected to be the next president upon his death. Hafez and Bashar al Assad of Syria are a good example. Saddam Hussein, with his sons Uday and Qusay, might have become such a dynasty had they not been killed by the invading Americans. But monarchy is bound to recur endlessly, as long as it remains part of the set of evolved social traits of the human species. Furthermore, it is part of a cycle.

Humans tend to develop large-scale, complex societies, which then all fail. A failed society fails to maintain a psychologically healthy sense of belonging to a greater whole, which gives rise to a certain consistent syndrome, first described by Wilfred Bion in *Experiences in Groups and Other Papers*.[25] When the dominant culture fails to produce a sense of belonging, the human mind regresses to a pre-verbal state, where it is ruled by innate, subconscious impulses that are common to higher social animals. Depending on one's personality and situation, one or another of three major impulses described by Bion may come to dominate the behavior of the individual, and, in due course, the society as a whole.

When it comes to aggressive young males, the sense of disconnection produces in them a heightened sense of insecurity and anxiety, which directly affects the sympathetic nervous system. This may cause an animal to behave more aggressively, or, in the case of the human animal, to gather rocks and to find and sharpen sticks, or, technology and finances allowing, to purchase semiautomatic assault weapons and lots of ammunition. This process may then progress through several stages. The end result is the spontaneous development of a warrior mentality—a cultural universal marked by a desire to prove oneself in battle, contempt for death and a tendency toward what Emile Durkheim called "altruistic suicide."

The pattern is the same among Homeric heroes, Mongol conquerers, Japanese samurai, European knights of the age of chivalry and Moscow's bandits and racketeers during the violent 1990s. Meaning is created out of meaninglessness through heroic acts of violence performed in keeping with a code of honor. Inclusion in the elite group is achieved via violent rites of passage and creates group loyalty and a sense of belonging. The gun cult in the United States is a strong precursor to this development, and the sporadic shooting sprees are its individual manifestations. This tendency may develop to the point of becoming a mass phenomenon. If it does, it will annihilate the current ruling class and the process of aristocratic formation will begin anew.

Another subconscious impulse takes over the minds of those who feel themselves to be weak and vulnerable. Here the subconscious urge is an infantile desire to find and cling to a strong, lord-like father figure. In the United States, this impulse finds its expression in widespread adherence to organized religion with its invisible yet omnipotent leader. The illusion of serving the leader, together with the conviction that all that happens is in accordance with his inscrutable will, helps to reduce the anxiety that is born of helplessness and alienation. Rhetorical or physical attacks on those who refuse to follow one's chosen divine leader offer a way to exclude those who do not belong, and to create a sense of solidarity, loyalty and belonging.

Lastly, there is a third subconscious impulse that has its roots in primate psychology, one that predominantly affects women: the impulse to ingratiate oneself into an imaginary group of superior individuals as a beta-female (or, in particularly sad cases, as a beta-male) in order to gain a sense of belonging. It manifests itself in the expectation of the emergence of something wonderful yet unborn, that will be the result of a successful mating between an alpha-male and an alpha-female. It finds its expression in the celebrity cult, via television programs and tabloids sold at supermarket checkout counters. Lower-class women follow with great interest the antics of the rich and famous: who is getting married, who is getting a divorce and, most importantly, who is pregnant, because, you see, one of these siliconed, Botoxed bimbos will one day give birth to our new Savior. Their sense of belonging, such as it is, comes from vicariously participating in the lives of people they consider their betters.

It is notable how smoothly the three impulses have repeatedly combined throughout history. In act one, our hero takes up arms against all who wish to oppose him and triumphs in battle; others eagerly fall in under his banner. In act two, our hero undergoes an instant and spontaneous metamorphosis from a rampaging bandit to an anointed sovereign and the people cheer and shout "Hail Caesar!" Optionally, the bandit is deified and temples are erected in his honor at great public expense. In act three, the anointed bandit takes a bride, and as they walk in procession women throw flowers at their feet and await with eager anticipation the arrival of their sacred progeny. In act four, the bandit dies and his degenerate, bickering progeny swiftly destroy the people's sense of belonging. The progeny are then butchered by the next hero/ bandit, and the cycle repeats.

What makes this cycle perpetual is that there isn't just one family, which at first produces a sense of belonging, then falls apart, goes through phases and comes back together. Rather, the family, or, in fact, many families, come together and break apart, but throughout the process they remain as families. Thus, the family can be viewed as a microcosm of society—or society as a meta-family. This line of reasoning leads to a radical conclusion: that family is society, while larger groups are illusory. At the rock bottom of human survival, there is no individual and there is no state; there is only the family, or, if there isn't, there is something that's not quite human—or there is nothing at all.

Case Study: The Ik

The story of the Ik offers us both a cautionary tale and a story of survival of an extreme kind—so extreme that it forces us to question the value of survival at any cost. Everything we know about the Ik comes from a single yet comprehensive source: the book *The Mountain People* by the British anthropologist Colin Turnbull,[26] who spent two years living among the tribe. (All page references below are to this text.) During that time, the Ik numbered some two thousand, living in the corner of northern Uganda where it borders (now South) Sudan and Kenya, in a number of small, temporary villages clustered between the Kidepo wildlife reserve and the mountains which fringe the escarpment that separates Uganda from Kenya.

While Turnbull's book found a wide readership beyond academia, his fellow-anthropologists found it extremist and biased. Bernd Heine, who observed the Ik some time later, found Turnbull's work unhelpful. Apparently, the Ik had been made aware of Turnbull's portrayal of them, and were less than pleased with it. Heine wrote that what he observed was at such variance with what Turnbull had recorded that he sometimes thought that he was "dealing with an entirely different people." So what we have here is a wonderful example of the principle of reflexivity that invalidates claims to scientificity within social sciences, from anthropology to finance—wherever the act of observing alters the behavior of the observed. Turnbull may have been biased against the Ik, but subsequent researchers dealt with Ik who were biased against Turnbull, and had modified their externally observable behavior in response to their unwelcome notoriety. Be that as it may; for my purposes Turnbull's book might as well be an impassioned work of fiction. But it is not that, for it is inconceivable that Turnbull wrote from imagination rather than from observation. To think differently is to claim that Turnbull had a very sick mind. Controversies over bias and objectivity aside, Turnbull told a unique and compelling story of cultural degeneration and biological survival.

Who are the Ik?

The Ik are rugged individualists. They are shrewd and enterprising, practical-minded and unsentimental, surviving by their luck and their wits. They inculcate the spirit of self-reliance and free enterprise into their children from a young age. They value privacy, believe strongly in private property and are scrupulous in repaying their debts. They are innovative, and augment their income by offering their neighbors a variety of products and services. They have pared down their social spending to the level of austerity required for survival. This has allowed them to survive in a situation where one would normally expect them to have gone extinct.

The Ik are a linguistic, ethnic and cultural isolate. Their language (Ichietot) is unrelated to any of the languages in the area, but is related to, of all things, classical Middle-Kingdom Egyptian. Under the permanent suntan their skin is not black, like that of the surrounding African tribes, but red. How or when a small group of Ancient Egyptians ended up in this part of East Africa is anyone's guess. For countless generations they lived as hunters and gatherers, circulating in a seasonal migration through large parts of what has since been carved up into Uganda, South Sudan and Kenya. But the place they have always considered their homeland is the escarpment. The Ik consider themselves *Kwarikik*, or "mountain people," different from the surrounding pastoralists who wander the plains with their herds, sustaining themselves on the animals' milk and blood. It is this that binds the Ik together as a people: their mountain habitat. Unlike their slow-paced, pastoralist neighbors—the Didinga, the Dodos, the Turkana—they are quick-witted, swift and agile. Their sacred source of historical identity lies within a set of caves carved into the escarpment, thousands of feet above the plateau that stretches toward Lake Rudolf in Kenya. These caves hold ritualistic objects decorated with pictograms that may be related to Egyptian hieroglyphics. (Turnbull stumbled upon them during a short follow-up visit, and was unable to pursue their detailed study.) The identity of the Ik is bound tightly to their inhospitable, mountainous homeland, and in Turnbull's estimation they would rather starve and die of thirst than abandon it. But everything else, as he soon found out, had become negotiable.

The Ik are a post-collapse society par excellence. They were once a carefree band of hunter-gatherers, and their former happiness could still be glimpsed among the Ik who temporarily wandered away from their homeland and crossed the unguarded border into Sudan, where they could resume hunting, although at considerable risk from the hostile Sudanese Arabs. (Perhaps now that South Sudan is independent and Arab-free they will be able to stage a comeback.) Disaster struck in 1958 when the British colonial government declared their main hunting ground of Kidepo Valley off-limits to them. After Ugandan independence, it was designated Kidepo Valley National Park, and got its very own police post. The police were armed with rifles and ordered to shoot any Ik they saw "poaching" in the park (trying to feed their families by hunting). The Ik were told to farm, but not anywhere near the park (where the police sent to guard them grew their plentiful crops) but high on steep, barren mountainsides. The result was intermittent famine.

It was the intermittency of the famine, combined with the certainty of its recurrence every three or four years, that progressively stripped away layers of Ik culture. The effects were plain to see even in their language, which lost all of its pleasantries and niceties, echoes of which Turnbull was able to discern. The most common Ichietot greeting became *"Brinji ngag!"* — "Give me food!" — with the standard reply *"Bera ngag!"* — "There is no food!" — followed closely by *"Brinji lotop!"* — "Give me tobacco!" tobacco being an effective palliative for hunger pains.

It is certainly questionable from a public policy perspective to put the interests of animals ahead of those of people who have been living in balance with these same animals since time immemorial without increasing in population or damaging the environment. These people now "sit in clusters and gaze over their former hunting territory, now a national park, and wonder at those who ordain that animals shall be preserved while humans die."[27] Nor is it particularly helpful that the internationally recognized borders between newly stillborn post-colonial nations carved up what up until then was a contiguous hunting range. "Mobility is essential to the hunting-and-gathering way of life, and nomadism is by no means the random, aimless meandering it is sometimes thought to be."[28] Hunter-gatherers like the Ik used to be the ultimate conservationists: "To overhunt is considered one of the major crimes, in the nature of a sin against divine command...."[29]

Nomadic mobility is important for more than just avoiding over-hunting or overharvesting in any one place: it also allows for realignment of human relationships and dissipation of conflicts before they can fully develop. Mobility provides for a constantly shifting locus of authority, making any movement toward authoritarianism impossible and preserving egalitarianism, cooperation and equality between men and women. The vegetables and grains gathered by women are just as important as the game hunted by men. Although men primarily hunt and women primarily gather, the two groups cooperate in setting up nets to catch game and beating the bushes to flush it out.

As nomadic hunter-gatherers, the Ik formed a fluid society, and their family structure reflected this same fluidity and freedom. To them, their family was primarily their community of residence. Kinship terms applied to present lines of responsibility and friendship, not lines of descent. Any adult was regarded as a parent, and any age-mate as a sibling. The downside of such a social attitude toward kinship based on freedom of movement is that, as soon as freedom of movement is taken away, family ceases to exist.

The list of basic human virtues, such as kindness, generosity, consideration, affection, honesty, hospitality, compassion and charity—for the hunter-gatherer these are not so much virtues as necessities for group cohesion, for there is nothing else to hold the hunting band together. Are these virtues superficial luxuries that one can afford during a time of plenty, or are they merely mechanisms for survival and security? As the experience of the Ik shows us, in times of extreme hardship, when there simply isn't enough to go around, such virtues must fall by the wayside, because the alternative is certain disaster, ruin and extinction.

The Ik probably had little or no experience of such extreme hardship while they remained on the move, taking only as much as they needed and moving on when conditions changed. "For the farmer the results of a year's worth of work may be destroyed overnight, whereas the most the hunter can lose is what he can replace tomorrow. Partly for this reason there tends to be little fear of supernatural malevolence among hunters; they live an open life untroubled by the various neuroses that accompany progress."[30] But this good life came to an abrupt end, and the effect on Ik culture was devastating. "The Ik, like all hunters, must have been as much a part of their natural world as the mountains and the winds and rains and the very game they hunted and wild fruits they gathered.... But when they were imprisoned in one tiny corner, the world became something cruel and hostile, and in their lives *cruelty took the place of love*" (my italics).[31] And yet they did not perish.

The aftermath of social collapse

The Ugandan officials and police who were responsible for coercing the Ik into their settled state described them as "troublesome, dishonest, elusive, tricky." All of the above terms seem apt, for the Ik came to practice lying and deceit as a sort of competitive sport, telling the truth only after succeeding at having someone accept a lie. Among the Ik, honesty comes down to making a dishonest effort to mislead: "While they still retain the quaint old-fashioned notion that man should share with his fellows, they place individual good above all else and almost demand that each get away with as much as he can without his fellows knowing."[32] Since you cannot possibly think that you own something if you do not know that it exists, the Ik make every effort to limit access to valid information by hiding things or by providing invalid information as a smokescreen. Ik village compounds consist of concentric circles of stockades penetrated by small and cryptic openings, and are designed not so much as a defense against an outside enemy as a defense against one's closest neighbors, who are the closest specifically because one trusts them the least and wishes to keep an eye on them at all times.

Turnbull describes the Ik as psychologically normal, socialized, well-adjusted individuals, not the least bit suicidal, and with a sense of humor that could, given their dire circumstances, be described as healthy. The Ik have taken *Schadenfreude* (German for "joy from someone else's misfortune") and improved on it, turning it into, to coin a term, *Selbstschadenfreude* (joy from one's own misfortune). "I think it was the laughter that disturbed me the most, and an indefinable absence of something that should have been there, perhaps in its place. Sitting at a *di* [an outcropping with a commanding view next to a village], for instance, men would watch a child with eager anticipation as it crawled toward a fire, then burst into gay and happy laughter as it plunged a skinny hand into the coals. Such times were the few times when parental affection showed itself; a mother would glow with pleasure to hear such joy occasioned by her offspring, and pull it tenderly out of the fire."[33] On another occasion, a blind Ik man was trampled underfoot while trying to reach a hyena carcass to scavenge some rancid meat—a situation he himself found absolutely hilarious.

Aside from such special moments of gruesome hilarity, Turbull found it difficult to detect any emotion among the Ik. When it was expressed, it took the form of artifice, its exact form depending on the immediate circumstances, and in relation only to the good of the self. The Ik are "temperless, cold-bloodedly surviving without wishing anyone else any harm or good."[34] To the Ik, good equals food. A good man is one who has a full stomach. There is no longer any such concept as *doing good*, there is only *being good*—specifically, being good and fat.

The Ik are a dismal failure at putting by and saving for a rainy day; their only savings are in the form of body fat. To this they take with great gusto, gobbling up any food that comes their way. This behavior is not unreasonable, given how uncertain their food supply is, and how limited their options for storing it. They are expected to farm, but one year out of four is a total drought, while in better years one field or another might produce something. Two drought years in a row spell famine, which no amount of preparation can avoid. Consequently, the Ik never count on producing a harvest and expend their energies accordingly.

Since the Ik are often on the verge of starvation, they are always on the lookout for more food, even during times of plenty when they are so full of food that they can hardly walk. Ik social occasions, normally held at the *di*, are usually silent affairs. Everyone sits scanning the countryside for any sign of death, which might promise food: a vulture dropping down and narrowing its circles or the smoke of a clandestine cooking fire after a successful poaching expedition. At the first sign of death, some number of people jump up and race off downhill in search of food.

Those who go out poaching share the kill with those who participate in the hunt, as well as those who find out about it and simply show
up, but they do not share the bounty with anyone else, even with their
own families. As a vestige of an old moral code, the Ik will offer food
if surprised while eating, and so they do their best to eat alone and in
secret, cooking meat as quickly as possible and wolfing it down quickly.
The men hunt and the women gather alone, and they eat separately and
away from their homes, to avoid having to share. The children learn to
feed themselves by watching the baboons and picking up the dates they
drop half-eaten. The old, their ability to find food dwindling over time,
slowly starve. There was starvation, even during times of plenty, but it
was confined exclusively to the aged.

Better living through mischief

With their old hunting grounds taken away from them, their movements restricted, and agriculture virtually impossible, the Ik were
forced to innovate, and hit upon the fruitful idea of encouraging, aiding
and abetting cattle raiding among the neighboring tribes. Their makeshift villages were strategically repositioned to allow the Ik to survey
all passes and approaches, giving them unique knowledge of the movements of the nomadic herders and their herds. They then sold this information to raiding parties in exchange for a share of the winnings.
Although they never kept cattle, their compounds often included a
boma—a stockaded area for hiding cattle away from prying eyes, where
the raiders could temporarily hide a herd. The Ik often poached and ate
some of the cattle entrusted to their care (something that is taboo for
the pastoral tribes, who do not slaughter except as part of a religious
ritual), then claim that the cattle died of natural causes.

Most of the cattle raiding episodes in the region were between
two tribes: the Turkana and the Dodos. The Turkana crossed the border from Kenya whenever their homeland was hit by drought. They
brought with them plentiful rifles and ammunition, but never fired
any weapons, watering their herds at watering holes owned by the Ik
and grazing their cattle in Kidepo park while the Ugandan police, out-
numbered and outgunned, looked on helplessly and did their level best
to keep their superiors in the dark. The Dodos avoided direct conflict
with the Turkana, but, just like the Turkana, took any opportunity to
abscond with the other tribe's herd. In doing so, both sides were aided

by the Ik, who were always forthcoming with intelligence and weapons. In spite of government prohibitions, the Ik made spears and knives with which they furnished the two tribes, often at the same time. Ik villages would split up according to which tribe they were aiding at any given time. The Ik are skilled blacksmiths, making charcoal and forging iron weapons using stone tools. This was one of the few activities in which the Ik cooperated (building houses and stockades was another) but even here they stayed aloof, concentrating on the work while avoiding communication and eye contact.

What holds a failed society together?

Other than their strong connection to the mountains that are their homeland, what bound the Ik together is a bit of a puzzle. Was it taking comfort in shared misery? Or was it the need to constantly spy on each other out of mutual mistrust? Turnbull eventually found the answer: "the only motive for working in company...was the pleasurable prospect of being able to enjoy someone else's misfortune."[35] The key element motivating cooperation among the Ik was *Schadenfreude*. Aside from the joy occasioned by someone's failure, during cooperative ventures such as poaching or gathering food or building materials, the operative forces were acrimony, envy and suspicion. "Economic interest is centered on as many individual stomachs as there are people, and cooperation is merely a device for furthering an interest that is consciously selfish."[36] Nor is there any trace of tribal solidarity in conflicts involving outsiders; in intertribal disputes, the Ik are very quick and eager to turn on their own. Such disputes are always settled locally, without involving any higher authorities.

The strongest form of contract among the Ik is *nyot*—an indissoluble lifelong vow of mutual assistance and aid with no right of refusal. It is entered into via a verbal agreement and an informal exchange of gifts, and is a common way of settling disputes. But as in all other instances, the Ik do their best to lie to their *nyot* about what they possess, to avoid having to share it.

There are instances where the Ik appeal to each other, as a group, to settle a dispute. In such cases, the judgment of the group is based "not so much on the nature of the action in question as to the circumstances in which the action took place."[37] Even in rendering justice, the Ik are guided first and foremost by their individual selfish interests. But the

most common way of settling disputes among the Ik is through voluntary relocation—to another village. Ik villages generally only last three,
at most four years, being rather shabbily put together and over time
becoming surrounded by a ring of human feces and infested with vermin throughout:"Roofs were alive with insects, including a particularly
unpleasant-looking white cockroach, and at night when sleeping skins
were taken out and unrolled, it was easy to hear the hiss and rustle
of the lice and roaches and heaven knows what else so disturbed."[38]
In making their living arrangements temporary, the Ik gave themselves
sufficiently frequent opportunities to start over, regroup and part ways
with their loathsome neighbors, human and otherwise.

Gathering building materials and constructing stockades and
houses were the activities in which the Ik came closest to something resembling communal labor, but this was only in appearance. In fact, the
institutions of gift and sacrifice were never used altruistically among
the Ik, but only as a means to build up obligations—which could then
be recalled as needed. The obligation incurred by receiving a gift could
be thwarted by its nonacceptance, and a great deal of ingenuity went
into engineering such situations, in order to benefit from a gift while
avoiding obligation. One effective but unpopular trick was to discharge
the obligation immediately, by offering food, which the Ik are incapable
of resisting.

Put out at age three

We might naively assume that the Ik must, at a minimum, show some
amount of altruism, albeit of a biologically motivated, ultimately selfish sort, with regard to their own children; if so, we would be disappointed. Ik mothers grudgingly take care of their children, toting them
around in a sling, breast-feeding them, handling them none too gently
and laughing at them if they cry. They put them down on the ground
while gathering food and are delighted if a leopard carries them off,
because then they can go and hunt down and eat the satiated leopard
sleeping off a big meal. Even this not particularly nurturing relationship is soon broken off:"children are not allowed to sleep in the house
after they are 'put out,' which is at three years old, four at the latest."[39]
Needless to say, this does not endear children to their parents. Rather,
it makes them quite happy to later see their aged parents slowly starve
to death.

Once "put out," a child has no chance of surviving alone and is forced to join a group of children roaming the mountainsides together in search of anything edible. There are two age bands: the junior (three to seven) and the senior (eight to twelve). The two bands do their best to avoid each other when foraging; more precisely, the junior band avoids the senior band, because an encounter normally leads to the seniors confiscating any food the juniors have gathered, accompanied by a beating. Even so, the older children seem to steal from the younger ones quite relentlessly, so the younger children do their best to avoid being caught out alone. Turnbull recounts one instance when an older brother snatched away from his younger sister a bag of charcoal that she had spent two days making, planning to exchange it for a bowl of porridge at the police station, beating her in the process. He found the situation quite funny; she not as much, perhaps because her Ik sense of *Selbstschadenfreude* was not yet fully developed.

Initiation into an age band and subsequent expulsion from it are the major rites of passage; both involve bullying. A child joins an age band as its youngest, weakest and most useless member, and is beaten on by the rest of the age band, but, having no choice, remains within it. Expulsion occurs when the oldest and strongest member of an age band is suddenly ganged up on by the rest of the age band and, having no choice, is forced to depart. The relationships within each age band are based on limited competition, maximizing individual benefit without detriment to others. Within an age band, a child forms temporary friendships whose inevitable destruction is a rite of passage in itself, teaching a young Ik the value of friendship. In Ichietot, the word for friend (*bam*) seems to carry an overtone of mockery.

All children play, but with Ik children nearly all of their games concern either food or sex. The younger children made mud pies, decorated them with pebbles—and then ate them. The older children hunted the smaller and weaker children with play spears and slingshots. In the older age band, sexual interest also played a part, and younger members won friends by offering sexual favors to older ones.

There no longer appear to be any rites of passage among the Ik beyond expulsion from the senior age band. The institution of marriage, which did once exist among the Ik, was via a very early tradition: marriage by capture. The young bride would venture outside the stockade at night to defecate, at which point she would be kidnapped by her groom and his accomplices and dragged to the groom's village. If she only whimpered, then her family would give a perfunctory chase, but if she screamed, they would be compelled to give battle and try to win her back. Certain taboos were observed: against drawing blood, and against visiting one's in-laws. But there were no marriages during the two years Turnbull spent with the Ik.

Instead, Ik girls, once they were expelled from the senior age band, universally turned to prostitution, finding their clients both among the Ik and the visiting cattle herders. Their professional careers were rather short, and they were abandoned to their fate after age eighteen, at which point they were no longer regarded as attractive. In another rare instance of cooperation, Ik girls joined forces to "go courting" to the herders' camps in groups of two. They found the work of prostitution rather boring, but group sex made it more entertaining and provided welcome opportunities for *Schadenfreude*. Beyond such casual encounters, there was a more institutionalized form of sexual relationship: Ik women were regarded as valuable commodities and were bartered as "wives" to visitors from other tribes. They exhibited their status by wearing a certain necklace—one for each such "marriage." Some Ik girls were "almost choked by such necklaces."[40]

Ik men valued their wives in other ways. A village elder sold the medicine he received for his sick wife, and when she died he buried her in secret within the walls of his compound, to avoid having to hold a funeral feast for the neighbors, but more importantly in order to continue receiving the medicine. When this was later discovered, he showed no trace of shame: "She was worth far more to him dead than alive."[41] Later, he went on to receive government famine relief on her behalf, which he, of course, ate himself. This, according to the values of the Ik, made him a fatter, and therefore a better, man.

In the past, the Ik had the institution of divorce. Divorce proceedings were initiated via ritualistic wife-beating with a thorny bush. There is a taboo among the Ik for drawing blood, so once blood was drawn, the marriage was dissolved and the wife returned to her own family's compound, to sleep on the ground outside the hut. There was also a taboo against visits from in-laws, which was quite useful in avoiding further conflict in case of separation or divorce. But by the time of Turnbull's visit divorces had become casual and informal and took the form of simple, unannounced abandonment by one spouse or the other.

It is remarkable that none of the above types of behavior had any repercussions. We would not expect hunter-gatherers to have a complex system of statutory and case law, but in the old days the Ik did stand united in defense of basic morality. They punished murder, incest and adultery by throwing the offender on a burning pyre, thus cleverly avoiding having to violate the taboo against drawing blood. But by the time Turnbull saw them, he found that "the almost universal practice of adultery was in a sense designed, or functioned, to complete the destruction of that useless and nonfunctional unit, the family."[42] According to his observations, most sexual activity among the Ik was of two kinds: masturbation and adultery.

For Ik men, seeking sexual relief through copulation was complicated by the fact that all Ik women required payment for sex, of food and possibly of money as well, and most Ik men had neither. In addition, it was their considered opinion that masturbation takes less energy, leaving more energy for looking for food. But as time, and famine, wore on, they were finding less and less energy for any sexual activity at all. Turnbull guessed that they regarded defecation and ejaculation with the same casual indifference—a question of ejecting some waste matter.

Considering the above, Turnbull comes to a provocative conclusion: "The Ik seem to tell us that the family is not such a fundamental unit as we usually suppose, that it is not an essential prerequisite for social life except in the biological context."[43] Within that very limited biological context, "the ideal family, economically speaking and within restricted temporal limitations, is a man and his wife and no children."[44] Why no children? "The children were as useless as the aged, or nearly so; as long as you keep the breeding group alive you can always get more children. So let the old [die] first, then the children. Anything else is racial suicide, and the Ik, I almost regret to say, are anything but suicidal."[45]

Further, this lack of family life was necessary because "there simply was not room, in the life of these people, for such luxuries as family and sentiment and love. So close to the verge of starvation, such luxuries could mean death, and is it not a singularly foolish luxury to die for someone already dead, or weak or old? This seemed to strike hard at the assumption that there are such things as basic human values, at the very notion of virtue, of goodness even."[46] The Ik force us to question what it means to be human, and the answer they offer is one that few of us like to hear: that being human is a luxury, not a necessity. But it is worse yet: when we cease to be human, we do not become animals. The Ik, degraded as their culture had become, still spoke Ichietot. They could reason about cause and effect, they had descriptive and narrative memory and communication, and they had the use of tools. This put them far ahead of other animals. When humans cease to be human, they do not become animals—they become cogs within a subhuman biological machine. Individually they are not to blame, for the potential for such inhumanity is present in every one of us. But basic human survival tactics make lesser animals seem more human in comparison.

"Kill them all!"

It is quite rare to have an anthropologist spend two years living with and studying an interesting and unique tribe, then come out of the bush and declare that this tribe should be killed with fire. Well, Colin Turnbull did not quite say that, but he did write a report recommending that the Ik be broken up into small groups and resettled in various places in Uganda far away from their homeland. But since, as he himself wrote, the Ik would rather starve and die of thirst than abandon their homeland, such a relocation would be equivalent to a death sentence. In any case, his prescription was ignored. I would guess that his colleagues and Ugandan officials suspected that Turnbull had been traumatized by his experience with the Ik. Like Kurtz in Joseph Conrad's *Heart of Darkness*, his methods were probably thought to have been unsound. And yet nobody else was in a position to make such incisive observations and to reach such damning conclusions about the Ik as he was.

But Turnbull went further. He pointed out that all of us have a bit of the Ik within us, as a potentiality, and observed that people in the developed world are becoming more Ik-like: "if any persist in feeling that I am overly pessimistic in my interpretation of the facts, there can be no mistaking the direction in which these facts point, and that is the most important thing of all, for it may affect the rest of mankind as it has affected the Ik.... [T]he symptoms of change in our own society indicate that we are heading precisely in the same direction."[47] "The Ik teach us that our much vaunted human values are not inherent in humanity at all, but are associated only with a particular form of survival called society, and that all, even society itself, are luxuries that can be dispensed with."[48]

Given the nature of his experience, Turnbull was forced to act not as an impartial, detached observer, but as a participant, for it was his own humanity that was on trial while he was living among the slowly starving Ik. He tried to care for them, only to realize that caring for people who are just days away from death serves no purpose but to remind them of a better time, a time when they cared for each other, and that this did not alleviate but exacerbated their suffering. In that situation, love equalled pain, and this realization forced him to acquiesce in his own hypocrisy: "At the time I was sure we were right, doing the only 'human' thing. In a way we were—we were making life more comfortable for ourselves, confirming our own sense of superiority."[49] He watched as humanity ebbed away, theirs and his, and even made a note of "the last Ik who was human."[50] She preferred being locked up in a Ugandan jail cell to the company of her own people, and upon release she immediately attacked a policeman in order to be locked up again.

Wouldn't it be nice if we could treat the story of the Ik as just a cautionary tale—something to carefully avoid—if it is at all avoidable, even at all costs, perhaps? But what if the Ik simply happen, as a result of circumstances beyond anyone's control? What if they represent a sort of perfection? What if we can perfect the system created by the Ik, and create an even better system of mere survival, one that treats each and every one of us "as individuals with one basic right, the right to survive, so that man becomes the perfect vegetable, no longer an animal, human or otherwise?"[51] The Ik seem to demonstrate quite conclusively that this is in fact possible: "the Ik show that man can do without society... for they have replaced human society with a mere survival system that does not take human emotion into account."[52]

Here is the ethical dilemma with which you and I must come to terms: is there value in preserving the lives of 6,973,738,433-and-counting humans alive on the planet as I write this—if to do so we must become like the Ik, or is it better for as many of us as necessary to die for the sake of preserving the culture that makes us human? Turnbull sees no value in such hollow, machine-like survival: "if there is no goodness...there is no badness, and if there is no love, neither is there any hate. Perhaps that, after all, is progress; but it is also emptiness."[53] The choice is a hard one, and wouldn't it be nice if, when the time came, merciful death descended upon us like heavenly grace? For the Ik, that time may not be far: "Luckily the Ik are not numerous—about two thousand—and those two years reduced their numbers greatly. So I am hopeful that their isolation will remain as complete as in the past, until they die out completely."[54] And should we be as hopeful for ourselves as Turnbull is for the Ik? Perhaps we already are, since "we say to ourselves that extermination will not come in our time, which shows about as much sense of family devotion as one might expect from the Ik, and as little sense of social responsibility."[55]

How do we know when we have become like the Ik? Or has this already happened, but we are so prosperous we can afford to hide the fact? Westerners do not "turn out" their children at age three—we send them to daycare and kindergarten. "We have shifted the responsibility from family to the state, the Ik have shifted it to the individual."[56] The Ik let their old people starve, while ours are fed, or are allowed to slowly starve in solitude, by the state. But take away the state, and what do we have? Is our intergenerational contract still intact or has our society "become a game that we play in our old age, to remind us of our child-hood?"[57]

The key to remaining human is in perpetuating the human life cycle, which involves children and grandparents: "the very young and the very old share one great belief in common, a belief in continuity, and a hope that is a hope for the past just as it is a hope for the future." With the Ik, this cycle has been broken: "Every one of the Ik who is old today was thrown out at three," breaking the link. "The system has turned one full cycle and is now self-perpetuating; it has eradicated what we know as 'humanity' and has turned the world into a chilly void where man does not even seem to care for himself but survives."[58]

If we say that we will not allow ourselves to become like the Ik, what exactly do we mean? Western society is able to "maintain order only through the existence of the coercive power that is ready to uphold the law, and by an equally rigid penal system."[59] The Ik, on the other hand, "have come to a recognition of what they accept as man's basic selfish-ness, of his natural determination to survive as individual before all else. This they consider to be man's basic right, and at least have the decency to allow others to pursue that right to the best of their ability without recrimination or blame."[60]

The state prevents us from becoming like the Ik, but what if the state fails or dissolves? What saves us then—love, perhaps? "The Ik offer us an opportunity for testing this cherished notion that love is essential to survival,"[61] says Turnbull. He went looking for love among the Ik and failed to find any trace of it: "if [love] was not among the Ik, it meant that, be it luxury or illusion, mankind can lose it, and that the very conditions pertaining in the Western world today are those that might make such a loss not only possible but inevitable; the process has already begun."[62]

Let us conclude then: we can survive cultural collapse, and the Ik show us how it can be done. Put their experience in your survivors' toolbox if you like, or just let events take their course. But as their experience shows, this sort of survival may be a fate worse than extinction. There can be no such thing as survival at all costs: whether you live or die, you pay with your life.

Afterword

Now that you have completed the arduous journey of reading this book, what are your "next steps"? By now you must have noticed that this is not a "We must..." book or an "Unless we..." book, or even a "We should..." book. There is no agenda here—just the assumption that collapse will happen, the conjecture that it can be analyzed as un-folding in five distinct phases and, based on quite a bit of research, the conclusion that each phase will require a different set of adaptations from those who wish to survive it.

This book is one long challenge to most of the notions we received as part of our schooling and socialization. To start with, it questions what being properly socialized means: is it being able to ignore the ob-vious signs of incipient collapse that makes you a well-socialized indi-vidual? It questions what being financially secure means: do numbers on pieces of paper handed to you by strangers make you feel safer than you should feel? It questions what participating in the economy means: is doing business with strangers you don't trust such a wonderful idea? It questions what being a patriot means: are a flag, an anthem and a few creation myths enough to tell you who your people are—the ones who are willing to die for you, and you for them? It questions what being part of society means: are you all fair-weather friends? Is society a game you play when you have the luxury of doing so? It even questions what it means to be human: how degraded does culture have to become to turn us into something significantly worse than animals?

Along the way, I introduced you to a cast of characters you would not normally meet. You met the Icelandic politician who declared that finance is politics, and who boosted economic growth and national competitiveness by destroying financial companies to free up skilled labor. You heard the story of the Russian mafia, with a happy end in which the Russian state turned out to be the best protection racket of them all. You met the Pashtun tribesmen, whose infallible sense of virtue makes them stick in the throat of any imperialist invader until he chokes to death. You met the Gypsies, with their ancient yet intact nomadic separatist identity and their exquisitely honed sense of the possible, anchored within a lifestyle that is non-negotiable. Lastly, you encountered the Ik, who force us to confront the uncomfortable notion that survival at all costs may be a fate worse than death. With the exception of the Icelanders, none of these, I would venture to guess, are people you would invite over for cocktails and hors d'oeuvres, hoping to pick up some hot tips on surviving collapse. Nor are you likely to tell your colleagues about the wonderful survival tips you picked up from a Russian mafioso, a member of the Taliban, a Gypsy or an Ik while standing around the coffee machine at the office. If you do, you will probably find that a thorough understanding of collapse is not helpful in ingratiating yourself into pre-collapse society.

If enough of the ideas in this book resonate with you and you absorb some of them, you may find yourself developing a secret post-collapse identity of sorts, like the internal identity of the Gypsies. You may turn into something of a social separatist, a bit like a Roma woman whose real name is Zemfira but who calls herself Cathy Smith when dealing with Gadje and who graciously accepts a gift of cupcakes from her Gadjo neighbors only to throw them in the nearest trash can, to avoid contaminating her household. Sometimes your secret identity might leak out. You might surprise a telemarketer by telling her that you can't do business with her because you don't know her personally. Or you might astonish a political campaign worker by telling him that you'd rather not vote for any American politicians because…you know what they are all like! Things will get really interesting if you ever run across somebody who knows what you know and is on the same wavelength. Should you automatically trust someone just because they have read their Orlov? You shouldn't. Trust is built on actions, not words.

But then why should you trust me? I can only assure you that I did not knowingly invent any facts and was reasonably careful in doing my research; but those are just words. The correct answer is that you should think for yourself, act on your thoughts and, if that works for you, learn to trust yourself. All I want to do is give you a gentle nudge in that direction. If this takes you far enough, you will become what is, in the eyes of politicians and educationalists—all those who wish to put specific thoughts in our heads—someone rare and dangerous: a person capable of independent thought. Along the way you will no doubt realize that you must keep your new powers secret from those you don't trust.

It would, I think, be helpful if more people internalized the message of this book and acted on it to the greatest extent possible. (From a purely self-interested perspective, moving forward, such people would make better neighbors.) But I am willing to set my sights much lower—even if most readers take this book as little more than a curious collection of opinion pieces, one idea might still rub off on them: that collapse is not a nightmare scenario to be avoided at all costs but part of the normal, unalterable ebb and flow of human history, and that the widespread tendency to block it out of our worldview is, to put it very mildly, maladaptive. Based on the feedback I've been receiving, this book might help a few people a whole lot; but I hope that it will also help a great many people just a little.

Because that's why I wrote it: to be of help. This book exists for one reason only: people have been asking for it. When I published my first article on the subject of collapse some six years ago, I never imagined that I was kick-starting an active (if nonrenumerative) career writing and speaking on the subject—yet, to my family's chagrin, that is precisely what has happened. Stopping, beyond a certain point, would have disappointed far too many people. But frankly, I prefer writing about sailboats, seafaring families, battling nature and technology, coastal redevelopment (houses will need to float, you know), perhaps with a bit of social commentary thrown in here and there, mostly focusing on funny things happening to happy people in idyllic settings: at anchor in a turquoise lagoon teeming with lunch and fringed by white sand and palm trees...anchor gets stuck in a coral head...hilarity ensues...you get the picture! As you might imagine, most books on such topics sell quite a lot better than the most fantastically excellent books on collapse. What, you might ask, has been keeping me from that other writing career? It is you; I wrote this book for you, so be grateful. And if you didn't like it, just wait for my next one; it will have hot salty breezes in it, and flying fish and coconuts, and the only things that will collapse will be iridescent, frothy waves on a sandy beach. Perhaps you will like that book better. Let's make one thing clear: there better be life after collapse, both for you and for me.

Endnotes

1. Richard Heinberg, *Peak Everything: Waking Up to the Century of Declines*, New Society Publishers, 2007.
2. Christopher O. Clugson, *Scarcity: Humanity's Final Chapter*, Booklocker. com, 2012.
3. Donella H. Meadows, Jorgen Randers, Dennis L. Meadows, *Limits to Growth: the 30-Year Update*, Chelsea Green, 2004.
4. Lucius Anneaus Seneca, *Letters to Lucilius*, n. 91.
5. Nassim Nicholas Taleb, *The Black Swan: the Impact of the Highly Improbable*, Random House, 2007, updated dediton 2010.
6. James Howard Kunstler, *The Long Emergency: Surviving the End of Oil, Climate Change, and Other Converging Catastrophes of the Twenty-First Century*, Grove Press, 2006.
7. Joseph Tainter, *The Collapse of Complex Societies*, Cambridge University Press, 1990.
8. Susan George, *Whose Crisis, Whose Future?*, Polity, 2010, p. 19.
9. David Korowicz, *Trade-Off*, p. 61. feasta.org/wp-content/uploads/2012/06 /Trade-Off1.pdf
10. Definition from Wikipedia, see en.wikipedia.org/wiki/Steganography
11. Michael Shuman, *Local Dollars, Local Sense*, Chelsea Green, 2012.
12. This and other quotes are from Adam Taylor's interview with Grímsson for *Business Insider*, published Apr. 15, 2012; see businessinsider.com/olafur-rag nar-grmsson-iceland-icesave-uk-banks- europe-2012-4
13. Volkov, Vadim, *Violent Entrepreneurs: The Use of Force in the Making of Russian Capitalism*, Cornell University Press, 2002, p. 17.
14. Ibid, p. 18.
15. Ibid, p. 15.
16. Ibid, p. 13.
17. Ibid, p. x.
18. Ibid, p. 35.
19. Ibid, p. 30.
20. Ibid, p. 28.
21. Ibid, p. xii.
22. Ibid, p. 22.
23. Frederico Varese, *The Russian Mafia: Private Protection in a New Market Economy*, Oxford University Press, 2001, p. 1.

24. Reprinted in 2012 by British publisher Green Books.
25. Basic Books, 1961.
26. Colin Turnbull, *The Mountain People*, Simon and Schuster, 1987.
27. Ibid, p. 123.
28. Ibid, p. 21.
29. Ibid, p. 25.
30. Ibid, p. 24.
31. Ibid, p. 259.
32. Ibid, p. 101.
33. Ibid, p. 112.
34. Ibid, p. 231.
35. Ibid, p. 241.
36. Ibid, p. 157.
37. Ibid, p. 155.
38. Ibid, p. 199.
39. Ibid, p. 121.
40. Ibid, p. 106.
41. Ibid, p. 86.
42. Ibid, p. 181.
43. Ibid, p. 133.
44. Ibid, p. 134.
45. Ibid, p. 131.
46. Ibid, p. 130.
47. Ibid, p. 289.
48. Ibid, p. 294.
49. Ibid, p. 228.
50. Ibid, p. 271.
51. Ibid, p. 290.
52. Ibid, p. 290.
53. Ibid, p. 286.
54. Ibid, p. 285.
55. Ibid, p. 293.
56. Ibid, p. 235.
57. Ibid, p. 291.
58. Ibid, p. 233.
59. Ibid, p. 182.
60. Ibid, p. 182.
61. Ibid, p. 236.
62. Ibid, p. 238.

Bibliography

Brooker, Paul, *Modern Stateless Warfare*, Macmillan, 2010

Clunan, Anne L. and Trinkunas, Harold A., eds., *Ungoverned Spaces: Alternatives to State Authority in an Era of Softened Sovereignty*, Stanford University Press, 2010

Durkheim, Emile, *Suicide*, Free Press: New York, 1966

George, Susan, *Whose Crisis? Whose Future?* Polity Press, 2010

Glass, James M., *Psychosis and Power: Threats to Democracy in the Self and the Group*, Cornell U. P., 1995

Hancock, Ian, *Danger! Educated Gypsy*, University of Hertfordshire Press, 2010

Hayek, Friedrich, *Denationalization of Money*, mises.org/books/denationalisation.pdf (accessed March 6, 2013)

Horsman, Matthew and Marshall, Andrew, *After the Nation-State*, Harper Collins, London, 1994

Kagarlitsky, Boris, *Empire of the Periphery: Russia and the World System*, Pluto Press, 2008

Kagarlitsky, Boris, *The Revolt of the Middle Class*, Cultural Revolution, Moscow, 2006

Kizilov, Valerii and Sapov, Grigorii, *Inflation and Its Consequences*, Panorama, Moscow, 2006

Kohr, Leopold, *The Breakdown of Nations*, Chelsea Green Publishing Company, July 2001

Koonings, Kees & Kruijt, Dirk, eds., *Armed Actors: Organized Violence and State Failure in Latin America*, Zed Press, 2005

Kristeva, J., *Nations without Nationalism*, Columbia UP, New York, 1993

Lacan, Jacques, *Language and the Self: The Function of Language in Psychoanalysis*, Johns Hopkins University Press, Baltimore, 1968

Lane, Frederic, *Profits from Power*, State U. of NY Press, Albany, 1963

Lindqvist, Sven, *Exterminate All the Brutes* (*Utrota varenda jävel*, 1992), The New Press, New York, 1997

Lutz, Chaterine ed., *The Bases of Empire: The Global Struggle against US Military Posts*, TNI, 2008

McLaughlin, John B., *Gypsy Lifestyles*, University of Illinois, Lexington Books, 1980

Meadows, Donella H., ed., *Limits to Growth*, Signet, 1972

Meadows Donella H. et al., *Limits to Growth: The 30-Year Update*, Chelsea Green, 2004

Modestov, Nikolai, *Moskva Banditskaya*, Tsentrpoligraf, Moscow, 1996

Newton, Michael, *Savage Girls and Wild Boys*, St. Martin's Press, New York, 2003

Okely, Judith, *The Traveller-Gypsies*, Cambridge University Press, 1983

Rotberg, Robert I., *When States Fail: Causes and Consequences*, Princeton University Press, 2004

Stewart, Michael, *The Time of the Gypsies*, Westview Press, 1997

Strange, Susan, *The Retreat of the State: The Diffusion of Power in the World Economy*, Cambridge University Press, 1996

Turnbull, Colin, *The Mountain People*, Simon & Schuster, 1987

Varese, Frederico, *The Russian Mafia: Private Protection in a New Market Economy*, Oxford University Press, 2001

Veseth, Michael, *Mountains of Debt*, Oxford University Press, 1990

Volkan, Vamik et al., *Psychodynamics of International Relationships*, vol. 1, Lexington Books, 1990

Volkov, Vadim, *Violent Entrepreneurs: The Use of Force in the Making of Russian Capitalism*, Cornell University Press, 2002

Index

A

Abramovich, Roman, 69
abstract markets, 90
Adams, Douglas, 204
addictions, 95
aerial attacks, 170
affection, 248
Afghanistan, 170, 174, 189, 191–193
Africa, 52
African-Americans, 168
agrammatism, 232–233
agriculture, 6
AIG, 27, 32
aircraft carriers, 171
airports, 8
al-Assad, Hafez, 160
alcohol, 37, 112, 114, 197
Alexander II, 115
Alþingi, 65, 67, 69
al-Qaeda, 65
alternative living arrangements, 208
aluminum, 7, 38, 68
Amazon, 178
ambulances, 198
Amish, 148, 206
Anabaptists, 148
anarchy, 125–139
Ancient Egyptians, 246
Android smartphones, 138
animals, 230–233
animal societies, 127–130, 133
anti-aircraft missiles, 193
anti-alcoholism campaigns, 112
anti-capitalism, 167
anti-imperialism, 189
antipodal episodes, 83–90, 102–103
anti-terrorism, 64–65

Apollo, 152
Apple computers, 138, 178, 186
arable land, 18, 31
Argentina, 76–77
aristocracies, 172
Aristotle, 74
armored cars, 47
arrest, 218
art and culture, 169
artwork, 87
Assad, Hafez and Bashar al, 241–242
assassinations, 170
assault rifles, 33
assembly work, 79, 176
asset stripping, 120
atheism, 204–205, 207–208
Athenian democracy, 191
athletes, 113–114
ATM machines, 47, 48
Austen, Jane, 95
axes, 82

B

bailouts, 26, 48, 69–70, 76, 135
Bank of Russia, 26
bankruptcy, 40, 100, 101, 166
banks: bankruptcy of, 29; branches, 47; closing of, 48; collapse of, 63–71; financing economic growth and, 29; foreign, 67, 161; fraud, 67; loans from, 19, 29; privatization of, 69; shares of, 63
barbarism, 156
Bardi, Ugo, 8
bargaining, 126
bartering: author's use of,

43–44; economic relationship hierarchy and, 86–88; preservation of society and, 31; private trading systems and, 89–90; Soviet Russia and, 98–99; strangers and, 99–100; survival through, 49; tribal lifestyles and, 83–84
bauxite, 7
Belarus, 185
belief systems, 203–208
Bell Labs, 137
belonging, sense of, 243
Berra, Yogi, 12
bicycles, 6
Big Bang Theory, 204–205
big box stores, 79
bike lanes, 197
bilinguals, 146
Bin Laden, Osama, 193
biological systems, 133–135
Bion, Wilfred, 242
birth rates, 218
black markets, 47, 198, 199
blackouts, 9, 186
Black-Scholes model, 26
blasphemy, 149
Bolsheviks, 131
bond investors, 20
bottlenecks, 8
Branch Davidian sect, 206
breast cancer, 153–155
Bregović, Goran, 216
bribery, 53, 94
bridges, 8, 169
British, 191–192
British Commonwealth, 150
Broca's aphasia, 232–233
Broken English, 236
Brown, Gordon, 64–65

BSD Unix, 184
bubble economies, 42
bulk shipping, 31–32
bullying, 254
bureaucracies, 173
burglaries, 121
Burkhart, Reed, 55
Bush, George W., 48
business owners, 119, 201
business revenues, 30–31
Byzantine coins, 36
Byzantine Orthodox, 148

C
cable news, 57
calculators, 237
call centers, 176
calligraphy, 144
campaign contributions, 180
campsites, 223
cancer, 153–155
Cape Verdean Creole, 235
capital: access to, 14; decay
    of, 8; expatriation of, 120;
    labor and, 177; shares of,
    196; universal mobility
    of, 135
capitalism, 66, 131, 166,
    167–168
captive markets, 50
carcinogens, 154
career abandonment, 2–3
careers, 10
cargo, 38, 77, 84
car registrations, 218
cars, 40, 81–82
cascaded failure, 75–78
cash, 39–40, 48
cashing out, 32–38
Catalonia, 68
catastrophic personal loss, 13
Catholic church, 137, 149, 205
cattle raiding, 251–252
cease and desist orders, 221
cell phones, 183, 184, 186
censorship, 186
central authority, 173–175, 189
central bank, 95, 101
central heating, 3–4

chainsaws, 82
chaos globalization, 137, 174
charcoal, 37
charitable donations, 100,
    208–209
charity, 196, 248
Chechen mafia, 115
Chechnya, 146
Chechnya conflict, 114–115
Chesapeake Energy, 33
Child Protective Services,
    206
children: abuse of, 3, 148;
    being "put out," 253–257;
    care of, 39; feral, 230–231;
    Ik people, 245, 251, 253–
    257; labor of, 176; lan-
    guage and, 232, 238–239;
    productivity of, 96; Roma
    people and, 216–222;
    violence and, 200
China, 157
Chinese writing system,
    143–144
chits, 46–48, 49
chlorophyll, 34
cholera, 198
Chomsky, Noam, 233
chores, 87
Christianity, 137, 147–148,
    149, 204, 215–216, 220
Christian Scientists, 206
Christmas, 203, 239
church restorations, 121
CIA, 181, 182, 193
circles of trust, 31
city-states, 150–151, 172
civil liberties, 207
clans, 84, 85–86
Clavell, James, 46
climate change, 13, 18, 164, 228
clinics, 162
Closed Border Policy, 192
closed-cycle systems, 104
cloth and fiber, 84
Clugston, Chris, 7
coal, 37, 140, 186
coal-fired steam, 75
coastal trade, 38

code of honor, 117
code-talking, 146
coinage, 51
Cold War, 44
Coliseum, 149
collapse: acceleration of,
    196; engineers of, 135;
    rate of deterioration and,
    10–12; stages of, 13–16, 31;
    taxonomy of, 13–14; as a
    transition, 14
"Collapse of Western Civili-
    zation," 13
collapse-preparedness, 14
collectibles, 87
college degrees, 10, 103
colleges, 203
Columbus, Christopher,
    83–84
commerce, 31, 105, 106, 183,
    229
commercial banks, 9
commercial collapse, 73–122;
    Greece, 9–10; occurrence
    of, 17
commercial credit, 75, 76
commercial culture, 202
commercial relationships, 58
commodities, hoarding of, 14
common identity, 172
communal necessities, 172
communes, 111, 131
communications technolo-
    gies, 168
Communism, 126, 131–132,
    156
community: activities in
    the, 201; alienation of
    a sick, 59–60; anarchy
    and, 127; choosing the
    right, 124; communism
    and, 131; family life and,
    41–42; identity of, 39;
    labor exchange in, 96–98;
    local, 173; new rules of,
    200–201; organization of,
    200; pre-collapse, 5; re-
    generation of, 201; trading
    systems of a, 46–50

community labor, 96–98
community planning,
  197–200
compassion, 91, 248
competition, 60
composting toilets, 197
computers, 237
computer technology,
  137–138, 183
confederations, 150
conflict resolution, 175,
  217–218
conformism, 5
confrontation, 219
Conrad, Joseph, 257
consciousness, 135
consideration, 248
conspiracy, 219
Constantine, Emperor, 149
construction, 96
construction sites, 77
consumerism, 14, 34, 80,
  96, 176
consumer items, 96
container shipping, 31–32,
  84
contracts, 105
contributions, 89
cooperation, 60, 92
cooperatives, 112–113
copper, 36, 38
corporatism, 156
corruption, 94–95, 109, 174
Corzine, Jon, 33
counterfeiting, 88–89
court systems, 120
CPSU, 112
creative sectors, 70–71
credit, 47, 48, 49, 75, 101, 102
credit cards, 39–40, 48
credit expansion, 18
creditors, 102
creole languages, 235–236
crime: burglaries, 121; clean
  living and, 113–114; disorganized, 121; fall in, 122;
  fighting, 124; incentives
  for, 174; market of, 102;
  money and, 53, 90;

organized, 106–109, 113;
  173; petty, 218; poverty
  and, 197–198; racketeering, 112–113; reduction of,
  197; street-, 121; thieves,
  109–112
Crimean Tartars, 89
criminal groups, 47, 57,
  107–110, 115, 116–120, 168,
  174, 199
crisis mitigation, 106
crisis task force, 48
crops, 19–20
cryptophasia, 232
cultural and historical preservation, 171
cultures: collapse and, 14, 15,
  227–260, 245–260; diversity of, 92; flips, 101–104;
  mainstream, 146–147;
  norms of, 83–90, 91
curfews, 124
currency: chits as, 46–48;
  control of, 36; denational-
  izing, 51, 165–168; foreign,
  26; Icelandic, 63; local, 101
customs duties, 69

D
Dante, 24
Darwinian evolution, 129
David and Goliath, 169–170
"Davos Class," 167, 168
daycare, 241, 259
death sentences, 111
debt: avoidance of, 41; crises,
  52; defaults in, 23–24, 29;
  expansion of, 85; growth
  of, 21; levels of, 75–76;
  as the "new normal," 100;
  perpetual, 20; printing
  money and, 166; risk of
  default, 24; risk premium,
  20, 24, 25; sovereign, 50,
  78, 178; violence used to
  collect, 121
deflation, 21, 29–31, 30, 31,
  34, 57
deforestation, 74

defunct states, proliferation
  of, 157–162
democracy, 66–67, 66–68,
  161, 175, 185
denial of collapse, 2–3
depression, 197
Deripaska, Oleg, 69
despotism, 50, 52, 67, 124–125
detachment, 5
detention, 124
development, scaling back
  of, 228
dialects, 146–147
diaspora communities, 204
dictatorship of the law, 122
dictatorships, 67, 122, 131,
  160–161
diesel, 37, 75, 80, 84
digital data, 182
disability, 126
disaster management, 196
discipline, 212
diseases, 168, 198, 228
disposable products, 84, 198
dispossession, 173
divorce, 222, 255
documentation, 218
Dodos, 251–252
donations, 89
doomstead, 196
drones, 170, 183
dropouts, 104
droughts, 18, 250
drugs, 114, 121, 168, 174, 175,
  197, 198, 200
Dudayev, Dzokhar, 116
Durkheim, Émile, 61, 242
dysentery, 198
dyslexia, 145

E
eavesdropping, 181
eBay, 167
eccentrics, 4, 5
eco-guilt, 34
economic policies, 174
economic relationship hierarchy, 86–88, 101–102
economics, 130

economies: activity of, 28–29, 174; collapse of, 103, 106; deglobalization of, 102; dislocation of, 196; disruption of, 164, 166; expansion of, 105; gift-based, 91–92; growth of, 18, 24, 29, 50, 102–103, 166, 202; illicit, 175; informal, 174, 195; insecurities and, 177; local, 101; market, 91–93; negative–of scale, 105; privatization of, 120; shrinking, 105; stagnation of, 164; steady-state, 74; underground, 198

education, 169, 171, 173, 197, 202

educationalists, 216, 218, 263

educators, 1–2, 4

efficiency, 78–83, 103

egalitarian societies, 128

Egypt, 179

elderly care, 39

elders, 41–42

electrical grid, 8, 31–32, 77, 169, 186–187, 198

emergencies, 198–199, 200–201

emigration, 29

e-money, 39

empires, 150, 189–194

employment, 43, 198

Enclosure Acts, 171

energy: access to, 124; availability of, 27; decrease in, 28–29; efficiency, 78–80, 84; expenditure of, 78–79; free, 140; in Iceland, 70; new sources of, 78; value of, 37

engineers, 1–2

English language, 143–145

enterprise control, 120

entrepreneurship, 97, 113, 168, 216–217

environment, 34, 168, 178

environmental calamity, 74

epidemics, 29

ethics, 91

ethnic designations, 117–118

ethnic groups, 146

ethnic identities, 142

ethnic mafias, 15

euro, 29, 52, 60

Euro Group, 18

Europe, 152, 171

European Central Bank, 52, 61, 165

European colonialism, 230

European Government, 18

European Union, 68, 157, 177–178

eviction, 219, 221

evolution, 3, 129

Executive Order 1602, 36

exiles, 204

expulsion, 173

"extend and pretend," 18

extortion, 20, 53, 111–113, 118, 120

F

Facebook, 179, 182, 185, 186

facial recognition, 183

factory production, 77

failed societies, 252–253

fairness, 91

faith, 14, 204, 208

families: cultural flips and, 102; extended, 239–244; financial resource pooling of, 54; free services provided by, 54; gifts and, 90–94; human interaction and, 85–86; life of, 2–3, 15, 39, 41–42, 241–244; raising children and, 202; reunification of, 43; society and, 209–210

famine, 250

farmers' markets, 197·

farming, 96, 140, 152

farming tools, 38

favors, paying for, 98

FBI, 182, 183

fear, 33–34, 92, 124

Federal Reserve, 61

feral cities, 168

fiat currencies, 19, 30, 38

finance, 9, 54–57, 61, 135, 229

financial bailouts of 2008, 26

financial collapse, 1–71; loss of meaning and, 60–62; occurrence of, 17–18; root cause of, 18–21, 24; of imaginary space empire, 21–24

financial crisis of 2008, 18, 61, 76

financial despotism, 50–54

financial elite, 201

financial fraud, 121

financial institutions, 14, 17, 32, 34, 50, 54

financial mediators, 39

financial taxes, 39

financial web sites, 57

financiers, 135

firearms, 33, 206

fire insurance, 12

First World War, 203

fiscal deficits, 51

fiscal policy, 166

fisheries, 31

fishing, 70, 79

flat Earth theory, 83–84

floods, 12, 18

food, 18–20, 82–83, 98, 124, 173, 198–199, 224

food guide pyramids, 85

force, use of, 165

foreclosures, 40, 79

foreign aid, 174

foreign banks, 67

foreign currency, 26, 43

foreigners, 202

foreign governments, 165

foreign occupation, 125

fortune-telling, 216

fossil fuels: access to, 228; collapse and, 75; decrease in, 28–29; depletion of, 18; imperialism and, 50; industrial economies and, 97; enabling globalization, 84; resource depletion and, 6, 140; restarting the industry of, 31–32; squandering the remains of, 78; steamships and, 84; use of, 27, 28

fracking, 186

fraud, 53, 121

freedom, 176, 207–208

free energy, 140

free markets, 56, 102, 169, 198

free services, 54

free speech, 124

free will, 135

freight, 80

French language, 158

French Revolution, 158

frictionless capitalism, 167–168

Friedman, Thomas, 167

friendships, 85–86, 90–94, 102, 197, 199, 254

fuel, 75, 77, 165, 166, 198–199

G

Gadje (non-Gypsies), 213–218, 219–220, 223, 224

gambling, 11, 53

gangs, 109, 198, 199

garbage, 198

gardening, 3, 197

gasoline, 33, 37, 56, 82, 122, 140

gas stations, 40, 49

gated housing, 174

Gates, BIll, 167

gathering, 246–248, 252

Gatlif, Tony, 216

Gazprom, 122

GCC, 138

GDP, 7, 28, 52, 63, 76, 119

General Public License, 138

generators, 198–199

generosity, 248

George, Susan, 26, 167

Georgia (former Soviet), 158

Germany, 29, 68, 169

Ghonim, Wael, 180

Gide, André, 157

gifts: advantages of, 90–94; anonymous, 94; economic relationship pyramid and, 86–87; economies based on, 90–94; economy of, 116; generous, 93–94; of money, 94; opportunities for giving, 96–98; preservation of society and, 31; reliance on, 101, 104; rules of, 93; selling of, 93; Soviet Russia and, 98–99; symbolic, 91, 100; tribal lifestyles and, 83–84

Glitnir (bank), 65

global economy, 9, 26, 32, 48–49, 76–78, 102

global finance, 135, 137, 167

global industrial civilization, 3, 6

globalization, 150, 169, 170, 236

global material living standard, 7

global population, 27, 28–29

global supply chains, 77

global trade, 9–10, 84

GNU project, 138

gold, 19, 29, 30, 35–37, 36–37, 116, 222

Goldman Sachs, 74

gold rush, 30

gold standard, 51

Google, 138, 167, 178, 180

Gorbachev, Mikhail, 112, 121

Götterdämmerung, 61–62

government: absence of, 108, 175; debt and, 166; disintegration of, 105–106; expansion of, 105; impersonal institutions of, 229; regulation of work hours and the, 176; self-, 108, 162, 175; services from the, 162–165, 168, 217; social spending by the, 177; strengths of, 168–169; weak, 108

government finances, 75, 102

government services: collapse and, 3–4; crisis task force, 48; lending at interest and, 19–20; loan guarantees from, 18

Government Short-term Obligations, 25

government workers, 177

GPS, 182–183

grandparents, 4

gratitude, 91, 208

Greece: collapse in, 9; debt in, 52; junta in, 67; national default of, 75; unemployment in, 52

greed, 20, 92

green technologies, 34

Greer, John Michael, 13

grief, stages of, 13

Grímsson, Ólafur Ragnar, 64–66, 70–71

Gryzlov, Boris, 69

guerilla weapons, 170

Gulag archipelago, 109–110, 111, 112, 168

gun cult, 242

gun running, 121

gypsies, 212–215

"gypsiness," 224–225

"Gypsy king," 220

H

Haarde, Geir, 65

half-linguals, 147

hand-made gifts, 96

Hangul national writing system, 143

hard drives, 184

hardships, 199–200, 248–249

Hatian Creole, 235

Hayek, Friedrich, 51, 88

health care, 126, 169, 171

heat waves, 18

hedge funds, 24–25, 69

Heinberg, Richard, 6–7

Heine, Bernd, 245

heresy, 205

hierarchy, 125, 136–139, 190, 194

Higgs boson, 206

high-efficiency lighting, 197
higher learning, 4
highways, 8, 31–32
Hispanics, 168
historical preservation, 169
high-tech sectors, 70–71
Hobbesian evolution, 129
Holy Roman Empire, 203
Homeland Security, 182
homes, weatherization of,
    197
homeschooling, 3, 211
homesteading, 3
honesty, 91, 248
honor, 191
horse-trading, 216
hospitality, 191, 248
hospitals, 77, 162
host-pathogen relation-
    ships, 87
house cats, 80–81
house of cards metaphor, 18
housing, 40
Hubbert Curve, 8
human interaction diet,
    85–86
human isolation, 239–241
human relationships, 85
human weakness, 136
hunting, 3, 246–248
Hussein, Saddam, 160, 241
hyperinflation, 21, 29–30,
    31, 57
hypnosis, 56–57
hypocrisy, 67, 208, 258

I
ICBM, 171
Iceland, 63–71, 77, 157
Icesave (bank), 65
Ichietot language, 246, 257
identification papers, 218
identity, 219
Ik people, 15, 228–229,
    245–260
illegality, 106–107, 198, 199
illicit economies, 175
illiteracy, 143–144
IMF, 61

immigrants, 124, 164, 198, 204
imperialism, 165
imperial languages, 142–146
imperial nations, 50, 131
imperial state, 139
imperial states, 172
impersonal systems, 100
import chains, 14
imported goods, 19–20
imports, 101
incarceration, 191
independence, 42
Indian Penal Code, 192
indifference to suffering, 5
indoor plumbing, 3–4
industrial civilization, 8, 126,
    157, 176
industrial economy, 8
industrial installations, 15
industrialized economy, 7
industrial machinery, 160
industrial model of work, 97
industrial personnel, 4
infants, helplessness of, 230
inflation: deflation, 21, 29–31,
    30, 34, 57; hyperdeflation,
    31; hyperinflation, 21, 29–
    30, 31, 57; Iceland case
    study of, 63; Maastricht
    treaty and, 52; rate of, 165;
    targets, 29
infrastructure, 169, 176
institutions, 104, 116
insubordination, 124
insurance, 12, 92, 99, 121
insurance policies, 40, 218
Intel, 167
interest, 19–23, 32, 47
international aid, 196
international investments,
    195
International Monetary
    Fund, 63, 69
international telephone
    conversations, 44–45
international trade, 19–20
international trading com-
    panies, 69
international wages, 79

Internet, 168–169, 171, 179–
    180, 182–187
interpersonal relationships,
    104
intimidation, 121
inventions, 138–139
investments, cashing out of,
    3, 202
investments, international,
    195
investments, private, 178–179
investor capital, 33
investors, 70
Ioseliani, Djaba, 121
Iran, 179, 185
Iraq, 170, 180
Ireland, 67
Iron Curtain, 44
Islam, 148, 149, 205
Islamic Courts Union, 174
Islamic Republic of Iran, 148
Isle of Man, 68–69
Italian language, 158
Italy, 52, 158

J
Japan, 143
jewelry, 222
Jewish religion, 149, 218
joblessness, 106, 178
jobs, 162
juice bars, 114
Juncker, Jean Claude, 18
jurisdictional arbitrage, 169
jurisprudence, 217
justice, 192

K
Karzai, Hamid, 193
Kaupthing (bank), 64, 65, 69
Kerensky, Alexander, 34–35
keystroke loggers, 184
KGB, 44–46, 121, 122, 181–
    182, 187
Khodorkovsky, Michael, 161
kindergarten, 259
Kingdom of Saudi Arabia,
    148
kiosk owners, 109

Knight Capital, 32
Kohr, Leopold, 151–153, 156–157, 163
Korea, 143
Korowicz, David, 29
kremlinologists, 13
Kropotkin, Peter, 60, 127–133
Krugerrand coins, 36
Kübler-Ross model, 13, 14
Kunstler, James Howard, 13

L
labor, 169, 176, 177
labor, community, 96–98
labor, manual, 140
labor camps, 110
labor exchange, 96–98
labor laws, 206
labor movements, 176–177
labor relations, 177–178
Landsbanki (bank), 65
land transportation, 75
land use laws, 206
language, 230–232, 231–232, 233–236, 236–239
Large Hadron Collider, 206
Latin, 145
Latin America, 52
law, 237
law and order, 171–176
law and politics, 218–220
law enforcement, 102, 105, 107–108, 165
lawlessness, 90, 106
Law of Diminishing Productivity, 152
lawyers, 201
Lebanese people, 225
legislation, 201
Lehman Brothers, 25–27, 32, 69, 76
Lenin, 137, 216
Leningrad, 211
letters, 44–45, 182
letters of credit, 77
liberal communism, 167
Liberal Democratic Party of Russia, 121

liberalization, 137, 167
Liberty Dollars, 51
Libya, 150, 160
lighting, high-efficiency, 197
Lindqvist, Sven, 230
linguistic identities, 142–146
Linux, 184
literacy, 143–144, 236–237
literature, 95
litigation, 201
littering, 218
loans, 9, 18, 19–20, 29, 40, 53, 54, 161
lobbying, 201
local businesses, 6
local power, 173
loitering, 218
loners, 5, 127, 239–240
"Long Emergency," 13
Long-Term Capital Management, 25–27, 32, 76
looters, 199
Lorenz, Konrad, 141
lose-find operations, 47–48
lumber, 116'
lumberjacks, 82
Luther, 137
luxury items, 83, 87

M
Maastricht Treaty, 29, 52, 177–178
Mac OS X, 184
madness, 74
mafias, 15, 113–115, 175, 198
Magnitsky Act, 43
magpies, 88
maintenance operations, 77, 198
malaria, 87–88
manual labor, 140
manufactured products, 50, 84
manufacturing, 70
manufacturing operations, 74
Manx operation, 69
Maple Leaf coins, 36

market, 90, 91–93, 120, 166–167, 169
market demands, 20
market liberalization, 112–116, 170
market systems, 57, 99–100, 103
marriage, 2–3, 220–222, 254–255
mathematical models of collapse, 7–8, 55–56
Mauss, Marcel, 91
McMahon, Kathy, 241
medical systems, 198
Medicare, 166
medicine, 10, 173
Medieval Europe, 151
Medvedev, Dmitry, 69
memory, spoken, 236–238
Mennonites, 148
metabolism, 134
metal ore, 6, 18, 31, 35–36
metaphysics, 131
Mexico, collapse of the peso in, 53
MF Global, 27, 32–33, 58
Microsoft Windows, 138
Middle Ages, 139, 151
migrant workers, 164
militarism, 141, 156
military: conflict, 89; expenditure of, 135, 141; force from the, 169; interventions, 169; interventions by the, 196; servicemen, 103; strategists, 13; violence, 171
military junta, 67
militia, 175
milk, cost of, 140
minerals, 228
mining operations, 74
Ministry of Defense, 121
Ministry of Education, 211
Ministry of Foreign Affairs, 121
Ministry of Internal Affairs, 121
minorities, 124

mischief, better living
    through, 251–252
Mishukov, Ivan, 231
mitigation strategies, 18
mitigation strategies of the
    US Government, 18
mobile devices, 81
Mohammed, 148
monetary mysticism, 54–
    57
monetary policy, 166
money. *See also* trade; ad-
    diction of, 53; alternatives
    to, 39–42; avoidance
    of, 102; communities
    running without, 53;
    concept of, 28, 52; control
    of, 36; corruption and,
    94–95; crime and, 53,
    90; decrease in, 28–29;
    devaluation of, 14, 34–35;
    disagreements over,
    52–53; end of, 26–32;
    exchange of goods for,
    74; exchange rates and,
    44; formation of a
    monopoly and, 88; gifts
    of, 94; investments of, 33;
    lack of, 53; laundering of,
    122; lawlessness and, 90;
    lending with interest, 19,
    25; printing of, 26, 27, 29,
    36, 51, 166; protection,
    118–119; reliance on, 104;
    social status and, 88–89;
    trading goods in exchange
    for, 51; transfer of, 43–44;
    universality of, 95; use of,
    50; value of, 31; working
    for wages paid in, 51
money-lenders, 78
Mongol Empire, 143
Mongol invasion, 89
monopolies: absence of, 118;
    failed states and, 165; gifts
    and, 92; maintenance
    of, 171; on military-style
    violence, 169; money
    creation and, 51; political,

155–156; profits and, 108;
    secret government, 174;
    trade and, 88–89; in trade
    and commerce, 172; on
    violence, 173
morality, 91, 256
Morozov, Evgeny, 185
mortality, spike in, 29
mortgages, 40
Moses, 128–129
Mubarak regime, 180
Muhammed, 149
municipal workers, 177
murder, 113
Musa I (emperor), 30
muscle power, 75
music, 216
mythology, 61–62

N
narcissism, 130
narratives, 236–238
national bankruptcy, 101
national borders, 162, 168–
    169, 200
national default, 76
national government, 164–
    165
national language, 142–146
national politics, collapse
    of, 62
national television, 122
national unity, 124
nation-states, 139–143, 150–
    151, 157–164, 168–172,
    176, 179
NATO, 64–65, 69, 117, 193
natural disasters, 77
natural gas, 140
natural resources, 7, 27, 31,
    75–76, 228
nature, laws of, 200
nature, student of, 127
Nazis, 218, 224–225
negative economy, 32
neglect, 197
neighbors, 102, 197
net worth, 60
"new normal," 99–101

Newtown, Connecticut
    school shooting, 33
NGOs, 196
Nobel Peace Prize, 112
nomadic people, 211–225,
    218, 222, 248
nonrenewable natural
    resources, 7, 74, 84–85
non-union jobs, 177
Norilsk Nickel, 69
Norse tribal democracy, 67
North Caucasian dialects,
    146
North Sea fishery, 68
NSA, 182
nuclear installations, 15
nuclear power, 140, 186
nuclear weapons, 170–171

O
Obama, Barack, 13
Obsessive-Compulsive
    Disorder, 224
occupational safety, 178
occupations, 216
ocean racers, 82
Oddsson, David, 69
OECD, 158
offshore industrial produc-
    tion, 79
offshore tax havens, 69
oil: companies, 69, 161;
    consumption of, 27–28;
    depletion of, 8, 28, 79; free
    energy and, 140; prices
    of, 80, 84; refineries, 8,
    32, 37; reserves of, 27–28;
    trade in, 115–116; oil-fired
    steam, 75
old age pensions, 173
Open Society Foundation,
    185
open-source warfare, 170–
    171
oral cultures, 116, 128–129,
    215–216, 238
organic agriculture, 6
organized crime, 107
orphans, 217

Ottoman Empire, 160
overpopulation, 164

P
Pakistan, 189, 192–194
Palestine, 149
panic, 25
parasites, 87
Pashtun tribal areas, 189–194
passports, 162
peacekeeping efforts, 196
peat moss, 75
pensions, 19–20, 126, 172, 177, 217
Persian coins, 36
personal connections, 119
personal efficiency, 82–83
personality types, 4–5
personal relationships, 58, 87
pesticides, 154–155
PFG, 27, 32
pharmaceuticals, 198
pharmacies, 9
phonetics, 142–146
phosphate depletion, 18
pidgin, 235
Pinsky, Robert, 216
pipelines, 8
Pirahã, 233–235
plantation economies, 50
poaching, 251, 252
police: distrust of, 119–120; lack of protection from, 197–199; protection from, 3–4, 47, 174–175, 217; secret, 181
Politburo, 13
political campaign funds, 33
political class, 201
political collapse, 123–194; Greece, 9–10; occurrence of, 17
political establishments, 15
political impotence, 13
political instability and upheaval, 18
political power, 174
political scientists, 135
political violence, 161

politicians, 1–2
politics, 14, 179–187
politics, law and, 217–220
pollution, 8
population, 67–68, 164. *See also* global population
pornography, 185
Portugal, 67
Portuguese language, 235
possessions, 20, 49, 88–89
postal service, 169
post-traumatic stress disorder, 114
poverty, 4, 79, 106, 124, 196, 197–198, 222
power, violence and, 178
precious metals trade, 115–116
predator-prey relationships, 87
predictions of collapse, 10–12
preparations for collapse, 2–3, 4–5, 123
primate psychology, 243
prisons: colonies of, 44, 111; control by gangs in, 168; escapes from, 191; illiteracy in, 144, 202; revolt in, 110–111; rise in population in, 122, 167, 218; Roma people in, 221; staying out of, 114
privacy, 223
privacy rights, 182
private capital, 51
privateers, 113
private institutions, 107
private investment, 178–179
private protection, 107–109, 122
private trading systems, 89–90
privileged communities, 4
production, 101, 151–152
professional associations, 201
profiteering, 98
prohibition, 173, 252
property law, 102

property owners, 201
property rights, 105
property taxes, 179
prostitution, 121, 199, 221, 255
protection, 120
Protestantism, 148
Protestant revolution, 137
psychiatric disorders, 224
psychology, 1–2, 4–5
public buildings, 197
public domain, 138–139
public education, 126
public health organizations, 85
public institutions, 107
public market mechanism, 89
public officials, 109
public services, 165
public transportation, 197
public utilities, 177
Putin, Vladimir, 69, 117, 122
pyramid schemes, 25, 135

Q
Qaddafi, Muammar, 160

R
racism, 142
racketeering, 112–113, 116–120, 120–122, 174
railroad tracks, 32
railways, 169
rate of deterioration, 10
raw materials, 7, 78
recessions, 13, 28, 29
reciprocity, 91
recognition, 92
recurring payments, 89
recycling, 216
Reddit, 187
refineries, 8, 32
reformation, 126
refugees, 164
re-gifting, 93
regulation, 173
religions, 147–150, 172, 203–208. *See also* specific religions

relocation, 59
renewable energy, 6
rental housing, 40
representatives, 68
repression, 173
reproduction, 240
Republic of Abkhazia, 158
reputations, 57–58
research, 169
resiliency, 80–81
resource use and depletion,
    8–9, 13, 106
retail chains, 14
retirement, 103, 126, 202, 217
retirement funds, 3, 32, 40,
    99
revenge, 191
revenues, 30–31, 121
reverse mortgages, 40
revolution, 92
Reykjavik protests, 65
Reinhardt, Django, 216
ride-sharing initiatives, 197
rioting, 48
risk-management, 27
risk of default, 24
risk premium, 20, 24, 25
rites of passage, 254
rituals, 104
roads, 169
robberies, 39–40, 48, 57–58
Roma, 211–225
Roman Catholic Church,
    148, 172, 206
Roman republic, 160
Rome, 203
Romneycare, 206
Roosevelt, Franklin D., 36,
    51–52
Rosneft (oil company), 69
royal family, 241
rules, new, 200–201
rum, 84
Russia: free markets in, 102;
    money of, 34–35; national
    default in, 76–77; sov-
    ereign default in 1998,
    24–25; Soviet collapse in,
    29; tributes and, 89

Russian Mafia, case study of,
    105–122
Russian Orthodox Church,
    121, 149
Russian Provisional Gov-
    ernment, 34
Russian Revolution, 89, 137

S
safety, improving, 197
safety deposit boxes, 36
sailboats, 82
sail transport, 38, 84
salted meat and fish, 84
sanitary conditions, 198
Santa Fe Institute, 133
savings accounts, 3, 14, 19–
    20, 32–38, 39, 41, 43
scale, excessive, 151–157
scams, 35
scavenging, 199
Schadenfreude, 249, 252, 255
Scholes, Myron, 26–27
school, 218
seaports, 8
sea transportation, 75
security, 164, 170–175, 198,
    223
seigniorage, 36, 51, 165
self-governance, 108, 162, 175
self-sufficiency, 98, 101
self-worth, 95
Seneca Cliff model of col-
    lapse, 8
Seneca (Roman philoso-
    pher), 8
separatism, 223–224
September 11th terrorist
    attacks, 183, 192
service personnel, 4
sewage, 198
shale gas, 33, 186
shareholders, 29
Shevardnadze, Eduard, 121
shipping companies, 80
shipping costs, 84
ships, 80, 84
shipwrecks, 5
shooting sprees, 33

shopping cooperatives, 96
shortages, 8
Shumacher, E.F., 152
Shuman, Michael, 53
Sicilian Mafia, 175
sidewalks, 197
silver, 30, 35–37
SIM cards, 184–185
single-handed ocean racers,
    82
single mothers, 83
skepticism, 7
Skype, 184
"Slacktivism," 185
slave labor, 84
slow steaming, 80, 84
slums, urban, 168
small businesses, 179
smartphones, 138
Smith, Adam, 167
social class, 95, 120–121
social collapse, 195–225;
    aftermath of, 249–251
social Darwinism, 4, 60
social harmony, 92
social inequality, 94
social inertia, 4
social institutions, 15, 203
social interactions, 85
socialism, 126
socialization, 96
social order, 39
social personalities, 5
social predators, 200
social reclamation, 202–203
social scientists, 1–2
Social Security, 166
social spending, 106
social status, 87–89, 90, 98
societies: characterization
    of, 55; collapse and, 14;
    deproletarianization of,
    97; existence of, 209–210;
    failure in, 196; healthy,
    85; modern, 105; sick, 85;
    turning your back on,
    202–203
socioeconomic complexity,
    105, 134

software updates, 81
soil erosion, 74, 164, 195
solar power, 78, 197, 198–199
soldiers, 198
solidarity, 92, 108, 172
solitary personalities, 5
Solzhenitsyn, Alexander,
    15, 112
Somalia, 174
Soros, George, 55, 167, 185
South Korea, 169
South Ossetia, 158
sovereign collapse, 24–25
sovereignty, 68, 118, 150, 157
Soviet collapse, 29
Soviet Eastern Bloc, 225
Soviet national anthem, 141
Soviet Russia, 98–99, 102,
    218
space colonization, 21–24
Spain, 20, 52, 68
specialty shops, 79
specie, 46–47, 49
speculation, 98
spices, 84
spies, 181–182
spoken memory, 236–238
Ssabunnya, John, 231
St. Matthew, 149
Stalin, Joseph, 112, 115, 168
Stallman, Richard, 138
Starbucks, 178
starvation, 29
state religion, 147–150
steady-state economies, 74,
    78–79
steam power, 186
steamships, 84
steganography, 45
Stockholm Syndrome,
    181–182
stock-in-trade, 46–47
stock market, 63
stock ownership, 120
stores of value, 37–38, 39–
    42
Strategic Defense Initia-
    tive, 13
street crime, 121

street vendors, 109
strikes, 126
student loans, 202
substanceless abuse, 95
subversives, 4
Sufi learning, 146
sugar, 84
summonses, 221
supermarkets, 49, 77
supplies, for crisis, 198–199
supply and demand, 167
surveillance cameras, 182–
    184, 183, 186
survival, 2, 14, 15, 33–34,
    87, 88
survival of the fittest, 4
sweatshops, 80
Switzerland, 172
Syria, 150, 179–180, 185
systems theory, 2

T
taboos, 224
Tainter, Joseph, 14
Taleb, Nassim Nicholas, 11
Taliban, 65, 174, 192
tankers, 31–32, 84
Target stores, 183
taxation, 206
taxes: avoidance of, 119;
    charitable giving and,
    208; imposed, 116; incen-
    tives, 179; levying, 51; local
    power and, 173; offshore,
    69; policies, 167; property,
    179; raising of, 106, 165,
    178; tribute as, 99, 100
tax havens, 69
tax receipts, 29, 218
tax revenues, 30–31
teachers, 177
technology: communica-
    tions, 170; computer,
    137–138; defense, 170;
    development of, 174; fossil
    fuels and, 238; green, 34;
    new, 80, 81; open-source,
    170; replacement of hu-
    man need and, 240

telephone conversations,
    44–45, 182
Tenth Commandment of
    Moses, 128–129
territory claims, 118
terrorism, 64–65, 148, 169,
    170
text messages, 182–183
Thames river, 75
Thatcher, Margaret, 68–69
theft, 88, 199
theologians, 135
thermodynamics, 2
thieves, 109–112
Tito, Josip Broz, 160
tools, acquiring, 3
Tor, 184
torture, 113
Torvalds, Linus, 138
tourism, 70, 197
trade: dominant position of,
    99; economic relation-
    ship hierarchy and, 86–
    88; efficiency and, 78;
    imbalances of, 50, 84, 86;
    liberalization of, 166–167;
    long-distance, 101, 108;
    meaning of, 73–74;
    monopolistic systems
    and, 88–89; shipping and,
    80; survival and, 88; tribal
    lifestyles and, 83–84; use
    of objects in, 50–54
1974 Trade Act, 43
trades, 46–48
tradesmen, 96
trade unions, 126
trading companies, 69, 115–
    116
trading systems, 46–50
tradition, 89
traffic jams, 8–9
tragedy, stages of, 13
transatlantic races, 82
transnational business
    environments, 137
transportation, 75, 77, 80,
    177, 197
trees, 34, 78

tribal communities, 83–86, 158, 189–194, 203, 211–225, 237, 245–260

tribal identities, 141–142

tribute: charitable donations, 100; communes and, 111; contributions and donations and, 89; economic relationship hierarchy and, 86–87; health insurance and, 99; preservation of society and, 31; retirement and, 99; taxes and, 99, 100; tribal lifestyles and, 83–84

trilinguals, 146

trust, 14, 57–60, 87, 108, 175, 229

Turkish language, 146

Turnbull, Colin, 15, 228–229, 245–260

Twitter, 179, 182

typhoid, 198

U

underage women, 206

underground banks, 115

unemployment, 10, 52, 63, 103, 164, 177

UN Habitat Report, 168

unions, 126, 156, 176–177

United Nations, 158, 163

United States Department of Agriculture, 85

United States Pledge of Allegiance, 141

unity, 156

Universal Grammar, 233–234, 233–235

universities, 203

University of Florence, 8

Unix, 137–138

unmarried men, 4–5

urban slums, 168

US debt, 165–166

US dollar, 29, 51, 52, 60, 63, 165

US federal budget, 165

US Federal Reserve, 25, 26, 76, 165

US government, 7, 165–166

US interstate highway system, 31–32

Usmanov, Alisher, 69

US mortgage crisis, 25–26

US sovereign debt, 165

USSR, 12–13, 112, 121, 158

US State Department, 162

US subprime mortgage crisis, 76

usury, 19–21, 24

utopians, 135–136

V

value, items of, 49

Vienna, 143

violation notices, 221

violence: avoidance of, 200; in communities, 175, 197; debt collection and, 121; end of law and order and, 171–175; fighting violence with, 199; intercommunal, 174; mental, 229–230; power and, 178; Russian Mafia and, 114, 116–117; strangers and, 57–58

virtualized politics, 179–187

virtues, 248

visas, 162

vodka, rationing of, 112

Volkov, Vadim, 108, 116

volunteering, 209

von NotHaus, Bernard, 51

W

wage laborers, 140, 176

wages, 79, 177, 178

Wagner, Richard, 61

war, 114–115, 180

warfare, 169–171, 206

warlordism, 15, 174

War on Terror, 184

water: fresh, 224; access to, 124, 228; crisis supplies of, 198–199; fresh, 6, 18, 31; pumping stations, 198

Waziristan, 189

wealth: abstract, 101; accumulation of, 173; concentrations of, 196; distribution of, 92; nation-states and, 164; offshore, 178; Roma people and, 222

weapons, 87, 115, 170–171, 174

weatherization of homes, 197

Weinreich, Max, 142–143

welfare state, 140, 176–179

Wells, H.G., 23

Wernicke's aphasia, 232

West, Geoffrey, 133–134

Western films, 113

Whorf, Benjamin Lee, 233–234

Whorfanism, 233–234

WiFi, 138, 184

wilderness survival training, 2

Windows operating system, 184

wind power, 75

women, 206, 243

word of honor, 47

work, 97, 176

workers' rights, 177

working class, 126

work weeks, 126

World Bank, 150

World Health Organization, 85

World3 model, 7

world wars, 29, 137, 156

writs, 221

written language, 238–239

Y

Yeltsin, Boris, 122

Yugoslavia, 160

Z

Zhirinovsky, Vladimir, 121

Zimbabwe, 29

About the author

DMITRY ORLOV has written extensively
on the subject of collapse, being first to
compare the collapse of the USSR to the
projected collapse of the world's other
Cold War superpower—the United
States. He is the author of numerous ar-
ticles and the award-winning book *Rein-
venting Collapse: The Soviet Example and
American Prospects.* Born in Russia, he
moved to the US while a teenager, and
has traveled back repeatedly to observe
the Soviet collapse during the late eight-
ies and mid-nineties. He is an engineer
who has worked in many fields, including high-energy physics research,
e-commerce and Internet security. For the past five years he has been
experimenting with off-grid living and renewable energy by giving up
the house and the car. Instead, he has been living on a sailboat, sailing it
up and down the Eastern Seaboard, and commuting by bicycle. Dmitry
believes that, given appropriate technology, we can greatly reduce personal resource consumption while remaining perfectly civilized.

If you have enjoyed *The Five Stages of Collapse* you might also enjoy other

Books to Build a New Society

Our books provide positive solutions for people who want to
make a difference. We specialize in:

**Sustainable Living • Green Building • Peak Oil
Renewable Energy • Environment & Economy
Natural Building & Appropriate Technology
Progressive Leadership • Resistance and Community
Educational & Parenting Resources**

New Society Publishers

ENVIRONMENTAL BENEFITS STATEMENT

New Society Publishers has chosen to produce this book on recycled paper made
with **100% post consumer waste,** processed chlorine free, and old growth free.

For every 5,000 books printed, New Society saves the following resources:[1]

27	Trees
2,447	Pounds of Solid Waste
2,692	Gallons of Water
3,512	Kilowatt Hours of Electricity
4,448	Pounds of Greenhouse Gases
19	Pounds of HAPs, VOCs, and AOX Combined
7	Cubic Yards of Landfill Space

[1]Environmental benefits are calculated based on research done by the Environmental Defense Fund
and other members of the Paper Task Force who study the environmental impacts of the paper
industry.

For a full list of NSP's titles, please call 1-800-567-6772 *or check out our website* at:
www.newsociety.com

new society
PUBLISHERS